Fairy Pudding

A Personal Opera

by

William Joseph Bryan

ROBERT D. REED PUBLISHERS   SAN FRANCISCO, CA

Robert D. Reed Publishers
750 La Playa Street, Suite 647
San Francisco, CA 94121
Phone: 650/994-6570 • Fax: -6579
E-mail: 4bobreed@msn.com
http://www.rdrpublishers.com

Text Designer: Marilyn Yasmine Nadel
Cover Photo: Jay Barrie

ISBN 1885003749
Library of Congress Card Number: 00-109045

Produced and Printed in the United States of America

Opera was invented by a group of Late Renaissance Italian intellectuals to describe their new art form that combined music, drama, scenery and movement. The word derives from Latin meaning "works" and in the minds of those Florentine gentlemen, the combination of those various endeavors might just as well be called "works", and since they were Italian, it comes out "OPERA"

To the above cited items I've added cooking and eating! Shakespeare wrote: "What a piece of WORK is MAN!" In American slang one hears now and then: "gimme the works!" It could just as well be:"Gimme the OPERA!" Here it is.

OPUS* ONE
PROLOGUE
The Mural

Walking along the school hall I could feel the tingle of excitement begin. We were about to go into the auditorium where something magical was going to take place. Sometimes someone would play the piano. Sometimes someone would talk, or a play might be presented by some other class. Whatever it was, though, it was going to take place in the auditorium and no matter what transpired on the stage, I could always lose myself in the wonderful world of the mural found on the wall.

High above the doors and windows was a mural that went around two sides of the large room. Starting stage-left a tiny medieval town, with church spires piercing the blue ceiling, gleamed from the wall as if actually twinkling with lights. As my eyes moved past the town and out into the meadow, a group of children appeared to be following a tall figure playing a flute. Dogs romped along beside the children and a great sense of excitement seemed to flow out from the scene. Anticipation, joy, escape from the ordinary welled up in my imagination. As the side wall was about to complete its length, a door was painted half open into the turn of the room leading to the large expanse of the back wall, larger because no windows took away from the space.

Where the village wall had been green and brown, the back wall billowed blue, a blue of all possibilities, of dreams and hopes of life yet to come. In the forest of blue-green trees rose a castle in the very center of the wall, the windows of which were the actual openings of the projection booth from which lights sometimes flickered out a story, but at other times were covered with colored paper allowing opaque colorations to twinkle through giving animation to the existence of that imaginary castle and all of what it might bring. Squinting my eyes more tightly made the light flicker expectantly and my enchanted existence would begin.

*Opus derives from the Latin meaning "a work", as in an amount or volume of work. Composers from Beethoven onward have used that designation in assigning numbers to their creative output (works) and I use that term in the same vein regarding the "chapters" of my life.

The auditorium floor was wooden. Metal framed chairs, bolted to the floor, contained contoured wooden seats that folded up so that people could more easily pass. The floors were well worn, but for their protection, were frequently oiled which gave off a faintly pungent odor of machine shop and wax works. When they had recently been treated they were dark brown and spicy. The hundreds of fresh footprints left slightly dusty imprints—those little feet carrying all the hopes of life yet to be revealed.

First grade at the public school was a bit of a bore following the more creative County Day school that had nurtured me for several years. My mother assisted in the teaching in exchange for my attendance, a precursor to the current use of mother participation in "day care." Everything there was friendly and interesting: rambling wooden buildings, outside ramps with our own tin cup and hand towel hanging on its own peg, the whole grounds interspersed with large pine trees. Huge piles of pine needles made wonderful hideaway places, secret nooks which pleased me more than running wildly around with the other children.

At any rate, all that freedom stopped when I went to the Florida "Cracker" public school to begin my "formal" education. Very little was learned, I'm afraid, except for an important social lesson, for the breach of which I was now sitting, a little terrified, in the principals office, which was stark and forbidding. Leaning against the wall in the corner was a large paddle. I thought that no one dared use it on me, at least I hoped not. The "problem": we had been sitting in a circle doing some sort of social interaction. A little girl sat next to me and kept pestering me...I can't remember how...but she kept doing whatever it was she was doing. Finally I hauled off and slapped her in the face, not hard, mind you, but enough to indicate my irritation at her continued annoyance.

Well! You'd think the end of the world had occurred. I was summarily plucked out of the circle and marched off to the principal's office where in no uncertain terms, I was told that little boys don't slap little girls. I intuitively knew that injustice was at hand. She was just as strong as I was, just as responsible for her irritating behavior and no different, in my eyes, as anyone else, pestering me too the point of physical response. I guess I did learn not to act out my frustration with pestering girls and it certainly helped me to be wary and defensive in my behavior toward females for the rest of my life.

I came home one day from the school principal's house down the street where the daughter, somewhat older than I, had been playing on a divine, tinkling instrument. The family was somewhat gypsy like, the father a scene painter and itinerant sign maker, his wife, with some official education, the local principal. From somewhere in their past came this circus-sized portable piano, somewhere between a toy piano and an ordinary upright piano, gaily painted with carnival scenes. The darkly pretty daughter played this charming, colorful thing and I don't know whether it was the brightness of the painted box or the cheeriness of the sound, but at seven years of age I went home to announce that I wanted to learn how to play the piano. My parents had no noticeable interest in music, save for my father's singing in the Sunday Choir. He had, as a boy, dressed like Teddy Roosevelt Rough Riders, sung with Telley's boy's choir in the Tabernacle at Ocean Grove, New Jersey.

Remarkably enough, a used upright piano was purchased and a piano teacher engaged and little Billy Bryan commenced to learn to play the piano.

I had been originally attracted to music back at the County Day school where once in awhile we were taken into the Headmistress' home for some "music appreciation." The only piece I recall hearing played was the *Sorcerer's Apprentice* by Paul Dukas. Whether it was the music or the action that attracted me, I'll never know. What I do remember is the headmistress sweeping back and forth frantically with a kitchen broom approximating the apprentice's attempt to get rid of the water. This took place, of course, many years before we were privileged to see Mickey Mouse do the same thing in Disney's FANTASIA to the same piece of music.

So my destiny of "teaching" music appreciation was set by these two momentous events: the tinkling of a gaily colored carnival piano and the sweep of a kitchen broom to music!

Many years later when Disney World first arose from palmetto fields and cypress swamps in Florida, I visited the Disney Museum. Memorabilia from years of Disney productions were admirably presented, but noteworthy to me was a prominently displayed letter from Leopold Stokowski, the world famous conductor for the film FANTASIA, regarding the overall tone of the film. Leopold began his letter by extolling the genius of Walt and in no way suggesting that any changes be made in the concept and execution of the film. But, Leopold goes on to say that perhaps Walt should re-think the advisability of having Mickey shown conducting an orchestra. OK for Mickey to be the Sorcerer's Apprentice, but perhaps a new character should be devised to serve as animated conductor. Walt's response was not shown, but we do have the results: Mickey Mouse conducts the orchestra!

My first recipe was acquired at about the age of 12 or 13. I was in charge of meals for a weekend of Boy Scout camping, not in tents but in cabins. There was a separate cooking cabin which became my domain. I must have had help from the Scoutmaster, but the first real meal I produced was a tuna casserole, later, when I "grew up", to be known as Fairy Pudding, in fact:

"FIRE ISLAND FAIRY PUDDING."

1 can of tuna
1 can of mushroom soup
1 small jar of Pimentos
1 package of wide egg noodles
2 times amount of grated cheddar than tuna
1/2 package of frozen green peas

Boil noodles in lots of slightly salted water until "al dente." Drain. In a baking dish, fold in all the other ingredients and bake in 350 degree oven until slightly crispy on top, about 40 minutes.

OPUS TWO

*J*uilliard in 1945 was up on 122nd street across the street from Grant's Tomb, adjacent to the Hudson River. I had to take a trolley from Yonkers, connecting to the furthest end of the A train, which by then was elevated and not a subway any longer. YONKERS! Well, long before "Hello Dolly", Yonkers was the only place where one could rent anything, anything for $18 a month, at least. War-time rent restrictions, plus no building during the early 40's, precluded any apartment being available down Manhattan way, at least for a music student.

That was the era of Rosina Lhevinne and her stable of future stars: John Browning, Daniel Pollock and, of course, Van Cliburn, soon to catapult America back onto the international map as a "worthy nation." I regularly ate one decent meal a day in the Juilliard cafeteria and over in the same corner always was Mme. Lhevinne surrounded by her bunch of prodigies. None of them had become famous yet, but she was the female half of Joseph and Rosina Lhevinne, duo pianists of great fame as well as soloists of distinction in their own right. As I was merely a freshman and of modest talent, I never was privileged to know any of them....then. But we did eat the same food! And eating, as well as preparing food, has been an interesting past-time (if nothing else) ever since.

Let's begin with Yonkers ("Zonkers" to my intimate friends). Upon arriving at the end of the Bronx line one had to continue by trolley into town, about three miles. I made my exit just as the low apartment buildings began to appear. A mere block and a half walk brought me to the four story, two-flats to a floor Italian tenement that was my home for nearly two years. It was the usual cold-water flat which meant no heat, no hot water, except this one did supply hot water. It was also what is known as a railroad flat, meaning you went from one room to the next directly with no hallway providing privacy. As I lived alone that was no problem. My flat was on the ground floor, as a matter of fact it was a little below street level so my front windows peered out at the legs of passerbys. During the winter I kept the front room mostly closed in order to conserve heat. Only in Spring did the first rays of sunlight enter through open windows. The back room was a large kitchen with a bath off to one side. The kitchen contained a huge iron kerosene cook stove. There was a side-burning compartment which supplied what heat I had during the winter which also, when fired up, heated an oven. Not being very proficient yet as a chef, it was used mostly for warming bread and the like. I don't recall cooking much of a variety but I do remember making large pots of lentil soup which lasted for a week and nourished me at night following the daily Juilliard lunch.

Once in awhile I'd have company and a great effort was made to provide an interesting meal. For those special occasions I'd approach my neighbor who lived directly above me and whose nightly rolling about on the floor after a day of drinking would sometimes keep me awake. He was an Italian by heritage as were all the tenants in our building, indeed in the entire neighborhood. Everybody called me "Little Toscanini" as I practiced the piano several hours each day— but not at night. Amazingly no one ever complained about the sound emitting from my flat.

My second floor neighbor made his own wine in the basement. Each flat had a chicken-wire fenced off area for storage in the communal basement. My neighbor used his space to make and store his homemade red wine. Annually, in the fall, flatbed trucks filled with boxes of grapes roamed the streets of the Italian neighborhoods offering both red and white grapes for sale, but mostly red was what the home wine makers wanted. You'd hear their hoarse cries crying "grapes for sale" or whatever it sounds like in Italian. That's how my neighbor obtained his grapes. On my special meal days I'd go up and knock on his door and ask to buy a bottle of his wine—probably for 50 cents: "but of course" he would reply and down we'd go to the basement, my clean bottle in hand to be filled at the tap of a huge old wooden vat. As the wine lessened in amount in the vat the more oxygen got in, so that the longer the wine stayed in the barrel the worse it got rather than the better. While the bottle was filling up he always made me drink a water glass full of the stuff right then and there, which was a bit hard to do notwithstanding that I was a novice wine drinker and the stuff was pretty frightful. He'd drink some himself and then always proclaim: "eata the spaghetti and drinka the wine and you'll grow up to be big man like me!" while pounding me a little on my chest to emphasize his point. My first wine experiences!

The corner grocery was a simple plate-glassed corner store with whole cheeses dangling from the ceiling, dried fish in bins, barrels of olives, boxes of spaghetti, etc., all smelling of oil and garlic. Behind the counter and down a little hall was a dining alcove for the owners to sit in. Almost always when I went by, a policeman would be sitting there sipping a glass of the shop-keeper's home-made wine. I'm sure he didn't pay for it, nor did the owner have a license to sell the stuff anyway, but that's how things were and that's how a shop owner kept the walking patrolman contented on their beat. A small price to pay for protection.

I had two used upright pianos, both from the Salvation army. One I kept on the glassed-in stairwell at the rear of the flat which I used in fine weather. The other was in the nearest bedroom to the relatively warm kitchen. I rehearsed the two-piano concerto by Mozart with a class-mate while the sounds ricocheted between us in the kitchen.

On Sundays my dancer friend came up frequently to visit. Following a walk around the fancier houses above the Italian ghetto where I lived, we'd return to warm up with a pot of tea and little thin slices of whole wheat bread warmed slightly in the kerosene oven and then spread with orange marmalade. I had a modest Art deco style radio, probably purchased from a thrift shop (wish I'd kept it) that we'd turn on for Phil Spitanly and his All Girl orchestra, to listen to the Sunday afternoon program entitled "Hour of Charm." This was a popular family program which gave us much merriment. Along with Evelyn and her Magic Violin, there were other regular items such as an orchestrated version of a well-known hymn. At the end of each phrase (about four measures of music) there is always a release point for singers and congregations to catch a breath. At those points the all girl orchestration always included the ringing of a single stroke on a chime. Upon hearing the chime we would collapse in a spasm of laughter, frequently rolling on the floor and holding onto our sides.

In a life-time of hearing and using the phrase "campy" (it takes a life-time of usage to understand the meaning of that word and its definition is not found in any dictionary) one realizes that it can refer to many situations. Certainly the ringing of a single chime at the con-clusion of each line of a hymn tune, and repetitively so, is "campy!" In fact one yearns to return to such innocent frivolity—they don't pro-duce such shows anymore. Mostly shows "shoot" people and that isn't campy at all!

In New York, music students attended concerts nearly every night. Of course from Yonkers it was a bit of a trip. But that's what we did. Even William Kapell, just starting his concert career, would be at all the Town Hall piano recitals. There were sometimes two and three a day: matinee, late afternoon, and then evening recitals. It was part of our training: to listen to other interpretations and to hear repertoire other than what we played ourselves.

A school boy friend of mine preceded me to New York the previous year and after studying at the Ballachine-Lincoln Kirstein American School of Ballet, landed a corps de ballet position in the new *Ballets International*, which the Marquis de Cuevas had put together with his wife's money. The company rehearsed all their newly commissioned works in a dance studio to the side of and in a part of Carnegie Hall. Many singing teachers had studios in this building and the hallowed halls were continually alive with the sound of vocalization. At street level to one side the still-fabled Russian Tearoom existed, filled with prima ballerinas and impresarios. But the corps de ballet as well as Philharmonic musicians dined at the Carnegie Deli on the west side of 6th avenue directly across from the hall. After sitting in the corner all morning long watching a rehearsal, a gang of us went to the deli for lunch. I was just new in New York and didn't know anything about menus or European food or...a real bumpkin. Sandwiches were ordered and then came dessert. I looked at the menu and rather loudly asked: "What is this apple strudel" (as in strut) to the dismay of my dancer-friend who hissed: "It's the commonest pastry in the world and its 'strewdel'!" I never ordered "strewdel" again, although I may have picked one up at a bakery now and then without calling it anything!

Following the failure of *Ballets International* my friend moved to Ballet Theater as a member of the corps de ballet but was given some chances as a demi soloist...most notably as the drunken bridegroom in the finale of Petrouchka. But Ballet Theater had fallen on bad times, having had to move their performances from the "old" Met (on 39th Street) to a theater on Broadway and playing to half empty houses. I often attended these performances free by running out to purchase last minute flowers for ballerinas at the request of Lucia Chase, the money-bags for the company. I was able to see legendary dancers in their repertoire of that era: Eglevsky and Markova in Giselle; Nora Kay, Anthony Tudor and Hugh Lang in Lilac Garden; even Agnes de Mille in her own Rodeo.

OPUS THREE

*O*n Staten Island lived the widow of my family's patriarch, William Bryan, surgeon and medical director of the Staten Island hospital during the first quarter of the 20th century. He died before I knew him, but his wife, Auntie Mae, lived on for many years in the large wooden turn-of-the-century style house, but it was not "Victorian". He had his nephews (my father and his two brothers for whom I am named, William and Joseph) dig and build for him—following World War I and the passage of the 18th Amendment in 1919—a wine cellar in his basement. He only allowed his nephews to do the work so no one outside the family would know. Then, through his Wall Street friends, he was able to stock it with fine imported wines, some of which were still there when I was attending Juilliard. I would be invited, along with my Cousin Don, who was like an uncle to me and of the same age as my uncles, for Thanksgiving and Christmas or sometimes just myself alone. Auntie Mae always kept a cook-house-keeper and tried to maintain the style of elegance of service she had been accustomed to while Uncle Will still lived. Upon entering the dining room she'd always exclaim: "I've had the wine opened so it can BREATHE!" Of course she was right, but at the time I thought she was just being eccentric.

Besides the beautiful roasts, turkeys, hams, etc. that graced the table, there was the cocktail time before the feast. This was her favorite time of day, more so than "breathing the wine." She loved Manhattans and always had a pitcher full even if it was just the two of us. Once served she would turn to me and say (in a marble-mouth sort of sound that only she could do): "I just luf cocktail time, don't you?" and laugh heartily as we clinked and downed the first glass.

I learned to drink under grand tutelage but with a kind of restraint that forbad "getting drunk" or acting so. In the Spring I'd buy a dollar's worth of lilac blossoms to bring her while enjoying the 5 cent ferry ride to Staten Island. The Statue of Liberty gleamed off toward the ocean, but I never dreamed I'd be sailing past her one day on my way to study in France...but that's later.

My Grandmother, whom I loved dearly, resided in her older years with her two sisters in Asbury Park, New Jersey. My mother had been born in East Orange, New Jersey, and her father was a partner in a building supply firm in Trenton, New Jersey, called Cook and

Genung, the later name being my Mother's maiden name, so there is a lot of "Jersey" in me. Mr. Genung was English born and his heritage was a considerable mystery as he was, supposedly, an orphaned infant emigre adopted and raised by the Genung family in Trenton. My Mother used to allude to the possibility that her father was of noble birth who happened to have been shipped to America for adoption in order to cover up some scandal. We'll never know about that!

In any case, for my Grandmother, what glamour existed in earlier, wealthier days, ceased to exist and she was reduced to keeping house for her two sisters in order to have a roof over her head. She was the chief cook and bottle washer, and probably laundress and house cleaner as well, although I was only present for festive weekends now and then, arriving by train from Penn Station in New York to the "shore." In those days —and probably still today—Asbury Park had a well-known boardwalk full of carnival-like amusements: miniature golf (which I adored) bumper cars, merry-go-round ,complete with gold ring, etc., and Salt Water Taffy! I saw my first live lobsters floating around in tanks in front of fancy seafood restaurants which I never entered.

Gram prepared all the meals and perhaps Aunt Diddy (Elizabeth) might possibly have set the table, while Aunt Jo (Josephine),being the artist of the group, was left alone to paint or write until time to dine. She was a splendid artist in the turn-of-the century, Impressionistic style. She had studied in both France and Italy prior to WWI. Fortunately, I own the majority of these lovely oils, the ones already received before her death. Although she bequeathed all of them to me, a Jersey neighbor stole them before my Mother could arrive from Florida to arrange for the funeral and to transport my Grandmother back to Florida. The neighbor wouldn't give them up when Mother came calling for them. Remember the scene in "Zorba the Greek" when the old lady lies dying and the neighbor women crouch in the corner waiting for her last gasp so they can cart off the bed clothes, blankets, and all? Well, it was something like that with the paintings.

Aunt Jo apparently had lost her sense of taste and upon sitting down at the table would immediately reach for the salt and pepper and sprinkle it all over her food. My Grandmother, who had spent the day preparing (and properly seasoning) the meal would remonstrate: "Jo! You know you can't taste anything! Why do you put all that salt and pepper all over everything?" To which Jo would reply: "but I can remember what it tastes like!" followed by a faint, crooked smile. This scene transpired daily.

During the first summer I was in New York, prior to"discovering" Yonkers, I rented the 2nd floor of a Brownstone on 52nd street between 5th and 6th avenues. It consisted of 2 large rooms and a bath. I shared it with my dancer friend who took the front room facing 52nd street while I took the quieter back room. I think there was a sort of kitchen in the hallway that connected the two rooms. Mostly I remember eating a lot at the Automat, the one up on 57th street near Carnegie Hall. I've just read (July 1999) that the last of the Automats has closed. That's too bad because they kept a lot of folks out of soup kitchens.

At the corner of 5th Avenue and 52nd street was the famous Stork Club. But down at the other end, just east of our flat was the egalitarian Leon and Eddies where Billie Holiday often performed. I remember seeing her name in lights larger than the name of the club. Each morning as I left for Juilliard one could smell the stale beer and cigarette smell emanating from the open doors where janitors were trying to air out the place for the next evening's frivolities. Around 3 a.m, I was awakened frequently by the voices leaving the closed club and the last were always: "Good night Leon", "Goodnight Eddie".

My dancer-friend was a favorite model for both George Platt Lynes, the great photographer of the first half of the 20th century, and of Pavel Tchelitchew (brought to America by Lincoln Kirstein at the same time as he brought George Ballachine) whose extra- ordinary painting "Tree of Life" occupies a room unto itself at New York's Museum of Modern Art. It still causes quite a stir among viewers. It was slightly damaged during MOMA's fire a few years back, but Pavlik was still alive and was able to personally repair it. Occasionally he took my friend to dinner at some little bistro and would order only a half bottle of Bordeaux for the two of them saying: "If we drink too much, we'll get tipsy!" (!!)

It was in theory class in August 1945 about 10 a.m. when someone somehow announced that an atom bomb had been dropped on Hiroshima and the war was about to be over. Instead of hurrying to Times Square when the war was over the following week, I, instead, hurried to Asbury Park to be with my Grandmother and great aunts. I walked the boardwalk amidst excited crowds and probably saw fireworks: it's a bit of a blur. I may have walked the boardwalk south to Ocean Grove where the huge Methodist tabernacle stood and where famous preachers as well as artists had performed for many years...from Jenny Lind to Marion Anderson! There was probably a joyous and prayerful service of Thanksgiving that the war was finally over. I often went there, so to remember if I did go there exactly the night of the war's conclusion would require carbon dating or the like.

As I have already mentioned, my father had sung in the Ocean Grove tabernacle "Rough Rider's" boy's chorus as a youth. He was often staying with his Aunts...Annie and Dora ...in Avon-by-the Sea where, in better days, my Grandmother had her home on Avon Lake. Her sister Jo also had a house in Avon, but closer to the ocean, about a block away. When my father and mother were teenagers they were great swimmers of the ocean as was Aunt Jo. One day she mentioned to her niece, Marie, that she ought to come swimming and meet the Bryan boys: Bart, Bill and Joe! Bart being the eldest (not necessarily the handsomest) but the same age as Marie, they soon became enamored of each other. Those were the halcyon days prior to America's entrance into WWI. Of course all the Bryan boys went off to war, but only my Dad experienced trench warfare in France. Mother's junior year at Smith College was to have been spent in France, a tradition in those days. But WWI smashed that dream, and the war pretty well smashed my father's body: he developed tuberculosis of the spine and upon returning to America, was one of the first persons to have a portion of leg bone removed and transplanted into his decayed back.

OPUS FOUR

After spending two years in New York City attending Juilliard, as well as attending many recitals and ballet performances, I left to continue my music studies at the St. Louis Institute of Music. This did not have the prestige of Juilliard. But I heard of a teacher, Maurice Lichtman, who taught a "weight and relaxation" technique based on his knowledge of Chopin's playing acquired from his teacher who had been a student of Chopin. Chopin pieces were used almost exclusively for instruction.

But upon arriving in St. Louis for the fall term in 1947, I discovered that Maurice Lichtman had been taken sick and had been replaced as artist-in-residence by Leo Sirota. Dr. Sirota had been Ferruccio Busoni's favorite student. He premiered Busoni's huge piano concerto for symphony and male chorus under the composer's direction. He also premiered the first performance of Stravinsky's reduction of Petruchka into a suite of piano pieces for solo piano. Artur Rubinstein was scheduled to perform the premiere in Paris, but as he hadn't conquered the material, Sirota gave the first performance in Paris at the Palais de Chaillot. Sirota may still be heard on a current CD release entitled "Busoni and His Circle" of which almost half of the recording is of Sirota's playing: (Pearl CD GEMM 9014)

As an Austrian Professor of Music, Sirota had been invited to become head of the Imperial School of Music in Japan during the 30's. Japan, having been rebuffed by America following WWI, wanted to Westernize, so it turned to Germany and Austria for guidance. They imported technicians from Germany to build many sorts of things including craftsman from Bechstein piano company who produced the Yamaha piano based on the German design. They also imported artists and professors. Sirota brought Russian pianism via Berlin, Busoni and Vienna to Japan and for ten years gave concerts and taught the best and brightest of Japanese talent. He had one daughter who attended the "American School" in Tokyo as a child and teenager but in 1941 she was ready for college. Sirota enrolled her in the well-known West Coast women's college, Mills, in Oakland, California. As he was friends with Darius Milhaud, who happened to teach composition there during the school season, arrangements were made for Beate to live with the Milhaud family. Sirota was also planning to immigrate to America following completion of the school year 1941-42. While bringing his daughter to California, he brought some household goods in preparation for their eventual immigration. In September, after delivering their daughter to Oakland and preparing to leave SFO for Tokyo, Mme. Sirota (Gisa) implored her husband (on bended knee she claims) not to return to Tokyo but he answered that he must complete his contract. Of course, by December we were at war with Japan. With a daughter already in America and the Sirotas also being on the 1941 immigration quota list, they were summarily interned (house arrest) for the duration of the war.

The Sirotas managed to survive: former students smuggled things to them including window panes to repair broken windows keeping them from freezing to death.

The war over, the Sirotas were some of the first people allowed to come to America. Japan's loss (sic) was our gain. Having musician friends in New York, they stayed there while he prepared for a Carnegie Hall debut. That took place with considerable success in the Spring of 1947, but that is too late in the season for engagements to be booked for the following year. Consequently , when the opportunity arose for his becoming artist-in-residence at a "piano school" in St. Louis, he took that position...one small step for Sirota...one gigantic step for St. Louis...and for me. In my study with Leo Sirota, I entered the real world of pianism. Despite my modest talent, I entered the world of Chopin, of Liszt and Schumann; even some of the great transcriptions of Busoni. When Sirota performed I was spellbound, having never heard such virtuosity in spite of the many piano recitalists I'd heard in New York. This was "Russian Pianisim". Rosina Lhevinne was teaching this to her students, including Van Cliburn, but they had yet to be heard in America. This was also the kind of pianism of Vladimir Horowitz, who at that time was in one of his several hiatuses. My meager ability tried to "catch up" to this brand new (for me) kind of piano playing. It took eight hours a day at the practice piano, besides attending regular conservatory classes, in order to play catch up. But that is what an inspiring teacher can do for you: make you want to work.

I played my first concertos while Sirota played the orchestra part on the second piano: Beethoven's 4th and 5th . Liszt's No. 2 in A major was my graduation piece two years later. The first piece Sirota gave me to learn was Beethoven's 32 Variations, a piece seldom played, but very worthwhile playing as well as listening to. I heard it for the first time in many years over the radio just recently and it was magnificent. That first year, along with Chopin Etudes, Schumann, etc., the signature piece for the year was Liszt's *Funerailles*, a work that Sirota would later say that with it, he "pushed me through the door of music." I remember his pushing me, literally, on the back when it was time to play the big chords while he simultaneously grunted.

The second year saw me learning the Bach-Busoni Chaconne, Beethoven's Opus 110, Chopin Ballade #4 in F minor as well as the Fantasie in F minor, both considered the masterpieces of that composer's work. Sirota would say: "If I can teach you how to play these, you will know how to play the others!" Yes.

At the end of the first school year in St. Louis, Mme. Sirota prepared a meal for a handful of Sirota's best students. In spite of the occasional opulence I had witnessed on Staten Island, nothing prepared me for the European touch experienced that night. This was 1948, not that long following WWII. People weren't overflowing with money or wine. She had a couple of bottles of white wine, but for an aperitif, she placed a little grenadine in the wine to give it a different look. She had been able to bring out a barrel of china prior to the war in anticipation of their immigration. There were beautiful Japanese platters upon which she placed the various courses. The first was Piroshki which are little meat-filled pastries. Then came a sliced meatloaf already cut into servings and surrounded by a julienne of kale and red cabbage creating a very decorative look. I never had before observed food "presented", so to speak, as a spectacle in and of itself. I cannot recall the rest of the meal, but that presentation remains always in my memory.

Mme. Sirota, a musician in her own right, was Augestine Horenstein, sister to the well-known conductor, Jascha Horenstein. As I chauffeured them often to the St. Louis symphony performances, I was privileged to eat with them more often than did other students. Being Viennese, she often prepared Wiener Schnitzel for a quick at-home meal. She knew how to buy the right piece of veal, to properly bread it and to quickly pan-fry it in butter. She always said: "Eat only butter; margarine is no good for you" (that said 50 years ago!). Note to hosts: Put out the best china, decorate the plates, color the wine (if necessary), make a feast to the eye as well as to the stomach.

I asked what Sirota ate on recital day in Japan (over a ten year period he gave 350 recitals or concerto appearances throughout Asia, but mostly in Japan). She said the refrigerator was stocked with everything so that Leo need only say what he wanted to eat and it was instantly prepared. His favorite luncheon was caviar.

Sirota took driving lessons, but for the symphony concerts I served as chauffeur. During the drive to downtown St. Louis and before entering any important highways, it was necessary to traverse various cross streets within the town of Clayton. Sirota had pre-determined which of these frequent stop streets were to be adhered to. Riding shot-gun as we proceeded along the way, he'd say to me in his accented English: "SHTOP!"; "DON'T SHTOP!" depending on his interpretation of how important the intersection was.

The symphony season was about 20 concerts long and brought many soloists to St. Louis. The most memorable for me was a performance by William Kapell. He made a very spectacular debut with the New York Philharmonic performing the American premiere of the flashy Khachaturian piano concerto. The critics all said it was very displayful, "but can he play anything else?" When he came to St. Louis he certainly proved he could play something else. In the provinces, artists frequently performed encores in those days. Following the playing of the concerto, Kapell performed a huge piece, presumably to prove he could "play something else." It was a Liszt transcription of a Bach Organ Toccatta and Fugue, one of the faithful-to-the-composer transcriptions Liszt could do and not a paraphrase as were his operatic transcriptions. It was a true rendering of the composition from organ to the piano and a major work to perform as an encore, requiring at least fifteen minutes to play. His performance was enthralling; so precise, so monumental, so moving. I was trans-fixed. Afterwards some fellow students said I played like Kapell. That was a bit of a stretch but it was nice of them to say so. A story that got back to me, however, was that they enjoyed the results of my labors, but that they would never work as hard as I in order to achieve those results.

Soon after, William Kapell died in a plane crash while returning from a concert tour in Mexico. It was a great musical loss for America, for Kapell was truly America's first home-grown concert pianist. He can still be heard on a Columbia disc "William Kapell Remembered".

The Institute did not provide housing. Instead, an enterprising couple (the woman mostly) ran two boarding houses, one for girls directly across from the school and the other for boys down the street a couple of blocks. Meals were taken by both boys and girls collec-

tively at the girls "dorm". There were about 25 students there (a freshman girls dorm was elsewhere in downtown St. Louis). Table conversation frequently centered on music. A few returning GIs had already
arrived back from the war and were using their GI Bill to continue
their education. I was slightly younger than they and a little intimat-
ed by their maturity. One day the oldest of the bunch pronounced:
"Beethoven is nothing but scales and arpeggios!" He knew I had
already performed Beethoven's 4th Concerto. I was speechless...then.
Since becoming a teacher of Music Appreciation these many years, I
often used as example what should have been my retort: "Yes,
Beethoven uses a lot of scales and arpeggios but watch where they
go!" The term "architectonic", a term invented by Beethoven biographer R.H. Schauffler to describe Beethoven's music, indicates that the
"architecture" of sound is where Beethoven's genius lay. It is the edifice of sound he builds which is its strength.

Following my graduation from the Institute, I no longer lived in
the boarding house, leaving behind the philosophical discussions
with fellow students. I found a third floor attic room in the old
Northeast side of St. Louis on Dodier Street which I pronounced in
the French manner—having never heard any of my blue-collar
neighbors pronounce it. The location was near a local brewery, one
not yet gobbled up by Budweiser (who, incidentally, was located in a
huge plant on the west side of St. Louis.) The vapors emanating from
a brewery are pungently sweet. A seedy park adjacent to the brewery
was graced by a bust of Beethoven. Undoubtedly the original inhabi-
tants of the neighborhood were German accounting for both the
brewery and Beethoven. Not having classes to attend and not receiving the personal guidance of Sirota, my eight hour practice schedule
diminished to two or three. One day in the Spring I took an extended
walk into downtown St. Louis, several miles at least. Wending my way
back at sunset time, I stumbled upon a little Greek cafe. In its window
was an old-fashioned gas-burning rotisserie filled with a whole lamb
slowly rotating against the flames. I couldn't resist the look of it (I'm a
sucker for Greek food) and went in and ordered the meal of the day.
It was a Saturday evening, the day before Greek Orthodox Easter, and
the special meal was in honor of that event. I had never tasted before
whole stalks of celery and carrots cooked along side the lamb on the
rotisserie. Nowadays the great vogue is to grill vegetables, but it was
in a Greek restaurant many years ago that I first tasted them.

After earning my Bachelor of Music degree and subsequent graduation, I gave a few piano lessons to a handful of adult students including Bill Bernoudy, the trendy Frank Lloyd Wright alumnus who was building exciting things in the suburbs of St. Louis, such as a party pavilion for Joe Pulitzer, Jr. west of Clayton. One of the society students he introduced me to was a young lady whose household still kept a butler, etc. When I appeared for the lesson and rang the door bell at the front entrance (at least not at the servants entrance as in the days of Haydn and Mozart) the butler (in a white coat) would open it and announce: "The musician is here". After a few times of this ceremony, the young lady , when I was announced, finally retorted: "He's not the musician ; he's the piano teacher!" I actually enjoyed being announced as the musician, and was disappointed when it stopped. But the lessons soon stopped anyway. Society ladies only think they want to play the piano. They don't want to work at it.

In a sense I was vegetating. Sirota heard of a newly organized scheme that William Fulbright, Senator from Arkansas, had thought up. He experienced, as a graduate student, the benefits of foreign study by being a Rhodes scholar. He proposed that in order to use up funds that were owed the United States under the wartime's Lend-Lease program, that a scholarship program be developed where host countries could "pay-off" their loans without having to use dollars to do so by hosting and paying a stipend to American students studying under scholarships in their countries. I had never heard of it, but Sirota had and encouraged me to apply, securing for me the necessary recommendations, etc. A performance tape was required from music students, so I recorded the Bach-Busoni Chaconne. My entry was post-marked midnight on the final day applications were accepted. Nevertheless I won a Fulbright Scholarship!

There was a long period of waiting to hear whether one had received a placement, (my application was for study in France). That is why, in my restless state, long walks into St. Louis from Dodier street and discovering little Greek restaurants occupied my time. But marvelously, the good news that I had won a scholarship was finally received and Dodier Street became 'Do-De-ay' for sure.

Leo Sirota
Artist Teacher
Internationally Known Pianist
Faculty, *St. Louis Institute of Music*
Teacher of William J. Bryan from 1947-50

Dr. Leo Sirota, Pianist
March 1948, *The Southwestern Musician*

William J. Bryan about the same time
he studied with Leo Sirota

Trunk Label to France

Brendan Robinson

Passport of
William J. Bryan,
return from France

The Pied Piper 1953

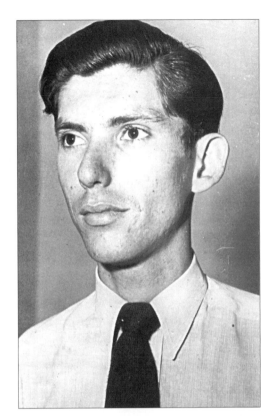

Nationwide Response

IN PUBLIC MEETINGS, LETTERS, TREATISES, EVEN POEMS

To National Purpose

AMERICANS EARNESTLY TAKE UP THE CRUCIAL DEBATE

LIFE

TIME & LIFE BUILDING
ROCKEFELLER CENTER
NEW YORK 20

This report summing up the reaction to LIFE's series was prepared by a group of staff members headed by Associate Editor Edward Kern.

The editors very much appreciate all your

assistance in LIFE's behalf, and thought you would

be especially interested in this issue.

Jean Bargos

Jean Bargos
For the Editors

JULY 11, 1960
CIRCULATION: 6,700,000

"Little" people - individuals - seem consc
ɡ caught up in the jaws of destiny and are
lized to act as a babe in a dinosaurs mouth
ɔses don't mean anything, if they can't mak
ɪe fury of   livi
ɪanity's s   .ife
order out

William J. Bryan, a student at the University of Southern California, thinks the problems of the world are just too big and confusing for individualism to cope with: "Little people—individuals—seem conscious of being caught up in the jaws of destiny and are as paralyzed as a babe in a dinosaur's mouth. If our purposes don't mean anything, if they can't make a sound in the fury of government, then the individual must, for sanity's sake, retreat to his 'private life' to make some order out of his existence. What is there left to do?"

WILLIAM BRYAN
Student

Excerpts from LIFE magazine, July 11, 1960 while living on
Kilkea and Melrose Avenue, Los Angeles, California

*I am the Poet of the body
and I am the Poet of the soul . . .*

Photo of Gerald "Rishi" Heard by William J. Bryan and as portrayed in
"WALT WHITMAN TODAY" with poetry by Walt Whitman

Paul Mayo and WJB in publicity photo for their recitals

OPUS FIVE

*T*raveling to France on the S.S. America was the first time abroad for me, and the first time on the ocean—first time for a lot of things! Crossings were still done by classes and we were definitely 3rd class or what they euphemistically called "Tourist Class." What it meant was that four persons were put up together per cabin, two double bunks and a couple of closets and sinks completed the floor-plan. One went down the hall to use the toilet and had to make an appointment for a shower! Our roommates were two Mississippians, one an already published novelist (Thomas Hal Phillips) and the other, a droll, Faulkneresque type of character (Charles Geyser) full of Southern stories who was a history major but should have been a writer. Once in Paris we would occasionally meet for dinner during the first month there because everyone stayed in Paris for a crash-course in the French language. After the first month both our Mississippi friends departed for other parts of France. Only the music students got to stay in Paris! Charles loved calling the waiters "garks", his shortened version of *garcon*, which, at that time, one still called French waiters. Whether they still call waiters in France "boy" anymore, I don't know, but I rather think not.

As we were landing in Cherbourg and preparing to disembark, I took one final look into our cabin mirror and muttered: "I'll never get past the gendarmes!" which amused my author cabin-mate immensely. He said he had to use the remark in his next novel. To my knowledge that never happened....so I'm telling it to you now!

PARIS! "the last time I saw..." was not then; I've been back several times since. But staying there for nearly a year under very *La Boheme* circumstances is a unique experience and not one obtained by tourist travel.

Following our auditions, I was admitted for piano study at the Conservatoire National de Paris (the Paris Conservatory) to take lessons from Lazare Levy, a legendary, quaint, white-haired little gentleman who, in addition to his own accomplishments as a concert pianist, had the distinction of being the teacher of the English sensation: Solomon, a pianist of phenomenal technic for 18th Century piano literature—faster, clearer, than anyone had ever heard before! Lazare Levy's other claim to fame was producing an exhaustive edition of the Czerny "exercises"; he must have taught all of them (several volumes) to Solomon in order for his prodigy to acquire such a fantastic technique.

For me, a Romantic neophyte from America, Levy placed me on a strict diet of Beethoven Sonatas save for the excruciatingly difficult Toccatta of Schumann, which is an absolute ball-buster for the hands. The one piece of French music I learned was Ravel's *SONATINE* which was a requirement by the Conservatoire for the Spring exam (concur). In addition, a Chopin Etude was required, one in the fall and one in the Spring, along with a movement from a Beethoven Sonata, all to be learned within a four to six week time-frame. No one knew what the pieces were to be until announced by the Conservatoire.

Paris, since it's a filled-in swamp, can be bitterly cold due to not only the temperature but the damp humidity. Before moving to the suburb of La Garenne following the month of language study in Paris, we stayed in a minus-any-star hotel near the Sorbonne, and around the corner from the Parthenon. We were renting by the week, but many of the rooms were used by "ladies of the night". Our male chamber-maid used to grumble everyday about "Whore-frost on the sheets!", as he called it, as he made his daily rounds. On the corner was a typical Paris cafe-bar. On more than one miserable penetratingly cold night we would stop in for a hot buttered rum, spritzed by the same espresso machine used for morning coffee. Nothing tasted better or was more warming than a hot buttered rum on a cold, wintry night in Paris.

Around another corner from the bar was a garishly painted Russian restaurant. There were three rooms all painted vividly from ceiling to the floors in wildly primitivo paintings, mostly in vermillions, rendered in a sort of Chagal-like manner, and reminiscent of his floating figures. In fact Chagal had just recently finished painting the ceiling of the Paris Opera and had possibly been the inspiration for the restaurant. Anyway, expatriate Russians all knew each other...Paris was their favorite city away from Mother Russia.

The food was delicious: Beef Stroganoff, Coq au Vin. In fact each of the three rooms had a different motif and one room featured large Coq's everywhere. A large, grandly dressed Madame sat on a sort of throne-dias by the kitchen door and inspected everything that came out. She was probably keeping track of the items for the bill because she produced those, also, by the time one requested: "l'addition, s'il vous plait". All the while a cat perched upon her shoulder looking like a fox muff.

Brendan accompanied me to Paris and was using his GI Bill to continue his study of music in France, (he had studied the past year at St. Louis with Sirota and had occasionally kept me company during the dreary year following my graduation). Following that first month in Paris, we moved from the Left Bank out to the suburb of La Garenne and no longer had the cute, little cheap eating places to go to as before. So we began to cook at home. "At home" was a closed-in garage containing no running water or hardly any other conveniences. It was owned by Madame Suzanne Zolla, a former *Opera Comique* singer who had placed a hand-notice on the bulletin board at the Conservatorie advertising her "converted" garage for rent to music students, only. During the war she had been reduced to bicycling to a factory for employment, which she was still doing even in 1950. Our cooking was done over two small alcohol-fueled burners. We learned to eat in courses because it was only possible to prepare one thing at a time. If we boiled potatoes, we always made a little extra to use the next day as a cold first course served with a little vinegar and oil and a wedge of tomato. The best red meat one could obtain at that time came from the Cheval whose shop was characterized by an iron cut-out of a horse hanging above its door. No other indication was needed for what was inside. However, at that point in time the best red meat was horse meat. I haven't had any since, nor would I eat any if it were offered today.

Another "Old World" novelty was the once a week (hopefully) trip to the public bath house. In Winter, especially, it was the warmest place in town. Once in a while we'd borrow the big, flat tub from the land-lady and pour warm water over each other. Remember, any warm water would have had to be made over two little alcohol burners. Hot water was better used to make coffee. I bought a French hand-cranked coffee grinder and several sets of the aluminum coffee filters than are used for making one cup at a time.

The Marquis de Cuevas had given up on America following the demise of his Ballets International and moved to Paris where he started a new company centered on his prima dona and his premier danseur: Rosella Hightower and George Skibine. Jean Babelais also danced for the company before forming his own experimental modern-ballet company. A great crowd pleaser was watching Hightower and Skibine perform the grande pas de deux from "The Nutcracker", complete with spectacular "fish-dives". It always brought the house down. My life-long friend, Roy Tobias, recently retired from his duties as Artistic Director and resident choreographer for the Universal Ballet, Seoul, Korea, writes regarding the famous fish dives: "Your description of the pas de deux sounds more like "Sleeping Beauty", dynamic and fish dives, more than "Nutcracker". A fish dive is a pose achieved after the ballerina, while spinning, is taken around the waist with her partner's left arm alone; lifted slightly from the floor, the force of the turn propels her into a position where head is perilously close to the floor while at the same time her legs are in the air, her feet close to her partner's left ear. The success of the pas depends on the rapidity of the multiple turns into the sudden fall and the ending static pose. It is not the original choreography, thus unknown in Russia, but was invented by Pierre Vladimiroff (School of American Ballet) and Nemchinova, probably the result of a mistake when Pierre saved Vera from an ill executed pirouette by lifting her off her leg. Diaghilev, standing by, was delighted and said: 'Keep it in, you guys', or words to that effect., for the famous 'Sleeping Beauty' in London, 1921 (?)" However, it could just have well been inserted into the grande pas de deux of "Nutcracker" since I'm quite sure I remember which piece of Tchaikowsky was being played.The performances took place in a re-done movie theater near the Arch de Triumphe transformed into a performance hall.

One evening I saw Jean Marais conversing with his young American ex-dancer friend during intermission on the staircase of the theater. The most recent film of Jean Cocteau,"Orphee", had only recently premiered the grand opening of a new movie palace on the Champs Elysees. Cocteau's films were all masterworks of invention, but the one still acclaimed for its special effects (even by Hollywood today) is *La Belle et la Bete* which was the film that first made Jean Marais a star. The story of his having to daily put on the beast's make-up was remarkable for the sheer unpleasantness that cinema artists must sometime endure.

In a magazine feature on George Skibine, he talked of his private life in Paris and his fondness for cooking and gave his recipe for Beef Stroganoff which I found very intriguing. I was determined to learn to make it when I got back to a real stove: (can't cook Stroganoff over an alcohol burner!). This recipe became my chief guest meal until I discovered moussaka, Beef Bourguignon and my own turkey-leg recipe. Stroganoff is easy except for all the chopping and sauteing that is required. According to Skibine, Colonel Stroganoff insisted that it be served only with home-fried potatoes, which is another time-consuming activity. Serving it with rice is the easy way out, but save the rice for a turkey or chicken dish.

BEEF STROGANOFF

two pounds of sirloin steak
2 large onions
l lb. of fresh mushrooms
l pint Sour cream
2 tbs. herb Province or a mixture of oregano
thyme and marjoram may be substituted
1 cup of beef bouillon

Chop onions and saute in heavy skillet until glassy, remove onions into holding dish and after slicing mushrooms, saute as well and set aside with onions in holding dish. Cut steak into one inch squares and brown well in the skillet. Add herbs, onions, and mushrooms, and half of the bouillon (use the rest as needed if mixture needs more liquid while cooking) stir and cook over low heat with a tight lid for about an hour. Meanwhile, peel and slice potatoes and brown in cooking oil (canola or olive)in another skillet, timing them to be done just as the Stroganoff is ready. Fold in sour cream to the mixture and serve with a green vegetable and salad.Red wine goes best with Stroganoff.

When Brendan and I would have a fight, which was frequent, I'd go off to Paris without him and spend the day alone wandering about and usually ending up at the Cite where the dormitories for the Sorbonne and the University of Paris were domiciled—many miles from their respective campuses of learning and, in fact, they had more of a college atmosphere. There was a huge student cafeteria where you went through the line picking up the various "courses" that suited you: soup (I peered into the kitchen once and was over-whelmed by the size of the kettle which was made of copper and sat on its own cooking dias all by itself), whatever meat and vegetables were being served (all pretty bland for French cooking), and con-cluding with a desert course of plain yogurt to which you added the confiture of your choice. All this, along with a quarter carafe of wine, came to about 75 cents, about 3 francs at that time.

After a day of sulking, I'd end up at the concert which Brendan and I had planned for that night and there he'd be outside the hall full of remorse for whatever altercation had ensued. Following the concert we invariably headed for one of the corner *Brassieres* that served sup-pers very late. Since concerts didn't begin before 9 p.m. and didn't finish until at least 11:30, we were always hungry. A French speciality for midnight suppers is cold sliced rare roast beef served with Dijon Mustard (but of course!), a little salad of rolled leaves of "bib" lettuce in vinegar and oil and concluding with a hot fudge sundae topped with *creme fraiche* which, unlike American whipped cream, has a slightly "turned" quality as in plain yogurt, but very delicious. I've haven't truly enjoyed an American Hot Fudge sundae since.

In the Spring, the *glace* shops became very active. Often we'd stop by one of these in the late afternoon and order up pistachio, or something exotic like that, and it was always served with tiny glasses of ice water—the only time water is automatically served in a French eating establishment. Brendan would always order "cafe filtre san sucre" to the astonishment of the server, for in France one never mixes hot and cold items simultaneously. I was usually satisfied to sip my ice water neat.

The film *Les Enfants du Paradis* had made Jean Louis Barrault famous. I was always impressed by the film as well as the meaning of it's title. "The Children of Paradise" are artists and students who can only afford the cheapest seats high up in the belfry of a theater and the film is about these *enfants* who are the true audience —understanders—of the proceedings on stage. Some few years later I opened a coffee house in Santa Monica Canyon, California, and called it by that title.I rented a small grand piano upon which I performed nightly, had interesting paintings on the wall, etc, and served ice cream and coffee!

Jean Louis Barrault had a theater right along the greenbelt besides the Champs-Elysees where he performed regularly in a season of plays. We went (Brendan was fluent in French; I wasn't). But I enjoyed the sound of the language and even dreamed in French by the end of a few months in Paris. Being taken up by the sounds rather than the meaning, I was enormously struck by the theatrics of the way J.L.B. began his plays: the house lights would dim and then three great thrusts of what must have been a sledge-hammer (more muffled as if you had used a tree trunk) plunked against the wooden stage floor. It certainly got your attention and an immediate hush would fall over the audience. At the fin de siecle of our age, over-wrought with "technical effects", such simple means are very dramatic.

Speaking of the French language and dramatics, no one was better at it than Jean Cocteau himself. He, besides being inherently poetic, relished in the sound of his native tongue, especially in the staccato effects possible. Listen to his declamations as he narrates his libretto for Stravinsky's *Oedipus Rex*. His sound is as exciting as the music itself. Jean Marais learned how to speak and act from his mentor and every film he appeared in bears the imprint of Cocteau's tutelage.

Edith Piaff and Cocteau died on the same day. Both obituary notices were on the front page of the New York Times. Cocteau was not bed-ridden or anything like that, just feeling aged, I guess, and was staying at his county house outside Paris. When the news that the legendary "Edit" had died was phoned to his residence in the early morning, caregivers decided to keep the news from him until about noon-time at which time they told him, whereupon he said: "the curtain descends". Reclining on the couch, he thence-forth died! If only all our passings could be so easy, and perhaps as simplistically dramatic. My brother John, who was a Medical doctor, certified Internist, always said that there is only a thin wire between life and death. I say that we dance on this "wire" for our length of time....

Maggie Tate had been the favorite interpreter of songs by both Debussy and Ravel even though she was English. She had a superb, flexible voice and, obviously, an impeccable French accent. Her recordings of both of those composer's songs, with Alfred Cortot at the piano, are still the definitive interpretations. Another singer of distinction was Madeleine Gray who gained American fame via a performance with the New York Philharmonic of the Canteloube settings of the "Songs of the Auvergne". Those performances—and an immediate recording release—made an absolute sensation in New York very soon following the conclusion of WWII.

By 1951 when I was in Paris, she was getting old but nevertheless gave a recital at least once a year.We would get and religiously read each week, Semaine de Paris, in order to pick out what concerts we were going to attend. Often there were matinees and late afternoon concerts prior to dinner. Concert times were always listed in military time: the full 24 hour count. For some reason we thought her concert was to be at 3:30 or 4 p.m. when in fact it was at 2:30 or "14:30" p.m. My G.I. buddy Brendan should have picked up on that but, alas, our sacred pilgrimage to hear the legendary Madeleine was fruitless— only an empty hall remained by the time we arrived.

The three famous German pianists—Edwin Fischer, Wilhelm Bachaus and Walter Gieseking—each gave three piano recitals during the concert season in Paris. The first was a mandatory all-Beethoven recital usually consisting of just sonatas. Wilhelm Bachaus played Beethoven for all three of his recitals, which were generally given by each artist a few days apart. Walter Gieseking, whose French music recordings are very famous, did play in his third concert some of these works. For the most part, the German repertory was what was played, with a little Chopin thrown in.

I saw the legendary Alfred Cortot, as an elderly gentleman, present a master class, but he did not play. There is an amusing story regarding Cortot: the famous violinist and composer Georges Enesco had a rich student whose father rented Salle Gaveau for a recital by his son and paid Enesco to accompany on the piano. On stage, Enesco realized he needed someone to turn pages and, seeing his friend Cortot in the audience, asked if he would oblige. A droll critic in the next day's paper wrote: "The accompanist should have played the violin, the page turner should have played the piano and the violinist should have turned pages!" Ah, *vive la France!*

OPUS SIX

What does one do following a year of study as a Fulbright scholar in France? I posed this question midway through the year to my novelist friend Hal who was more experienced with academia than I was and he said: "Apply for a teaching fellowship back in the States." So I investigated the various universities that offered music possibilities, and sent about eighteen letters from France. I received about three positive offers and had either the fortune or misfortune of selecting the University of Colorado in Boulder for two reasons. First, I knew a former St. Louis Institute student who had married a previous Institute student who was now teaching piano at Boulder.I also thought that knowing someone in such a "far-off" place (being Florida born) would be helpful. Second, the head of the piano department, with whom I would study, was Storm Bull, grand nephew of the 19th century legendary Norwegian violinist, Ole Bull. Storm had studied with Bela Bartok and seemed very solicitous of my coming to Boulder. So I went to Boulder, Colorado in the fall of 1951.

Unfortunately, after having studied with Leo Sirota and Lazare Levy, Storm Bull only managed to live up to his first name!: (one of his practice recommendations was to place a book to read on the music rack while practicing scales and exercises—and God knows— maybe even pieces of music!). The less that can be said about my musical experiences in Boulder the better. The only fun relationship from those two years was being a regular Sunday evening companion to Cornelius Van Vliet, cello instructor and alumnus of the New York Philharmonic under Toscanini and a former First Chair Cellist for the Minneapolis Symphony before "retiring" to the University of Colorado. He was a widower living alone up near the "Flatirons", famous totem of the Colorado "Buffaloes". On Saturdays he would migrate to Denver in his old square box of a Dodge to purchase either a whole rabbit or chicken, salad, vegetables, etc and Cresta Blanca white wine—about the only wine (besides Virginia Dare) one could buy nationally in the 50's at a supermarket. Mid-afternoon on Sundays I would appear to "cook it" under his guidance. I had never cooked whole chickens or rabbits until that time. He liked the chicken lightly stuffed with celery and onion, etc., and roasted while the rabbit was to be broiled, but neither one to be overcooked. Indeed, unlike today's admonitions, he preferred both to be done "rare" (it was delicious and neither one of us ever got sick!). The evening meal began, after I started the food cooking, with an aperitif of Dubonet mixed with vodka. One or two of those, and dinner followed along with a whole bottle of Cresta Blanca Chenin Blanc (fortunately not too sweet: one couldn't buy anything drier in those days). Following dinner we retired back into the living room where Cornelius would consume a beer or two and smoke a cigar. I tried to stay sober for the walk back home to the boarding house where (again) I was domiciled.

Yes, the "boarding house". It was a block from the University of Colorado campus entrance and had about six or eight rooms rented out to male students. I stumbled upon it by chance and offered to clean the rooms of the other students, change sheets, vacuum, etc. for my room and board which the "landlady" accepted. As an "artist", I've endured my Bohemian experiences. One of the students had extremely foul smelling feet and when it was time to "do" his room, change the sheets, etc., it was almost too much to bear. Having only a scholarship to cover tuition, it was necessary for me to earn my keep somehow. And this is how I did it. I had told my father some years before, that if he would see me through music school, I'd earn my living by music somehow: teaching a few students in St. Louis following graduation, then the Fulbright Scholarship which gave me a stipend and travel, now Colorado with a teaching fellowship and room and board by cleaning rooms...and waiting tables for the boarders. The landlady had several "successful" friends, one who was a marvelous entertainer-singer at the piano who regularly performed at a club in Denver, but during the summer, at the "Bloody Face on the Floor" saloon in Central City, Colorado. The opera house was just starting it's revival and tourism was beginning to take shape. One couldn't buy anything there today without being someone like Bill Gates. The landlady ran a restaurant there during the summer where her young chef could sear a steak on a metal slab as good as a grilled steak in his estimation. Occasionally he would come by Boulder and grill steaks for us students, usually venison, on his "metal slab":(an institutional flammed "grill" which all restaurants use for cooking meat.) He always claimed it was as good as grilled over charcoal. I don't believe it, but in those days I was hungry and it tasted fine to me.

I had my first true Boeuf Bourguignon in Boulder. There's a marvelous restaurant up in the hills above the old Chautaqua site and along side the famous flatirons. It's still there, I'm told: Hilltop Restaurant, and it's run by a Swiss couple who migrated to Colorado because it reminded them of home. They would fix bourguignon if you ordered it a day ahead, because the meat needs to marinate, of course, in Burgundy wine or any decent red wine, along with garlic and French mustard. They used a very good grade of beef cut into fairly large chunks. Being more frugal, I use a tip roast or bottom round cut of beef , cut into one and a half to two inch chunks and marinated for at least two days. I learned my recipe from an Alsatian chef who had a very good restaurant in Borrego Springs, California named for himself: Bernard's.

BEEF BOURGUIGNON

2-3 pounds of tri-tip roast or bottom round
2 carrots
2 celery stalks
1 large onion
3 cloves garlic
2 tablespoons of butter
2 tablespoons of flour
2 tablespoons of Herb Provencal
Marinade: one cup of red wine, dash of soy sauce,
tablespoon of Dijon mustard all well stirred.

Prepare meat by trimming off all fat and cut into one and a half or two inch squares. Place in heavy crock (with lid) and pour over the marinade as well as the chopped garlic cloves. Place in refrigerator for two days. With the three vegetables you will create a julienne. Chop onions and place in separate frying pan from that to be used for the meat. Make glassy over moderate heat, chop carrots and celery and add to onions (one wants to mingle the flavor of the onion with the other vegetables; that is the secret of a julienne.) Add another clove of garlic or two, finely chopped, to the julienne, reduce heat and cover, adding a little balsamic vinegar to create steam. Drain meat and brown in an iron skillet, lightly oiled, over high heat. Set browned meat aside. Melt butter in meat skillet and dredge in flour to make a roux. When pasty, add marinade slowly while stirring it in the roux . Place meat back into crock, one layer at a time, sprinkling each layer of meat with herbs and cover with julienne. Do this after each layer, depending on the size of crock. Pour roux over the contents and add more red wine to cover (as needed). Poke through along side the meat to ensure the roux has saturated everywhere. Bake in oven starting at 350 degrees and after one half hour reduce to 325 and cook for two and half more hours. Serve with baked or boiled potatoes, salad and more red wine! (Baking potatoes may be added into same oven an hour and a half before finish time).

One of the boarders at the house in Boulder was a law student majoring in water rights—a big topic in the West. He knew something about the then emerging Aspen colony as a Mr. Pepicke from Chicago had recently bought the Jerome Hotel and helped host the 150th celebration for Goethe bringing artists from all over the world including Artur Rubinstein. From that auspicious debut, the Aspen Festival was conceived as an ongoing summer conclave of primarily musical endeavors, although a few enlightening lectures were included in the format. Of course, Aspen has become a paramount encampment for the nurturing of young music talent as well as being a high-end ski resort in the winter. Prominent professional musicians from various orchestras of the world sit as "first chairs" while students fill the rest of the seats. The proximity to professionals for these students is a great inspiration for the future orchestral players of the world. Just as all this was in its early stages, my lawyer friend introduced me to Aspen during the Thanksgiving break. I was eager to find a place where I could still perform, but also provide an outlet for all the great student talent that was present all summer long.

Off into the snowy regions we went and ended up staying at the Jerome, maybe for as little as $5.00 a night! The original board sidewalks were still in use and most of the buildings were derelict. There was one modern edifice on the west side of the "park" and it was for sale (as was most everything in those days!) It contained a semi-circular bar with restaurant and kitchen which was perfect for what I envisioned. Above were six rental units, one of which could become my future home. It was built, I'd say, only ten years before and seemed well constructed of cement blocks. The asking price was $32,000. Granted, a bit of change in 1951-2 but not astronomical. I could foresee the piano, the restaurant, students performing during the summer, ski-guitarists during the winter...the whole ball of wax.

My millionaire Uncle Joe was in charge of investments for the Jefferson Standard Life Insurance Company located in Greensboro, North Carolina. I sent him photos of the building, the prospect of what I wanted to do, etc., hoping that his company would make a

loan on the property. When no word came back from him after a reasonable length of time, I called "long distance" (kind of special in
those days) which brought him out of a meeting. He told me that
"Jefferson Standard didn't invest that far west", only to find out later
that they invested as far West as San Francisco. End of dream. Of
course, Aspen today is (and has been for many, many years) an
investor's paradise! Oddly, no one has done what I envisioned as an
ongoing showcase for up and coming talent. I've been back to attend
the festival at least three times over the past few years. There are no
longer any board side-walks, but "my building" is still there essentially as it was when I could have bought it.Whom ever owns it now
has added a high-rise lodging building behind the original, and I'm
sure the entire project is worth millions—if you could buy it! (Rich
relatives, Ugh! I wasn't looking for a hand-out, but for a legitimate
business loan.Of course, if I had been more experienced, I would
have sought a loan elsewhere...but I still had Storm to put up with!)

One of the current, hottest international violinists is Joshua Bell
(sound-track for THE RED VIOLIN) who was in one of those "training" orchestras at Aspen as a student and very likely would have performed at "my" cafe. And countless others exist. Joshua performed
for my adult class in Palo Alto some years later and is a friend of my
traveling companion, Robert Wood, whom you'll meet later.I never
confronted my uncle regarding the immense success of Aspen. He
was rich, but not in imagination—nor in kindness to kin.

My "relationship" with Storm Bull was so unsatisfactory that I
invented ways of intriguing myself musically. One way was as pianist
for the local ballet school. We made several performances, even traveling as far as Colorado Springs to present our spectacle. Brendan
had joined me in Colorado and began composing some interesting
music to which the dance instructor choreographed a ballet—and I
played the piano score.

One Sunday while wandering around the streets of Denver, following discussions about opening an arts academy within Denver by
our troupe, I happened to pass the Children's Art Museum which was
a division of the Denver Museum but housed in a former department
store. All the former store windows had been transformed into settings of the various objects that the museum contained: dolls, toys, a
toy piano, little drums, etc. I was fascinated by the displays and
immediately began imagining piano pieces to go with the objects.

As part of the teacher-training at St Louis, we were instructed in the Progressive Series of Piano Education that the Institute was, in fact, a training institution for the publisher of the Series. These editions were from the very beginning of piano training all the way to the major compositions of Chopin and Schumann, the latter being specially edited by Leopold Godowsky, the original editor-in-chief for the Progressive Series of Music. But for beginners, special compositions had been commissioned to be composed with titles like "Dance of the Grasshopper", "Toy Piano" and the like. As I was acquainted with these pieces, I began to associate them with the objects in the Children's museum. I also thought back to my childhood to think of a favorite story, and of course, the WALL from my elementary school days came to mind with its depiction of the Pied Piper leading the children away from the city and into an enchanted new world. With movements from Schumann's "Kinderscenen" and his "Carnival" and "Papillions", I sketched out a rendering of the Pied Piper story interspersed with piano interludes to dramatize the story-line. I also decided to call myself THE PIED PIPER PIANIST.

After feverishly putting the ideas together, I went back to the Denver museum, walked right in and made my proposal: a piano program built around the objects they already had in their museum, (at no fee from me). I wanted the experience of doing it, not quite knowing where it might eventually go, but just wanting to do it. They said "yes", and a date was set for about six weeks later. Naturally, that gave direction to my piano practice, again, and it didn't have anything to do with the university!

Someone made a swallow-tail coat from green corduroy, beneath which I wore a checkered vest. This costume was completed by a fantastic peaked green straw hat. I was the Pied Piper, all right, and the program began with my sitting at the tiny toy piano and playing "The Toy Piano." The program was a success. More importantly, it finally gave a direction to what I was going to do with my piano training and might indicate a way to earn a living.

J went home to Florida for the Easter break planning to present an evening adult concert, but it was to be publicized through free Pied Piper performances at several of the elementary schools. So that was the beginning of presenting the Pied Piper in a school assembly. My father had been very active in the local chapter of the Optimist Club and through his contacts, I appeared as the PPP at the Optimist International Convention that summer in Washington, D.C.I performed Chopin's Polonaise in A flat for the entire convention which is a daunting task without "warm up" pieces played in advance. The next day I performed a Chopin Waltz (also in A flat) before a ladies luncheon which included the Vice President's wife, Pat Nixon. The intention was to promote the idea that Optimist clubs could present me in their various schools as a contribution to the community and then present me in an evening adult concert for which I'd get paid. Only three clubs responded and sponsored me in their communities. But it was a start.

Dad, as a newspaper man, (known in St. Petersburg as "Mr. Times") knew all the various organizations in town, including the local chapter of the International Platform Association, which was a clearing house for various performers that presented school assemblies and women's club appearances. It was the residue of the old Chatauqua circuit days concept. They held annual conventions which were primarily showcases for new talent. Dad arranged that I be presented. I prepared a sophisticated presentation designed for the Woman's Club market entitled "Kitchen Koncert"(!): here I was combining music and food, a life-long activity. Again, much preparation was necessary. In July of 1954 Dad and I drove to Ohio, where my presentation was made. I received an invitation to present the "Kitchen Koncert" to a group of club presenters in Chicago, but the real accomplishment was landing a three year contract with National School Assemblies whose specialty was school programs throughout the United States. I signed the deal, but also learned that it takes two years before it takes place due to the fact they need that time-frame in which to advertise and book a person into workable tours. One learns the ropes one step at a time. As many of the appearances would be before high school audiences, I also had to devise another program appropriate to that age group. This became my "Shipboard

Impressions": an imaginary journey of various entertainers performing aboard ship. I had never seen that sort of thing (certainly not as a
3rd class passenger going to France) but I could imagine it and that's
what I made up for a show, concluding with an impersonation of
Liberace! The show's premise was that I was a waiter on board a ship
and that's how I'd seen these various entertainers. After performing
pieces such as Malaguena, Country Gardens, a short version of
Rhapsody in Blue, some Chopin, etc., I had a candelabra stowed
behind the piano as well as a tail coat.I'd turn my back to the audience, slip off the waiters jacket, slip on the tail coat and turn around
with candelabra in hand and a big smile on my face. It always
worked!

But the time I was to do that was two years later, so I still had to fill
in the time with activity. I didn't want to spend two years more in
Florida, so I migrated north to Detroit where my brother John was
practicing medicine and raising his young family. I started off by
going to my nephew's school and approaching the principal about
presenting my PPP program. They were interested. Then she sent me
to other principals around the area where more programs were
arranged . I spent six weeks booking programs and the next six weeks
presenting them. I charged $25.00 per school for two programs: one
just for the kindergarten and first two grades, and another for the
upper grades through sixth. I booked one school in the morning and
one in the afternoon, making a take-home pay of $50 a day!

The favorite story by then had become "The Little Elephant Child"
by Rudyard Kipling. I accompanied the telling of that story with
Charles Gounod's composition "Funeral March for a Marionette"
which Alfred Hitchcok was to use later as intro to his TV series. When
I did the program for the experimental school of the University of
Ohio at Columbus, the music teacher criticized my use of that piece
as they taught it with its "original" programmatic meaning. (Hitchcok
wasn't concerned about that when he used it.) Furthermore, music
can "mean" whatever you want it to mean and, in fact, the Gounod
fits the "Little Elephant Child" like glove to hand!

Through some very nice contacts I was able to achieve, word
spread about my program.The Mellon Foundation presented me in
all the primary schools of Pittsburgh and the Frick Foundation did
the same for the schools of Flint, Michigan. It was during one of my
stays in Pittsburgh that I heard Van Cliburn as a 19 year old pianist
perform the Brahm's 2nd piano concerto with the symphony. This is

prior to his winning the Tchaikowsky International Piano Competition in Moscow in 1958 which catapulted him to world-renown. I remember thinking how huge his hands looked on the keyboard, (I was sitting in the mezzanine very near the stage and had an excellent view). I also thought him a little young to be attempting the most profound of the concerti literature. I was only a few years older and probably profoundly jealous. After all, I was only giving school assembly "shows"! I can say, however, that once the bookings by National School Assemblies started, I received, at the end of that first year's tour, the "Best Music Program" award from the International Platform Association for 1957. I received a watch and a little statue, a little bit like an Oscar, but as any Oscar winner will say: "I earned it! (and it's mine!")

National School Assemblies started my fall-1956 tour in Utah, Idaho, Wyoming, ending up in Western parts of Colorado. From my box-like Jeep station wagon, which I used in my early days of school assemblies when I was booking myself, I had advanced to a Ford station wagon in which I carried my props: an ice cream table and chair (scene de effect!) for "Shipboard Impressions", along with the Pied Piper Pianist's costume and white tie and tails. Oh yes, I carried a few "traveling clothes" as well. The tour began in Idaho where I saw for the first time the great piles of buried potatoes harvested and waiting to be shipped. Any meal in Idaho is accompanied by the biggest serving of potatoes ever seen anywhere else in the world. For breakfast, massive amounts of hash browns are served. For dinner an enormous baked potato arrives, but fortunately, I'm very found of potatoes, so it was OK. If you ever need a potato-fix, head for Idaho.

Proceeding next to Utah was memorable for several reasons. The first was coming down from the mountain and seeing Salt Lake City lying below and encountering the plaque commemorating Bringham Young saying: "This is the place!" I also realized they had endured untold hardships reaching that point, including the murderous reason they had left Missouri in the first place.

Secondly, in all of my many school performances, none were better received (and perhaps better understood) than in Utah. Mormons know how to "teach" and to appreciate what is learned.

The third memory is of Crenshaw melons! I went into a little cafe for breakfast in S.L.C. and saw this fabulous looking slice of pale, peach-colored melon in the refrigerated display and decided to give it a try. I had never heard of or seen a crenshaw before. Then the first sensual passing of taste to pallete ensued. It was an initial discovery of a food that has hardly been more pleasantly duplicated. Another taste sensation, for a neophyte drinker, was having an Olympia beer for the first time. While it was probably in Wyoming instead of Washington, tasting it and then reading on the label: "Made from Tum Water" (as it heads for the tummy) made me think: "What a great slogan !"

The Fall school assembly scene was rewarding.My Spring season was spent in Kentucky, Tennessee, Mississippi and Louisiana. Talk about "culture shock!" Some of the worst "pianos" (some mere boxes of wires) I ever experienced were in the South. On occasion I encoun-tered hostile all-black student-bodies who weren't interested in what a "white-boy-classical-pianist" had to tell them. I endured.

When I got further south into Mississippi, it was close enough to slip into New Orleans for week-ends; great solace for the un-Mormon like reception I received in the South. Some people build their entire lives around preparation for Mardi Gras, designing and making cos-tumes for more than one change throughout the pre-Lenten season of partying. People migrate to various cities for various reasons. New Orleans in the 50's (before muggings, etc.) was magical. I was there on the weekend before "Shrove Tuesday" (Mardi Gras) and there were several parades and much hilarity. Can you imagine having to go back to Pascagoula, to perform school assembly programs after Mardi Gras weekend? Like anyone else that has to go back to work after such frivolity, I did it.

The best thing about touring the South was staying in true "board-ing houses" where one had a room to sleep in and partook of the meals for one inclusive price, usually no more than $5.00 and some-times as little as $3.50 per night. The food was spread out, buffet style, on a big serving table: massive dishes of pork chops; cooked green beans with bacon sides; squash, rice, lentils, fried okra, platters of sliced tomatoes, Jello salads (!) etc. That's before anyone knew what the word cholesterol meant.

I failed to mention that during the Fall tour I had stayed in funky, little hotels with lumpy beds, but the hotels usually served a several course dinner that was quite good: it just wasn't done "boarding-house" style.

I was under contract for two more years with National School Assemblies, but all the traveling to different places every day plus presenting multiple programs daily provided me with a bad sinus infection by the end of the tour. I went to Los Angeles to stay with friends for the summer and to have my sinuses drained. Under the doctors advice, I cancelled my contract with the agency. Furthermore, the tour was to begin in Alabama in the Fall and I didn't want to go there with or without a banjo on my knee. Those were the years of the racial confrontations in the South and my sinuses didn't need further aggravation. The Pied Piper Pianist era came to an end, in spite of having received the Best Music Program award for 1957 from the International Platform Association.

OPUS EIGHT

*N*ot having to go back on the road in the Fall required that I find something else to do! If you recall, I had tried to establish a coffee-house, restaurant-bar in Aspen, but without any luck. The coffee-house fad was just getting under way in Los Angeles and since I'd had my taste of Paris, I felt qualified to start such an enterprise! I spent quite a bit of time searching for a suitable (and cheap) location. I found two funky locations near the Westwood area which I wanted due to their proximity to U.C.L.A, where I hoped a lot of customers might be found. The two places I wanted required too much reconstruction in order to meet Los Angeles health requirements for a food establishment. I ended up locating a vacant store a half block from the Pacific Ocean in Santa Monica Canyon. Thus began my coffee-house era and the establishment of *LES ENFANTS DU PARADIS*. After painting the walls red, buying used bentwood chairs which I painted black, and having iron table bases made from old ice cream table moulds I found in an iron works establishment, I then rented a medium-sized grand piano and opened for business. You'll recall the meaning of the title: the "peanut gallery" where the students and artists gathered for performances as "the children of paradise."As time grew closer to opening, I placed ads in the "Daily Bruin" hoping to catch the college crowd with my explanations regarding the meaning of Les Enfants du Paradis. I performed each evening beginning the opening set with Ravel's *SONATINE* which I had learned in Paris. Somehow that tied it all together in my mind.

What didn't tie together very satisfactorily was the amount of business—and the amount of merchandise—I had to sell in order to pay the rent, no less pay myself. The year was mostly a frustration of trying to make ends meet.

Some good things came from the experience, however. Most notably, the meeting of Gerald Heard, the well-known religious and philosophical writer. He lived at the top of the canyon near where Aldos Huxley lived (until his death) and below, nearer to the coffee-house, lived Christopher Isherwood. All three of these Englishmen had come over at each other's behest. I think Christopher Isherwood was the first, but I'm not sure about that. I do know that he is responsible for the arrival of Gerald, for he wanted him to engage in the Verdanta experiences he was enjoying with Swami Prabhavananda.

Isherwood lived with his friend Don Bachardy, the portraitist. The two often passed by the coffee house on their way to the ocean and were always very much engrossed in lively conversation. To see them go down the street together was like watching a scene de ballet as Bachardy literally danced beside, in front of, and around Christopher as they engaged in animated conversation. I thought of the famous legend which followed a performance of the Ballet Russe in Paris as Diaghilev , Nijinsky and perhaps Stravinsky walked down the Champs Elysees together. The young Jean Cocteau had involved himself with the company by at least producing a program cover, but wanted to do more. As the group walked, Cocteau kept attempting to insert himself into the conversation as he desired to be commissioned to provide a ballet scenario for the notable company. Finally Diaghilev stopped in his tracks and, turning to the "dancing" Cocteau, exclaimed: "Astonish me!"

Cocteau may or may not have gone on to astonish Diaghliev, but he did go on to astonish the cinematic world. His first film Blood of the Poet is viewed regularly in Parisian University gatherings (where I saw it for the second or third time) and, more remarkably, his masterpiece, La Belle et La Bete is still making heads wag in Hollywood.

Don Bachardy was probably astonishing Isherwood without admonition, as he danced beside him in front of my "Parisian" coffeehouse in Santa Monica Canyon.

While Isherwood enjoyed more secular pleasures, Heard remained a strict vegetarian and maintained a more monastic existence in keeping with his Verdanta experiences, and his generally religious bent. I had the opportunity to sit at the feet of Guru Heard but my head pounded from the pain of all the information about the cosmos that he was pouring into my brain. I was receiving a wild mix of Christianity, Buddhism, science, human evolution, etc.

When Maharishi Mahesh Yogi first came to America, he stayed in Los Angeles with the family of Roland and Helena Olson. Helena wrote one of the first books to be published about the Transcendental Meditation movement which really started in their home at 433 Harvard Boulevard. Following that memorable year, Helena wrote "Maharishi at '433'" from which I have permission to quote the following passages.

"I opened the door to meet Mr. H.— and his secretary. His secretary, a young man, introduced Mr. H.—and himself to me. I was not at this time familiar with this gentleman's literature or lectures...but

Maharishi seemed to be expecting him. Maharishi exclaimed: "Mr. H.—is the first person to be instructed in the new Meditation House.' Looking at Mr. H.—at this lean, acetic face which acknowledged many years of life, the face of a scholar and teacher, I was puzzled. It was a countenance which showed spiritual fulfillment, but his eyes expressed fatigue. Much depth was in the serious face; but childlike joy, something of the bliss we saw constantly, was lacking... As spirals of incense rose, I could see Maharishi escorting Mr. H. through the garden, a gesture I had never seen before. Aspirants always wait for a Master, and the time spent in waiting is significant. Mr. H.—was not required to wait....The two men emerged from the Meditation House.Maharishi looked enraptured. As for Mr. H.—, his face was illumined. Now his blue eyes were shining with the light we saw so often on new meditators. In less than one half hour his face seemed to have become younger, less lined....Sensing that this was a most unusual occasion, I quietly asked the photographer to take a picture of the two men. Both were talking and did not notice, but as a flash was used, they both glanced up and Maharishi seemed a bit displeased. Very gently (he) said: "I do not think Rishi H.—cares to have his picture taken."

"After the photographer left I lingered in the little house. It was there I realized Maharishi had called Mr. H.—'Rishi'. In discussing the significance of Maharishi's name previously, it was disclosed that 'Rishi' meant a sage, a very wise man. It seemed so right for the gentleman with the lean, acetic face, and the now shining blue eyes, to be called 'Rishi'. Whatever was the significance of that day, I do not know, as I have never seen Mr. H.—since, but I have always felt it was a great privilege to have been near and to have witnessed that rare occasion."

Yes...Gerald 'Rishi' Heard. Take a look at his marvelous face and elegant talking hands in a photograph I was allowed to take of him a few years later from the time-frame of his meeting with Maharishi.

My encounter with Transcendental Meditation came later. And it saved my life!

After a year of attempting to make a go of the coffee-house, I quit and moved into West Hollywood taking a job as a waiter. Now I was the "gark", the garcon . It was at a non-union restaurant in Glendale, California: "Pike's Verdugo Oaks", a full-fledged dinner house, serving luncheons as well. It had a long bar, a club-style front room for patrons who preferred waitresses and a bit of the action as they viewed the bar area. Then a main room where only male waiters served. The entire room was surrounded by handsome leather banquettes, leaving the center for regular table and chairs, which were all arm-chairs. There was a Captain for each room and one Maitre d' overseeing all of us. He was a suave Greek who would escort the best patrons to the waiter he thought should handle them. The clientele was mostly made up of repeat customers. Sally Rand and her husband, by now long retired from her unique show career, was a frequent customer...and the Captain always made a point of telling me she was present. "Bob", one of the first franchisers of restaurants, was also a regular customer. He always arrived with only his young son. No questions; just serve.

The philosophy of the owner, Mr. Pike, was that a non-union waiter could be trained by the Captains and Maitre 'd to serve in the manner the house desired. The service was full-course American food. Soup was always served, as was salad. All side dishes (potato and vegetable) were each presented in an individual dish, which made for heavy trays. The baked potato was opened at the table by the waiter and allowed to "breath" (like wine) before butter or anything else was added. Prime Rib was a frequently ordered item and if one had four or more orders of prime rib for a table, the chef layered them on a serving platter and the waiter took the whole thing (along with all the side dishes of potatoes and vegetables) to a rolling flaming table. That's when the Captain shone, for he would then appear to serve the prime rib onto plates which the waiter was dutifully holding ready. The Captain was also very useful when it came time for fanciful desserts, two of which were often requested: Baked Alaska and Cherries Jubilee. The latter is where the Captain really shone for he would render the cherries with all his various liquors, then, heating the 150 proof rum in a special ladel over the flame allowing it to ignite, poured it over the cherries. This was then ladled out over ice cream.

Since retiring, I've been on many cruises where, for the Captain's Farewell dinner, the waiters all parade in bearing what appears to be flaming Baked Alaska. In fact it is nothing more than Neopolitan ice cream covered in a sticky white covering meant to pass as meringue. At Pike's Verdugo Oaks, real Baked Alaska was served and properly prepared. Obviously, layer cake must be baked ahead of time, but when an order is received for the dessert, the Chef mixes up a batch of meringue, then slices the cake in two so he can place a variety of ice creams in the center. Completely encasing the cake in meringue, the Chef then pops it in a very hot oven for a few minutes in order to quickly glaze the meringue. This is rushed to the flaming table by the waiter as the Captain further anoints the dessert with liquors and the afore-mentioned 150 proof rum and pours the flaming liquid over the Baked Alaska. He then slices it into servings, but always leaves a little on the tray for the waiter to enjoy back in the kitchen. That's how I know what real Baked Alaska tastes like!

In the beginning of my stint as a waiter, the hardest part was taking drink orders, and in those days nearly everyone had cocktails when they went out dining; even children were served "Shirley Temples" or "Roy Rogers": cherry flavored syrup placed in ginger ale with a cherry stuck on a tooth pick. Having drunk only red or white wine until that time, I was perplexed by orders such as: "Cutty Sark with a water back"; "Jack Daniels neat"; "perfect Rob Roy"; "Canadian Club"; "Four Roses on the rocks"; "Three Feathers high"! Or something with "a twist": (a twist of what?)

I could remember a simple Bloody Mary or vodka and tonic. But all call-name drinks (none of which I'd ever heard of at that time) had to be written down and then "discussed" with the bar-tender. Fortunately he was very nice and would give a little laugh but help me through it. He was particularly amused by my ignorance of what Cutty Sark or Jack Daniels was. The remaining challenge was to get the drinks, unspilled, back to the table and distributed to the right people. "Straight up" Martinis or Manhattans were delivered in little individual carafes and then poured out into cocktail stemware at the table, which avoided spillage.

Waiting on tables was not meant to be for the rest of my life. After the fantasy of a musical coffee-house failed to be profitable, and artistically speaking, not very rewarding, it was inevitable that I began thinking about a more appropriate career. Obviously, music had to be in the center. I didn't know very much about West Coast academia, but somehow I had heard that the University of Southern California had a good music department, especially in piano.

OPUS NINE

*J*ohn Crown was the head of the piano department at U.S.C. and I went to his home in the Hollywood Hills to play for him. He, very nicely, advised me to see Ralph Rush who was the head of the Music Education department, saying, that with my background of school assembly performances, etc., that my future lay in teaching more than in performing. Little did I know that the likes of Michael Tilson Thomas was a student there at that time who was also pianist for the Master Classes of Heifetz and Piatigorsky! Only later did I encounter M.T.T. as a performer when he appeared at several of the famous Monday Evening concerts held in a community center on Santa Monica Blvd. My funky little apartment was only a few blocks away on Melrose Avenue, just down from Melrose Place, yet to be known by its TV series.The apartment was above an old-fashioned pharmacy and across the street from a plumbing yard, whose trucks frequently parked directly in front of my building.But as I was the only residential occupant of the building, I didn't have to worry about disturbing neighbors with my piano playing...nor the plumbers!

Instead of becoming a Piano Major again, I became a Music Education major. I enjoyed learning something about how to look at a score, conducting and thinking about all of music as a listening and learning experience rather than just piano.By the second year of my two-year Masters degree program, I was ready to practice teach. The first semester was devoted exclusively to elementary teaching. I was assigned one school in what is called South Central Los Angeles today, but I was allowed to visit other elementary schools within that area due to my previous school experiences. I even resurrected my costume and did a Pied Piper performance for my school. These were all black schools, with mostly black principals and teachers. And they were wonderful. Children were orderly, polite, clean, and respectful of their teachers. The burning of Watts had not yet occurred. Nor had forced busing begun. The schools were proud of what they were doing and were probably better able to do so because of their homogeneity. It will take many generations before that kind of pride can return.

By Christmas time I was well established in my practice teaching. My "Master" teacher prepared her children in a Christmas program for which I acted as accompanist. When the assembly took place for parents as well as the rest of the school, I performed carols on the piano as a prelude to the program as people entered the auditorium. I used a typical song-book, as I'm not a "by-ear" pianist. I was able to add a few flourishes to the music which dressed up the basic four-part harmony, and, of course, I displayed a trained pianist's "touch." Following the program, the elementary supervisor for that district of Los Angeles came up to me to say that she had never heard Christmas carols played so beautifully. Nothing like a little study in New York, St. Louis, and Paris to help one's touch!

My second semester assignment was divided between a Junior High and a High school, the latter being Westchester High near the Pacific coast in a predominantly white enclave of upper middle class residents. The "Master Teacher" was Robert Wood, choir director, who was adept at putting on adaptations of Broadway musicals as well as appearing successfully with his choir at the various festivals in Southern California. While I had been presenting school assemblies following the two year's spent in Colorado, Robert had earned his teaching credential and gone to work for the L. A. school system. Although we were the same age, I became his "apprentice," (The Sorcerer's Apprentice?) and we have been friends all these years.

Having completed practice teaching , I was ready for the job-market. I found a position in the district of El Monte known for its music. Each of the three high schools of that district had three music teachers: a band director, a choral director and a class piano and glee club teacher. At Rosemead High I became the latter.

The spring I was hired for the coming school year, the department Chairman, Gerturde Kleecamp, told me about the summer music camp that she attended as a choral section coach and suggested that I get in touch with the camp's founder-director, Max Krone, and inquire about coming up. I did and was welcomed for the final two weeks of the summer to assist with the high school choir that always closed the season at the Idyllwild School of Music and the Arts, otherwise known as ISOMATA. Ralph Rush, my mentor-advisor during some uncertain days at U.S.C., conducted the orchestra, so the experience made for a well-oiled slide into public school teaching. For a near penniless "music student" the free room and board plus $15.00 a week was vacation enough prior to the arrival of the first pay-check in the fall, another month away! That check was for $350 and since I paid only $75.00 a month for Melrose "Place", I began to feel "ahead of the game."

Melrose was a plebian street in 1960, although some attempts at chic were tried. There was a tented restaurant-bar behind the hamburger stand at the corner of La Cienega and Melrose which was popular. Then a designer-jean store opened up on the corner of Cresta and Melrose. Between Cresta and my street, Kilkea, Kenneth Kendall had his hidden art studio. He was an eccentric draftsman who had become completely enamored with one of the early "Mr. Americas" who went on to become a "Mr. Universe" as well as a movie-star for Italian-made films based on the old Classics: Hercules, Ulysses, Cyclops, etc. Steve Reeves (no relationship to the later Superman film-star Christopher Reeves) was quite handsome as well as being well-built. Kendall created a series of astrological drawings creating the "signs"of the Zodiac out of images of Reeves. He also made quite a few sculptures of Steve and behind his dusty little store-front window were exhibited a few fragments of his rich imagination. I eventually ended up acquiring two of these lithographs (signed and numbered) which I have subsequently given to ONE and its amalgamation with the Gay and Lesbian Archives now housed by U.S.C.

During that first year of high school teaching, I realized that teaching class-piano every day for five days in a row to three sections of beginners is draining! I also thought they didn't need five straight days of it weekly, either. So on Fridays, I started giving "music appreciation" lectures, and often played concert pieces for them. I usually spent the last period of the day plus another hour after school practicing the piano.

The supervisor, who had made the nice comment regarding my "caroling" for the elementary school, had predicted —when it became time for me to choose between elementary or high school teaching—that, in any case, I would never be musically satisfied by whichever grade-level I taught. She was right! Even later, at the college level, this was true. Only by my dogged desire to keep performing while inventing new avenues for musical display, kept me practicing and trying to perfect what art I had.

The first result of this was a program presented for ONE entitled: "Music, The Hermaphroditic Art." (Appendix A) The concert was a huge success, garnering the largest crowd they had ever had for one of their monthly lectures. Word was that people were crying in the men's room during intermission, so moved were they by the program. My monologue, which preceded each piece, was subsequently printed in the ONE INSTITUTE QUARTERLY in their Spring Issue of 1964 under my *nom de plume*: Brian Jennings, a name suggested by the director of "ONE", Dorr Legg. Dorr had already won a battle with the Supreme Court over the mailing of his news- letter ONE and that was long before the Stonewall riots in New York City had begun to turn the tide for gay rights. His suggestion that I twist aspects of my name into a pseudonym was appropriate for those times in as much as I was a neophyte public school teacher. "Don't ask, don't tell" didn't exist then, if it exists at all. I used it thenceforth for other writings and photo stories which appeared in early editions of the newspaper THE ADVOCATE.

While working the second summer of my high school teaching days as assistant to the founder-director of ISOMATA, Max Krone, I developed a passionate interest in photography. There was an active photo department at Idyllwild, (Max loved photographs of every thing that took place) where I began to learn about picture-taking and what kind of camera to buy, etc. They even knew of a very good used Lica camera with several lenses available in a photo shop in Hemet at the bottom of the mountain from Idyllwild. I drove down the mountain and purchased it and it has been my one and only camera ever since.

As assistant to the director, I was there for the entire summer. The season began with a two-week junior high school camp: band, orchestra, choir, dance, art. The middle six weeks of summer was devoted to adult workshops: art, ceramics, folk-music weekends, folk-dancing weekends, etc.The climax of the summer was the high school encampment which featured a large choir and orchestra. A major work would be prepared for the final Sunday concert. The last year I was there a very ambitious performance of Verdi's *Requiem* was put together with the solos being performed by the teacher-coaches. My sometime concert partner, Paul Mayo, sang the incomparable tenor aria *Ingemisco* which is one of Verdi's finest utterances. Paul sang it beautifully in that lyric tenor etherealness that is so right for that aria just as it is needed for Puccini's *Nessun Dorma*. As a matter of fact, Puccini may have been thinking of *Ingemisco* when he composed his final aria.

Paul auditioned for Zubin Mehta singing the impassioned tenor aria from L'Africaine by Meyerbeer. I accompanied. The audition went very well, but Mehta said he wanted a "bigger" voice as he was just starting his concert versions of opera with the L. A. Philharmonic... Zubin's loss, I might add, in not taking Paul.

Meanwhile, back in Idyllwild, I was busy taking photographs. I started taking pictures with a particular project in mind: that of photographing images to coincide with passages from the poetry of Walt Whitman. My intention was to show contemporary versions of what Whitman was "singing" about one hundred and fifty years ago: the ploughboy (they ride tractors today); the carpenter (they probably appear pretty much the same, shirts off and up on beams); the delivery boy (Pizza Hut?). In fact the title was WALT WHITMAN TODAY and I made a deadline for myself of producing the book by his 150 birth anniversary in 1969. I acquired my camera in 1963 so there was plenty of lead-time for the project and in Idyllwild there were plenty of attractive, actively involved subjects to photograph, especially for: "I Hear America Singing"!

Many passages of Whitman's poetry reverberated in my head and whenever I saw an image that might be a prospect for a passage, I clicked away. Gradually I began to organize how I wanted the book to evolve as more and more pictures began to accumulate. The first section was to be: "Poets to come, orators, singers, musicians to come! Not today is to justify me and answer what I am for; but you, a new brood, native, athletic, continental, greater than before. Arouse! For you must justify me. I myself but write one or two indicative words for the future; I but advance a moment to wheel and hurry back in the darkness. I am a man who, sauntering along without fully stopping, turns a casual look upon you and then averts his face, leaving it to you to prove and define it; expecting the main things from you."

If that isn't a call to the future —almost a specific set of directions for going on from where he left off—then I don't know "nothing!" He left it to us to "prove and define it" and that was what I was attempting to do through my photography. It was a wonderful journey. It took several years and occupied a great deal of my attention; this in spite of the fact that I had a new job and was about to embark on my most important venue. I had been asked to teach music appreciation and piano at the foremost community College in America at that time, Foothill College, located in Los Altos, California. It served students from that community and neighboring Palo Alto, home of Stanford University and a community having the highest educational background per capita of any area in the world. It's no wonder that Silicon Valley grew from such roots.

OPUS TEN

The offer to teach at Foothill College came in the Spring of 1965 during my fourth year of teaching at Rosemead High School. John F. Kennedy had been assassinated in 1963 and for the first anniversary of that event, I prepared a fifty minute program entitled *A Pianist's Requiem for JFK* which I performed five times throughout the entire day from the Choral Room, live, in front of each of those regular classes, but broadcast throughout the entire school via closed circuit TV. A week before the broadcast, I recorded the program on the fine concert grand piano at the Beverly Hills high school where my friend from Idllywild, Robert Holmes, was chairman of the Music Department for all Beverly Hills schools.

Following the broadcast, I wrote-up the experience about using TV to communicate within an entire school and published it in the California Journal of Music Educators. Using TV as an educational tool was just beginning to be acknowledged as a possibility.

Armed thusly with a recording and a published article, I ventured forth for my interview with Foothill's President and Dean of Instruction. Although there were sixty-five applicants for the position open at Foothill, I managed to beat out several PHD's already teaching music history at good universities. But Foothill wanted a pianist as well as a teacher of music appreciation and since my Masters project had been lesson plans of what I was already doing in the way of teaching "appreciation", I landed the job! Obviously, the recording *A Pianist's Requiem for JFK* (Appendix B) helped immeasurably in securing the position.

November 22, 1963, the day of Kennedy's assassination, I was "directing" boy's glee, one of my two choral assignments. Around one p.m. the announcement came over the intercom that JFK had been shot during a motorcade through Dallas. Very quietly I said to my various ethnic-origin group: "You'll remember this date and where you were when you heard the news for the rest of your lives!" And so we have. The death of JFK happened over the weekend prior to the Thanksgiving four-day school vacation. We had already planned an Americana Thanksgiving assembly program with my playing Rhapsody in Blue as a solo, and accompanying and leading the entire school in some American songs. On that Sunday following the assassination, the principal of Rosemead phoned me imploring my opinion on what we should do with the Thanksgiving assembly.I counseled that we should go ahead as planned and that I would make a dedication statement at the very beginning of the program regarding the need to go on with life as that would be what JFK would wish: "What can we do for our country?"...The principal was greatly relieved and I was relieved to find another job the next year!

I spent my last summer as assistant to Max Krone at ISOMATA working up the lesson plans for the forthcoming music appreciation lectures which Foothill chose to call "Music Comprehension". In fact, it is a very good title for Music 101: how to comprehend what you are hearing in the most abstract of the arts: music.I also spent a lot of time thinking about and writing the opening lecture which I felt had to be the *raison d'etre* for taking such a course. Its thoughts are fundamental to my being and teaching. (Appendix C)

And so from 708 Kilkea, just off "Melrose Place", came Bekins to move me and my Bechstein baby grand piano (my pride and joy at that time) to its new location in Northern California. Along with the piano, went the Oriental-style orange colored couch which had been my first purchase (other than the piano) that I had made for the apartment on Washington's Birthday during my first year of teaching. Later, that became a tradition: to buy something for the house on "President's Day", the only free weekday a teacher has between Christmas and Easter. Since I never took "sick leave" to go shopping, when I retired I had an entire year of unused sick-leave to apply as another year earned to the time working.

Along with some clothes, the only thing I carried was the fragile Cocteaueske candelabra that had figured so strikingly in the coffee house in Santa Monica Canyon and which, by now, has gone into many new abodes, but always by my own hands. (See cover photo).

Although I was to be paid twice what I was receiving as a high school teacher, I still hadn't received a pay-check, and therefore needed rather modest living arrangements. Foothill had a newsletter for faculty which contained a classified section. From that source I was able to rent a wing of a private home from "Biz" who ran the box office for the college and who lived only a mile from the campus. The "wing" was a single large square room with a little Pullman kitchen off to one side. A little hall connected to a small bath which also connected to a narrow bunkroom for sleeping. Not as spacious as Kilkea, the main room was nevertheless adequate for my piano, my couch, and contained enough hanging space for my budding art collection.

Following the reading of my opening lecture on the very first day of teaching at Foothill, I sat down to the 6 foot Steinway and played Debussy's *L'sle Joiuse*, a very difficult piece to start with and one of the showiest Debussy ever composed. It would be suitable for closing a program rather than starting one, but I was determined to make an impression. Fortunately, I was in good enough practice to pull it off and word spread quickly that a concert pianist was lose on campus! At that time it took three classes to complete the first "lecture". As word spread that "the pianist is playing today", auditors would drift into the small hall where the classes were held to listen. One of these was Marina Derryberry, an ethnic Russian woman whose parents had fled the revolution and had grown up in Turkey and attended the state conservatory there. She had eventually migrated to America and married a Mr. Derryberry. It was about this time, as she was dropping in on my lectures, that she rather reluctantly began teaching a six year old ethnic Japanese boy named Jon Nakamatsu how to play the piano. In June of 1997, Jon Nakamatsu won the Gold Medal at the 10th International Van Cliburn competition and since has gone on to make a fine international concert career. During the semi-finals of that competition which Robert and I attended, I went back-stage to greet and congratulate Marina. When she saw me coming down the hall-way, she turned to the guard saying: "Oh, he's a very good pianist!" Well, I was, at any rate, back in the earlier days at Foothill. Perhaps, by osmosis, I can take some credit for the "formation" of Jon's talent!

At the conclusion of my first year of teaching at Foothill, during a year-end cocktail party for faculty, the conductor of the college-community orchestra asked me to perform with the orchestra during the following Fall season. Naturally the prospect of playing with an orchestra instead of a second piano accompaniment thrilled me considerably. I chose the Grieg A minor concerto for several reasons: I had frequently played the first movement in an unaccompanied version during my assembly touring days which left only the second and third movements to learn. Although considered a "war-horse" of a concerto, it nevertheless is a very good composition. Artur Rubinstein, during his 90th birthday TV appearance, performed and defended it against its critics. I have frequently lectured about this work and the first thing to say about it is to comment on its remarkable cadenza.

The primary difference between a symphony and a concerto is that the listener gets two versions of the thematic material: the symphonic and the soloistic. Grieg captures this difference notably by having the piano mimic the orchestra's presentation of the principal themes in a dialog manner. It is only in the massive cadenza (another unique feature differing from the form of a symphony) that the piano, out of the mist of rumination, decides that what has been the important material offered —in this case, the first theme—proceeds to render a massive, pianistic interpretation of this theme. In this manner, Grieg set the way for all future concerto cadenzas. Listening to the wonderful, but infrequently performed, first piano concerto of Rachmaninoff, one realizes what a great influence Grieg's A minor concerto had on this work. It's as if Rachmaninoff had it on the music stand alongside his writing desk. It is not a copy of the concerto thematically, but only within its construction. Here, too, the first theme finds it's most complete utterance in the remarkable cadenza. Rachmaninoff was observing an age-old learning technique known by painters for centuries: "If you want to know how to do it, copy the masters!" Would-be artists have always set up their easels inside museums and learned by copying.

By the next Fall, the Foothill orchestra had joined with the community orchestra to form the Nova Vista Symphony and I was the soloist for the debut performance playing the Grieg. The performance went well—I had only a slight memory slip in the final movement where I missed the proper modulation in the recapitulation. But I was able to recover quickly and unless someone had actually played the work themselves, would not have known of my error. This is the pitfall of single performances: it's make or break it—there are no second chances. I had to experience this over and over again with my single performances of works. But, traumatic or not, I had the opportunity to perform concertos with an orchestra nearly every year thenceforth.

The Pullman kitchen in the Los Altos house wing I rented was only big enough to serve up one basic meal and one that I ate daily, believe it or not. I had concocted it back in the "mouse-kitchen" on Kilkea. It consisted of an avocado half filled with cottage cheese, a serving of tater-tots from the freezer warmed up in the small gas oven and a piece of sirloin tip steak, pan-fried rare. That was the meal for me and anybody else who happened to be invited for dinner. Up until now cooking had been done, first on a kerosene stove in Yonkers; then alcohol burners in France; the "Mouse-kitchen" on Kilkea (which had at least a small gas stove with oven) and now, a two-plate electric burner (no oven) in Los Altos. It was time for a real house with a real kitchen and to start cooking real food!

Performing with the Nova Vista Symphony at Foothill College

 A Community Service of
De Anza and Foothill Colleges

SUNDAYS,
7:00 to 10:00 p.m.

GREAT
MUSIC
EPOCHS

The most listened-to music today comes from five great epochs of musical history. Using live and recorded performances of the master-works of the era, each of the five sessions of this class will study in depth the major forces of each of these epochs. Special emphasis will be placed on the music of Beethoven to coincide with the spring performance of several of his works. The Master Sinfonia will present all five Beethoven piano concertos; the Nova Vista will perform his Sixth Symphony and The Schola Cantorum will offer the Missa Solemnis. (Class registrants are not required to attend the concerts, but may obtain tickets at half rate.)

Instructor: William Bryan

Mr. Bryan is a popular music instructor at Foothill College. He is also well known in this area as an exciting performer on the concert piano. He has studied at the St. Louis Institute of Music, the Universities of Florida, Colorado and Southern California and at the Conservatoire National in Paris. He has been the recipient of a Fulbright Travel Grant and Scholar-ship, plus a Best Music Program Award by the International Platform Association for programs presented in high schools, and has published articles on music and music criticism. Mr. Bryan has been critically acclaimed in his several concert performances with the Nova Vista Symphony.

OPUS ELEVEN

I never had a proper kitchen until I moved to Los Gatos at the conclusion of my second year at Foothill. During that Spring I increasingly had a longing for a place of my own. I perused the newspaper home section, checking out the ads, answered some and more likely, in the middle of the night, drove by to look at places I'd read about. One of the advertisements was for a house in Los Gatos that would only be shown by a realtor, so I made an appointment to see it. Realtors insist that they take you in their car to view a property; it's part of their selling technique. The realtor announced prior to our arrival that the house didn't "show well" from the front. What she meant was that it didn't look like all the rest of the houses on the block. We entered what is called a pie-shaped lot: a long driveway nestled between adjacent properties which fans out toward the back with fencing on both sides. We entered the house via a carport and into an entry hall where one could either turn left or right leading into adjacent rooms. But once into the rooms, an immense wide-open view overlooking a swimming pool led the eye beyond over a canopy of green all the way to the beginning of the Santa Cruz Mountains. In other words, there was complete privacy and an unobstructed view of nature once inside the house and its "compound"! I had been looking at houses on hillsides which only looked down on roofs of other houses, etc. Here, I realized, was a calming view of nature with no other houses to look at. I knew instantly that this was the kind of "view" I really wanted and it came with a house that didn't "show well" from the front! I wasn't interested in showing well anyway. What I sought was privacy without being required to nod to my neighbors as soon as I stepped out of my front door each morning. It was the perfect house for me.

The largest room was one of those 1950's "innovations" where the kitchen was an island within a huge "family room" complete with brick fireplace as well as built-in cabinets topped with bookcases. The other room, into which the entry hall could enter in the opposite direction, was a smaller room used as a formal sitting room. It also contained a fireplace. Of course I had a grand piano to place and the larger room also had a half-Cathedral ceiling which made it more suitable in containing the sound of a large piano. Realizing that if I moved the island-kitchen from the "family-room" into the "sitting room", I could create a delightful country kitchen. Since there was room for a dining table as well that would allow the larger room to be the central living room. The piano would occupy the space that the kitchen occupied before and nearer the fireplace I would arrange the couch and chair group.

During sleepless nights, I was in heaven dreaming of all these possibilities and changes as I plotted and planned for the purchase of my first home. One is terrified thinking whether he can qualify for a loan, meet mortgage payments, etc. Also, before the big inflation of the 1970's, offer and counter-offer was done in the hundreds, not in the thousands of dollars that would have been necessary at a later date. Announcements were printed to look like wedding invitations proclaiming the date for the close of escrow. I thought if ordinary folks could squeeze friends and relatives for gifts when they got married, that I might try the same. After all, I was marrying a house!

It was a great marriage. It lasted for twelve years. I had many great parties there: recitals in the winter; pool parties in the summer; and that is where I finally learned to cook. When I needed to go to Florida to visit my father and aunt there was never any problem securing house-sitters as it was like a vacation to stay there. I admit that during the first few weeks the old standby meal of avocado and cottage cheese, tater-tots and fritzed tip-steak had to be the mainstay for a little while longer. I had made up my mind that I wasn't going to get used to the house as it was. I wanted to change the kitchen immediately for more reasons than one. I couldn't place a grand piano into the living room until the island kitchen was removed. And where the kitchen cabinets had been built against the wall in the "family-room", the wall had to be resurfaced with new Phillipine Mahagony paneling to match the rest of the room. The carpet was taken up from the "sitting-room" floor and more appropriate red-brick linoleum (to match the fireplace) laid to complete the "kitchen-look". With more wall space to cover, I needed more pictures, so hunting for new ones became a part of my day while the contractor worked on the kitchen. Keeping busy when acquiring a new home is not difficult.

During the previous summer I had kept busy another way. In the school business, one achieves pay-grade levels based upon education beyond whatever degree one already has. At the conclusion of my first year at Foothill, I needed only two more college units to achieve an entire "column" change which would greatly increase my salary-scale. In order to achieve that increase I enrolled in a graduate seminar on 20th Century piano music offered at Stanford University and taught by distinguished visiting professor -pianist Grant Johansen. There were about two dozen pianists enrolled in the course in which I participated by playing some Debussy and Satie, while others performed Schoenberg, Stravinsky and Prokofief. Johansen played an evening concert in which he performed the very difficult piano sonata by Aaron Copland. His performance was stunning, as was the music—electrifying actually comes to mind.

With these exhilarating weeks of exposure to 20th Century piano music I was able to earn my column change, which helped pave the way to qualifying for the purchase of the house in Los Gatos.

In addition to creating column changes (which don't happen very often: one must do the equivalent of another master's degree of education before one receives a column change, but I was only two units away from that point when I enrolled in the Stanford summer course), one needs to continue any sort of education to maintain his "step" increases, which are yearly upgrades in salary within one's column. Following the first year in Los Gatos, I decided to spend the summer in Mexico taking a gringo course in Spanish offered by the University of Gradalajara. I chose to stay in a hotel which included demi-pension: breakfast and lunch or dinner. Quite a few of the Gringos stayed there, and as our classes were only in the morning, we would assemble around the pool and be served drinks and snacks, ostensibly to study, but mostly we were having a good time drinking cerveza and eating nachos. Thusly my "step" increase was achieved.

More importantly, I achieved a liking for Mexican food and margaritas. I had driven down in my precious 1964 Riviera (!) which was probably a mistake. Riverias are built low to the ground and since the entire road from Arizona to Mazatlan was under construction, I ended up losing most of the exhaust system. Mexico's idea of a detour is to barely bulldoze a path alongside the highway being re-built: up one palmetto root and down another! The main reason I had taken the car was that my dancer-friend was to join me at the conclusion of the course and we were to drive to Puerto Vallarta and on to Acapulco as we both wanted to "discover" these two places. We also experienced Ziwatanejo, which my friend's dog fancier friends raved about, only to experience Montazuma's revenge, the only time that happened to me that summer. We hurried back to Acapulco where I got better as soon as I was again on La Condessa beach sipping rum punches.

Acapulco was a dream. It was not yet run over with high-rise hotels, only a few that stood like sentinels along the beach, each famous for its particular time of day and the kind of crowd it attracted. There was Morning Beach, Afternoon Beach, and best, Condessa Beach just below the hotel of the same name. That was where all the hustlers went, male and female alike, looking very delectable as they posed and oiled their beautiful bodies. Actually, it is more fun to be solicited by a pretty body than it is to be continually approached by the shirt, hat, skirt, belt and souvenir vendors. Meanwhile, one sprawls on the beach sipping rum punches from enormous over-sized, massively built "cocktail" glasses.

I've always been fascinated by glassware, especially the drinking kind: I have three houses and each is filled with complete sets of wine glasses of all sizes and dimensions. The advantage of having the car was to fill it up with goodies before returning to the States. I definitely wanted some of those over-sized "cocktail" glasses, but gift shops didn't carry them. I found them, eventually, in a restaurant supply house where I purchased six or eight of them for, I think, about a dollar apiece. I was already envisioning my pool-side parties back in Los Gatos (The Cats, by the way, in Spanish). To further take up the back seat of the Riviera, I purchased two of those marvelous leather and shaved-timber "tub" chairs one sees in South Western bars and in Mexican restaurants. I may not have learned much Spanish during the span of the summer but I sure learned to enjoy Mexican furniture, food and drink! I also advanced my "step" on the pay scale!

There was wonderful wall-space in the house at Los Gatos on which to show paintings. Although I already had quite a collection of art work, I could accommodate more. I went purposefully to two public galleries to see if there was anything that would appeal to my taste. In a Mountain View store-front gallery, next to Sears (!) I found an original oil by a Southern California artist depicting a marvelously muscled youth in the throes of extending his arms into the classic "Iron Cross" position, showing a marvelous torso. It looked also as if he could be plunging into the sea. At another "fly-by-night" shop, a merchant had imported a bunch of Italian canvases and was busily stretching them onto Baroque-style Mexican frames. The one I chose came with a description of the young man who was portrayed in pink and blue tones reminiscent of those periods of Picasso's oeuvre. Although I have given away many paintings to ONE over the years, those two remain in my collection and on my walls.

In moving to Los Gatos, I had decided instead of paying a mover to take down, transfer and then put back up the Bechstein piano, I would trade it in toward a new and bigger piano. The new Department Chairman promised that I could pick out a new piano for the lectures in Appreciation Hall at Foothill, so off I went to San Francisco to inspect what was available. The man at Steinway didn't bother to get out of his chair when I told him I was authorized to buy a piano for my college, merely saying that none were available for at least six months. Next , I went to the Baldwin agency and was able to play the one six foot piano they had set up. It was brilliant sounding—like all Baldwin grands—but I said: "I'd think about it". I had already made an appointment to see the Yamahas and they had set up two 7 foot, 4 inch grands side by side to choose from.I loved both of them and offered to buy one of them for myself if they'd give me the same price as they were giving to the college. In as much as a teacher is constantly asked: "what kind of piano should I buy?", they agreed to my terms, as well as giving me some credit for the Bechstein. They also made arrangements to pick-up the one and then deliver the other at a later specified time. I didn't want the Yamaha sent until the kitchen had been moved and the new living room made ready. One doesn't very easily move a large piano around in a house, especially over rugs and while living alone. So, by the Fall semester I not only had a new piano at college but also a new house and piano for myself.

Soon after moving to Los Gatos I read an article in the Los Angeles Times by their wine columnist, Robert Balzer. I had met him when he tried for a season or two to have a fancy restaurant outside of Idyllwild in the San Jacinto mountains above Palm Springs. I think he imagined his tony friends from the desert would make their way up for his elegant meals. A few did, but not enough of them to keep such an extravagant affair viable. He retreated to Los Angeles and continued to write his wine column, in one of which he advised never to drink red wine from the store shelf, but only after keeping it for awhile: "in the back of a closet, under the bed, or wherever it might rest for awhile". He even went so far as to say that Gallo's Hearty Burgundy would improve with age!

With that in mind (I never cellared Hearty Burgundy!) my wine friends in Northern California and I frequently went wine tasting at the local wineries. There was one in Mountain View where the grapes were brought in from Southern Santa Clara county ranches, but produced into wine in Mountain View. Gemello made big, red wines, generic blends for the most part, and sold them in gallon jugs. We'd taste and if we liked, would buy some. I liked what they called "Claret" (which is what the English call wine from Bordeaux) and bought a couple of cases, planning to re-bottle them into fifths, recork and cellar a la Robert Balzer's recommendation. I purchased a small hand-held corker and one of my wine friends, who worked at San Jose's Mirrassou Winery, gave me cases of used bottles from the tasting room as well as corks which I boiled and re-used. For home cellaring for a beginner, the used bottles were a Godsend. I soaked the labels off, gave them a good bath, sterilized them in the dishwasher (I had a dishwasher in Los Gatos!—a far cry from the "mouse kitchen" of Kilkea) and proceeded to refill them. Then I placed them in the crawl space beneath the house to age. In this manner, I started the first of what was to become three wine cellars over the years. There were some wine bargains in the local liquor stores and for awhile Los Gatos even had a wine discount store from which I added bottles to the crawl space. Always remembering Balzar's admonition to not drink red wine off the shelf, I began to collect red wine to enjoy for the future. Oh, the optimism of youth: the future is forever. Whether the future is forever or not, having a wine cellar, or some appropriate way to keep wine aging, is a good idea.Remember, the venerable winery, Paul Masson, had as their slogan: "No Wine Before its Time!"

OPUS TWELVE

$\mathcal{W}$hen I first started bottling wine, the bottles were one-fifth of a gallon and as I purchased Gemello "Claret" by the gallon, I could expect five nice bottles of liquid enjoyment. Then something funny happened on the way to the International Forum: the U.S. decided to join the rest of the world and go metric. After much propaganda, a few road signs were placed with both kilometers and miles posted—not many, mind you, but some. There were a few magazine articles about converting from inches, feet and yards to meters. The only thing that really took hold was moving alcoholic beverages from 5ths, quarts, and gallons into liters and milliliters. An ol'fashioned "5th" became 750 ML—I guess ML stands for mini-liter! Suddenly, all wine appeared on the store shelves in these sizes. The alcohol industry jumped on the metric band-wagon realizing that they would get the same money for a "bottle" of wine as before but without divying up as much liquid beverage. Suddenly, alcohol was being sold like petrol in Europe: by the liter, or mostly by a portion of a liter. It was like the 5 cent Mars bar becoming 25 cents and half its former size.

Nowadays, because of "metrics", I have more glass to recycle and less liquid pleasure per bottle. The glass folks probably loved the metric change over, once they got their re-tooling costs back. More glass, more paper, more labels, more cardboard boxes for a less amount of liquid. (At any rate, cellar your reds and drink your whites.)

Meanwhile in Los Gatos, we had lots of fun sunning and swimming, often not bothering about clothes because the pool area was completely private. Margaritas were not often served in those gorgeous Mexican goblets—one would get drunk way too quickly. But rum punch with lots of ice and a piece of fruit on top was just the ticket pool-side. The party would sometimes get out of hand when somebody would throw the empty goblets at whomever was in the pool. They were easily retrieved due to their size: none ever became broken.

Ah, life just seemed to roll along from lecture, to party, to concert, to occasional trips to a bar in San Francisco...My favorite was the Buena Vista at the end of the Hyde Street cable car line, at the west end of the Embarcadero-Fisherman's Wharf area. For 85 cents one received an entire cocktail shaker of either a Manhattan or Martini. It was served in a classic stemware cocktail glass garnished with your request. The entire shaker was then placed by your glass. If you drank fast enough, you had two full cocktails and another half-glass before it became too watery from melting ice. I believe that when I first went there the cost was 60 cents. It gradually rose to 85 cents!

I discovered the Buena Vista not by word of mouth —which is the way most people have found it —but through an accident of fate. It was during my first solo visit to "The City" before I had moved north from Los Angeles. My friends and I were house guests of dog clients in Santa Cruz and I got away on my own for a Saturday night "on the town". I had only been there once before and had yet to explore Chinatown, North Beach, or go up to Coit Tower. I was enjoying the view of the Bay from Coit when it sounded like the entire town was on fire: there were sirens coming from all directions. I could see a great cloud of black smoke rising up from the area below the Presidio and the Golden Gate Bridge. Since the fires of San Francisco had been such legendary stuff, I thought I'd better check this one out. I threaded my way down the hill from Coit Tower and eventually found myself on Beach Street where I miraculously found a parking space and walked toward all the commotion and smoke. Diagonally across from the Buena Vista was an old warehouse and this is where all the smoke was coming from.The entire block surrounding the ware house was filled with fire trucks. I slipped into the bar which I soon learned was the birthplace of "Irish Coffee", which I ordered in as much as it was a little early for cocktails. The famous beverage was its main seller. There was one bartender designated for only making Irish Coffee. Since there was always more than a single order for this beverage, the attendant lined up a row of the stemmed coffee glasses and poured hot water into the number of glasses he needed to produce. Following the heating-up of the glasses, he emptied out the water, inserted a single cube of sugar in each glass, and then, with inverted bottle of Irish whiskey in hand, go from glass to glass dispensing just the proper amount without ever up-righting the bottle. The coffee was dispensed in a similar manner, i.e. without stopping from one glass to the next...just pour. He then stirred each glass briefly and completed the drink with a carefully spooned gob of freshly whipped cream (no pressurized canister here) for topping. The cost: 60 cents.

While the fire raged, the occupants of the Buena Vista, with glasses in hand, stood by the door cheering each new piece of fire equipment that appeared on the scene. The biggest applause came forth for a single, gigantic nozzle-piece that looked as if had not appeared since the earthquake and fire of '06. It was of no use but I think the San Francisco Fire department decided to bring out every piece of equipment they owned. There it sat at the end of the cable car line as if, in fact, it might have come by cable itself.

That's how I discovered the Buena Vista and it has continued to be my favorite San Francisco bar. (One still has a Manhattan or Martini served in a full shaker: only the cost is a little higher.) The fire, by the way, smoldered on for several days. Following the clean-up, the eastern end of that block was transformed into what is now THE CANNERY, an upscale boutique and restaurant mall similar to the Ghirardelli Chocolate factory mall which is just at the other end of the block from the Buena Vista. The "Beautiful View" overlooks the Golden Gate Bridge to the west, Alcatraz dead-on, and Sausilito and Tiburon twinkling in the distance across the bay.

Tiburon was the place where Rodney Strong first started his wine business. He was ensconced in a gingerbread house back from the docks where he sold his wine either directly from there or via his mail-order business under the label of "Windsor Winery". For a few bucks more, he would personalize labels so one could have "Bottled for the Private Cellar of..." or Happy Anniversary, Birthday, or whatever. It was a great gimmick and I had some made for my growing cellar as well as ordering cases as gifts for family and friends. It was great fun and I'm sure impressed the recipients. Rodney Strong and his wife had been a dance team who I'm convinced are the couple Brendan and I entertained for a midnite supper of curried eggs following their performance at the University of Colorado during those "ballet school" days. Rodney eventually formed a real winery between Windsor and Healdsburg where he kept a "public" label called Sonoma Winery while still maintaining the mail-order "Windsor" label. After several restructurings, he now has a label of his own called "Rodney Strong."

OPUS THIRTEEN

$\mathcal{W}$ hen I moved to Foothill College I was able to take with me, not only four years of teaching experience (helpful on the salary ladder) but unused sick leave and retirement credit as well. By 1974 I had been teaching for thirteen years and was eligible for a Sabbatical leave. My department chairman had taken his the year before, spending it in Rome while studying conducting. He was a good correspondent and wrote me very detailed letters regarding their adventures in Italy.I had traveled to England, France and Austria on a piano teachers course the previous summer which had wetted my appetite for further travel. My first thought was of studying for a portion of the Sabbatical in England since I had been stimulated so by the teacher's symposium at Kent University that summer. However, when the Sabbatical was granted, I was so thrilled to be free for a whole year with partial pay, I dreamed of going around the world instead of taking more piano lessons!

Following the example of what my department chairman , John Mortarotti, had done when they went abroad for a year, I listed my house for rent with Stanford University, as they were always needing houses for visiting professors staying for an entire year. This sort of "exchange" system works very well: a sabbatical-bound family from one University uses the residence of another sabbatical-bound house-hold which in turn keeps the mortgage paid. Interestingly enough, my "tenant" was a music professor who needed a house with a piano so that he could continue composing as well as teaching at Stanford. He also needed a good school system for his three daughters. Los Gatos, for them, was a perfect fit.

The other thing that had to be arranged was the storing of my burgeoning wine collection which, up to then, was on the floor of closets or in the crawl space beneath the house.

San Jose had a State university and was surrounded by old-fashioned residences, many of which had outside entrances to basements. I thought that I might purchase one of these, fill up the house with student-renters and store my wine in the cellar. I kept imagining that if the students knew I stored wine beneath the kitchen floor, that they might use a circular saw to get at the wine. I looked at several listed houses but was not too impressed. A young woman realtor, new to the business and eager to make a sale, said she would search the multiple listings for the kind of property I was seeking. I agreed and with the guideline to find an older house containing an outside entrance to a cellar within proximity of a college, she went to work searching. Within a short time she called to say she'd found a place near the University of Santa Clara rather than San Jose State, that had the required cellar, a cottage and a barn on a large lot. She said: "Drive by and see it and if it interests you, I'll make arrangements to inspect it."

The house at 1365 Bellomy Street was a late 19th Century farm house, but not Victorian in style. It had a small bay window in front, a cottage in back, and a half-Cathedral shaped barn. Unfortunately the barn had gaping holes in its roof and a dirt floor. It had been a real carriage barn with a hay loft above and horse tethering below on one side and carriage space on the other. The two sides were separated by a wall of unfinished redwood unsullied by sun for over 100 years. It was about that time that California was re-discovering "barnwood" for furniture and other trappings. The cottage was slightly connected to the main house via an Italinate glassed-in gazebo alongside of which was the outside entrance to the small cellar which was dug just below the kitchen. All the requirements were there except that it was obviously going to take a lot of work to put into livable shape.

I had a colleague at Foothill who taught three dimensional art as well as drawing. He was in the process of getting a divorce and was sleeping on various friend's couches during the upheaval. He'd lean out of his classroom door whenever I passed by (the art rooms had huge plate glass window-walls so lots of light could get in but it also meant passerbys could see and be seen) and Mike Cooper would say: "Bill, why don't you find me a place where I can work and live?" In as much as I was the bachelor on the faculty without wife and children to support, it was thought I was rich! When I saw "Bellomy Street", I thought of Mike immediately. I knew I couldn't make this run-down place livable, but he could, and if he would cope with fixing up the barn, then he'd have his space for work while living in the house. I called him on the phone and said: "You better come look at it; I'll buy it if you'll fix it!" He came over. It was pouring rain. The lesbians who lived there (one of whose parent's owned the property) tried to discourage us by showing the rain coming into a back closet room. Obviously they didn't want to move.

The month was March, 1973, and I had just been granted my Sabbatical for the following year. The oil crisis had not yet begun and inflation had not yet taken hold of the economy, so property values had barely budged—one dickered over a few hundred (or less) dollars in making offers and counter-offers. The owners wanted $21,000 for the place. I offered 20K and asked them to hold a $4,000 second mortgage as it was difficult to get more than a 60% loan on such an old house built on "mud sills", i.e. redwood beams that rested directly on the ground as supports to the structure. When the broker went for the closing of the sale he told the seller: "You better take this offer because that house is a wreck and you won't get a better one!" They took it and I had my second property with the potential for a beautiful wine cellar for 20K!

When Mike Cooper met me at the house that day in the rain he didn't commit himself immediately. I said I wouldn't buy it if he wasn't interested. I couldn't fix the place up myself. In a day or two he called to ask if he could have a roommate to help pay the rent (all of $150.00 per month; just enough to pay the mortgage). We agreed on a deal and he moved into the "cottage" even before escrow closed. He began work on the barn immediately in order to turn it into a viable sculpture studio. There was a huge hole on one side of the barn's dirt floor where car-junkies apparently used to work on cars from their "earth lift". This had to be filled in with new dirt, then a whole dump-truck load of gravel was spread and then cement poured. I paid for the materials, but he supplied the labor...with a lot of student help. He removed the center divider of redwood barn material (carefully) as he was going to "decorate" the interior of the main house walls in kitchen and living room with barn wood. He even built an art-deco frame for the bath tub complete with swirling curves along the tub top. He actually needed more barn wood for his project than what came out of the barn. I found a collapsing barn in Southwest San Jose whose owner allowed us to take another load of wood for Mike's decorations.

Meanwhile, my student-assistant (who turned out to be my best piano student) helped me move my cases of wine into the cellar for their sabbatical rest. I wanted to turn the basement into a proper wine cellar, but that had to wait until after the year abroad.

Mike built new slatted redwood cellar doors just like they are in Kansas tornado country (a la" Wizard of Oz"). I felt my wine would now be safe and that Mike would not saw a hole in the kitchen floor and drink my wine, although if anyone would have known how to saw through a floor, it would have been Mike!

OPUS FOURTEEN

*A*round the World on multiple airlines with multiple stops for $1,700. The one rule was: keep going forward, no backtracking and decide your route to begin with. Dates could be changed, but not routings. The "ticket" was written on Pan Am stock as that was the airline I began on and the carrier for at least half of the distance. Those were the good ol' days when Pan Am was king of around-the-world airways. As I wasn't planning to start my trip until school started, I planned to go the Pacific route in order to stay in Spring and Summer as long as I could while postponing arrival into Europe until April. Also I was eager to explore English-speaking New Zealand and Australia just in case I ever felt the need to migrate. After spending a year in France coping with a foreign language and studying some Spanish in Mexico, I thought that if I ever moved away from America it had better be to where English is spoken.

On about the first of October, 1973, I embarked on my odyssey from S.F.O. with too much luggage (I learned that quickly), a $1,700 ticket good for a year, and Arthur Frommer's "Europe on $5 & $10 A Day"! First stop: Hawaii—after all, isn't a Sabbatical supposed to rejuvenate you? My budget, not counting the air ticket, was $500 a month. Therefore, YMCA's were in, Marriots were out. Even reluctant to take taxis to and from airports due to their cost, the very first stop in Honolulu, I boarded public transportation with two pieces of luggage and a shoulder bag, then transferred buses in downtown Honolulu in order to get to the "Y" at the edge of Waikiki. I already knew that I had packed too much stuff. I stayed three or four nights at the "Y" until I found a hotel in Waikiki that had a little pent-house room complete with refrigerator and hot-plate for $55.00 a week. Fourteen stories up, while not having an ocean-view, it overlooked instead the green mountains which turned out to be a very restful view. The ocean was only a block away and each morning I started with a swim in the Pacific, followed by breakfast at one of the many seaside restaurants. As an around-the-world ticket holder, Pan Am had provided special coupons for Hawaii which included one moderately priced day's use of a rental car, and many two-for-one dinner coupons. I had made the acquaintance of a young guy at the "Y" who happened to work nights which gave him freedom during the day. We planned the car rental day on his day off in order to go around the whole island of Oahu. Besides swimming along the famous "blow-hole", we stopped at the Polynesian Cultural Center for the river parade depicting the arrival of King Kamehameha of ancient times.To maintain a semblance of sabbatical integrity, I planned to attend as many music activities as presented themselves throughout the trip.For Honolulu, that meant going to the opera's production of Boito's Mefistofele which I had never heard before and was quite thrilled by the exciting performance; the production and singers came from the New York City Opera and were very good, (The Metropolitan Opera has waited 75 years to revive it in 2000!) It was amusing to get dressed up in tropical heat to attend an opera amidst palm frond trees. I remember stepping outside during intermission and being rather overwhelmed by the heat. Ordinarily one thinks of opera season and fur coats going hand in hand.

Hawaii is very beautiful, especially up in the mountains where the vines, flowers, wild coffee trees, mahoganies, ferns, and orchids are all entangled together in lushness. There is a charming residence which has been turned into a small art museum nestled up against such hills that offers, in addition to indigenous Hawaiian paintings, some of the loveliest views of Honolulu spread out below. This is the Honolulu Art Academy built on the residence of Mrs. Charles Cook.

After savoring paradise for two weeks, I left for New Zealand via America Samoa. I'm afraid I'd been swayed to stop there by a beer commercial that went something like: "and as the sun sets on Pago Pago, I reach for a San Miguel..." Pago Pago (pronounced: "Pango Pango" which sounds better with "San") is not very romantic with or without a beer in hand. It was the only place during the entire trip in which I had to take my luggage apart for a customs inspection. Of course, it was the era of long-hair and since I had some, the bureaucratic "American" Somoan wasn't going to let a snotty-nosed "mainlander" go unnoticed.

Once in New Zealand, the Auckland airport bus took me downtown to the foot of the wharfs where cruise ships park right at the end of the street. I had never seen such beautiful ships. Then and there I started planning what I was going to do come retirement! (The ship in port was the brand-new "Royal Viking"). Meanwhile though, it was off to the local YMCA via public transportation, not exactly a simple feat in unknown territory. First, while struggling with too much luggage, one has to find out where the Y is, and then what bus-route gets you there, and then, when on the bus: "Please, Mr. Driver, let me know when I'm at the Y!" Then get off with luggage as well as psyche intact. The world, on $5 & $10 a day, ain't easy.

The "Y" in Auckland was inhabited by a lot of interesting guys who, for the most part, had jobs, but lived there for economic reasons. Unlike in the States, the room came with meals as in a pensione and it was interesting to hear all the chatter and opinions expressed by table mates as they discussed current topics. For the first time I heard the term "rubbish" used to describe some politician's utterance or policy. The English-New Zealand inflection to that word gives it an emphasis that can only be equated with the flushing of a toilet. It's definitely dismissive.

My travel-plan was to go from country to country by air, but within each country, to travel as much as possible as the "natives" do: i.e., public transportation, not only for economic reasons, but also because I wanted to feel a part of the life as they lived it. I traveled within the two islands of New Zealand for six weeks and wrote a travel article describing these weeks spent on every kind of public transportation: day-boat between Auckland and South Island; buses and a train around South Island; steamship back to Auckland; ferry to Bay of Islands, etc. I never submitted it, but it appears here as Appendix D.

At the "Y" one of the assistant directors was of Maori heritage. As a preservationist of that heritage, he instructed Maori youths in the dance rituals native to New Zealand. He invited me to attend a rehearsal one evening, which I accepted with pleasure. The Warrior dance comprises a lot of menacing stances while exaggeratingly extending the tongue. It's meant to be a scare tactic, but ends up being rather amusing to watch. The youths were encouraged to be serious about their efforts in order to convey the true menacing they were attempting to portray. The entire group was most cordial to me, their American visitor, and were especially pleased that someone was interested in their traditions. I was assured that Maoris were very friendly and if I met any and said certain words in greeting, that I would be welcomed most hospitably. The words were: "qui hora."

A few days following the Maori rehearsal I made my pilgrimage to the Bay of Islands, a marvelous series of islands, some inhabited by single houses, others not inhabited at all. I had arranged a motel stay on the largest of the islands and, after arriving to the Bay, took the fast ferry to get there. Having partaken of several glasses of sherry on the bus (New Zealanders make and drink lots of sherry and have special bars which only serve sherry—there was one near the Y in Aukland which I visited frequently!), I was feeling particularly cheerful and upon exiting the ferry, saw at the end of a long dock, a very attractive couple sitting on a bench watching the harbor activity. The male looked very much a Maori warrior type and since I was a little tipsy, went right up and spoke the magic Maori greeting. Well, nothing happened. I repeated the words and quickly told them about being told to use them, etc. (Bay of Islands was all Maori before the English arrived and that is where the last battle and eventual peace negotiations were held which forever gave Maori equal rights to the "white" man). Well, the guy said he didn't know what the words meant because he was a Japanese-American from Hawaii! Since I had recently come from Hawaii and knew the difference between a Luau and a Hukilau, I said: "Well, let's have a Hukilau, then" and rushed off to buy two beautiful fish from the boat that was tethered next to my recently departed ferryboat. (The difference between a Luau and a Hukilau is that the former is pork cooked in a fire pit while Hukilau is fish cooked over coals.) The guy and his girl-friend were helping to sail an American yacht around the world for a family that contained a normal daughter, but the two twin boys of around 14 years of age were mentally retarded. The parents thought that, instead of just trying to keep them in some sort of a school, that the whole family would be better served traveling the world for an "education" rather than staying home in Oregon. The father had built his boat himself, and, as a fine cabinet-maker, worked for whomever needed his talents whenever they stopped in a port. They were in no hurry to circumnavigate the globe.

On the bench with the twin boys and the guy with his girl friend, was an Englishman of about 35 years of age who was traveling around New Zealand in a "caravan" (European for a small house-trailer). He had painted it like a big bright bee as well as his old model "Humboldt" car with which he dragged the caravan. With this group, I was taken to the yacht and introduced to the father and mother.

My first meal at the Bay of Islands was on the yacht during which we planned the Hukilau for the next evening at the campground where the caravan was parked. The next night we gathered for the feast, other food having been procured, etc. My caravan-friend had a record player and speakers which he rigged up outside his trailer and put on Rachmaninoff. By then much sherry had been consumed as well as other wine and I began to expound on what was happening in the music, (one of my first "extemporaneous" lectures on music). I get very excited and enthusiastic when I talk about music, and unbe-knownst to me, they were all having a little pot while I'm raving on about the music. The next morning, when I found out that they had been smoking pot, the caravan-friend said: "We were just trying to keep up with you..you didn't need any pot!" The "high" of music.

In Wellington, on the southern tip of North Island, lived a former young adult couple whom I'd met in Los Altos. He was a genius math-ematician whom the U. S. government sponsored in graduate work at Stanford University. He was quite possibly involved in the Linear Nuclear testing tube built by the government along a mile course next to Stanford for atom-smashing research...all very top secret. Both husband and wife were amateur pianists and while he "worked" for the government, she enrolled in classes at Foothill where I met her. They had returned to New Zealand by the time I was there on Sabbatical. They had purchased a new home outside Wellington in a little suburb and graciously invited me to come stay with them while I was in Wellington. Her parents lived on a farm outside of Masterton, having acquired the land from the government as a reward for serv-ing in WW ll. Along with raising some cattle, they were avid home winemakers. That is where I had my first experience with Elderberry wine which I later incorporated in my own wine making experiences, most notably in creating late-harvest port-style wine. The mother's specialty was Elderberry wine which she made from the berries of wild bushes growing along the roadside. That is exactly how I found them some years later in Healdsburg. The first home wine-making book I read was by an Englishman who always suggested for nearly any red wine, the addition of Elderberries into the crush. Those recipes called for cans of condensed grape extract which , coming from California, I never needed to use.

As my young couple both worked and I was on "holiday", I stayed out of there way as they prepared to leave each morning for work (only one bathroom). Dawdling in bed until after they left, I would then get up, fix myself breakfast and put something on the record player. They owned a copy of Sibelius' 2nd symphony, although well known, I had not become acquainted with it. The 5th had been one of my romantic memories from St. Louis days and I knew the first, but not the 2nd. From the house one caught a glimpse of the fjord that flowed south from the interior of the island into the Wellington Bay. I could just see it off in the distance. By the time the last move-ment arrives with its magnificent melody— and I'm sitting mesmer-

ized by sabattical idleness and looking out toward the fjord—I understood Sibelius in all his "Finnishness" while realizing those majestic
sounds are not limited to the vistas of Finland. It was a very powerful
experience: I had Sibelius for breakfast ever morning for the rest of
my stay (sic).

From Rotorua, to Queenstown, to Napier, Mount Cook, Dunedin
Christchurch, etc., New Zealand is a lovely place, containing many
natural wonders in a relatively small area. In my imagination, it
seemed what America might have "felt" like at the turn of the 20th
century—slightly quaint. One little episode represented this feeling:
Early on in Auckland I read that a concert pianist was presenting a
recital in a hall not too far from the Y. Upon entering the hall, I saw
that the seating was on a flat floor with individual chairs lined up in
rows. I approached a row mid-way in the hall where two ladies were
seated on the two end seats with empty seats beyond them. I indicated that I wished to enter the row. They made no effort to adjust
their bodies to my passing, nor did they get up. I finally squeezed by
as their rigid, straight-out-of Kansas garbed knees pressed against
my flesh. I'm not sure whether they had ever been to a concert before,
but I thought: "This has to be prairie-ville 75 years ago!"

The best lamb dinner I've ever had was, however, in New Zealand
while visiting the seismic eruptions at Rotorua. Following a day of
inspecting the sulphuric bubblings, I strolled around the small town
and came upon a simple store-front restaurant whose window-sign
announced the evening special as roast leg of hogget. After consum-
ing my usual dosage of sherry back at my hotel, I returned for the
most delectable roast of "between lamb and mutton" dinner I've ever
encountered, not withstanding the Greek dinner in St. Louis. New
Zealanders, I was told by the manager, like their lamb more mature
than do Americans, so it has a stronger flavor. Along with roast potatoes, carrots, and natural gravy, minus the unseemly American habit
of serving a mint sauce, it was a most memorable dinner. Meat and
Potatoes: the English invented it. (See Appendix D for a description of
my tour of South Island.)

OPUS FIFTEEN

*A*fter six countrified weeks in New Zealand, I boarded another plane for my continuation of country to country flights. Before leaving Auckland, however, I visited the Botanical gardens which were busting out all over with their Spring spectacle. To my knowledge, I had never experienced a Wisteria-covered arbor before and I was overwhelmed by its full-bloom beauty. Florida doesn't grow Wisteria and Southern California is also too warm for it. But I swore one day I'd have a Wisteria arbor, and I did, later, in Healdsburg— when the Wisteria blooms in early Spring in wine country it's like a good omen for the forthcoming grape crop as their luscious purple flower clusters hang like bunches of grapes from the vine portending great vintages to come.

Upon arriving at the Sidney airport, I took my first taxi into a city as it's a long way in and it was already night time when I arrived. Sidney is also a lot bigger than either Auckland or Honolulu. From then on, the "expensive" taxi ride from the airport into town became the norm, particularly since future arrivals would be in foreign-tongued venues (one can't just go up and ask which local bus to take, although I did just that when I finally arrived in Rome!) In Sydney, I asked the cabbie to take me to the Y, but when we arrived it was full. He drove me to a cheap hotel the Y suggested that I go to just down the street, but inflation thusly commenced for The World on "$5 & $10 a day!"

My first full day in Sydney was spent finding better accommodations.I had heard about the King's Cross area from someone in New Zealand and so taking the subway to that area, I began my search.Among charming older buildings mixed in with newer ones, I found a renovated hotel-apartment building with a vacancy sign in the window. The rental was for a month at a time and as I expected to stay at least that long, I took it. The converted hotel room had a closet-kitchen with a sink and utensils which meant I didn't have to take all meals out. The shower and toilet were community affairs at the end of the hall. Thusly, I began my sojourn in one of the most beautiful cities in the world.

The endless harbor makes it one of the most spectacular cities in the world. The proximity to the ocean via a ferry-boat ride is as unique as going to a place called "Manly Beach" in the first place! The

Sydney Chamber of Commerce issues the following statement regarding the latter: "Captain Arthur Phillip, Commodore of the First Fleet and later the first governor of New South Wales, sailed near the site of Manly during an inspection tour of Point Jackson in January, 1788. So impressed was Phillip by the proud bearing of the Aborigines there that he named the place 'Manly Cove.'" The mind-blowing Opera House, built out onto a spit into the harbor, is now as famous a world-wide landmark as the Eiffel Tower or the Golden Gate Bridge and in fact is more spectacular than either of the aforementioned. I can't say how many rolls of film I took of that building, but I took them from every imaginable angle: from ferries on the bay; from the beautiful bridge to its left; from the heights of the neighboring park; from its front incline of steps; from the tall tower building behind it in the city; etc. Naturally, I attended several performances there in all its venues: movie theater, opera house and concert hall, as well as frequently having lunch or breakfast at its outdoor cafe water-side. Luckily, King's Cross was within easy walking distance and so my frequent visits simply added some aerobics to my trips. The Sydney Symphony also performed in a hall within town which provided a more intimate sound than the one heard in the vast opera house.

As it was Christmas time in Australia, "Messiah" by Handel was the featured concert at the opera house's concert hall (different than the hall in which operas are performed). Having grown up in Florida, which also had a tropical Christmas- time, it was somewhat nostalgic to be celebrating Christmas amongst palm trees while Santas, ringing bells at the Salvation Army kettles, wore shorts.

Prior to leaving California on my journey, I had become a Limited Partner in a new vineyard venture called Monterey Vineyards which was put together by a well-known Central Valley farm family by the name of McFarland...there is even a town near Bakersfield named for that family. They had not grown wine grapes before, but were convinced, because of their agricultural experience, that they could grow grapes in Monterey county. Mirrassou and Paul Masson had already developed vineyards there and McFarland wanted to develop vineyards with rows of one mile in length to facilitate machine harvesting. By this time I was buying more and more wine and wanted somehow to become more involved with wine production. My becoming a limited partner in a new venture seemed, therefore, appropriate. Knowing at that time that I was going around the world,

I decided to have business cards printed indicating that I was a limited partner in Monterey Vineyards so that I might gain entry into some wineries during my travels.

Brandishing my newly printed business cards, I proceeded to the offices of one of the biggest wineries in all of Australia's burgeoning wine industry, McWilliams. (The names of wineries in Australia are all startlingly Anglo sounding, unlike California titles which sound more Italian or French. It was hard to take generic Anglo names seriously—until one tasted their wine!) Great strides were being made by them to make Bordeaux style reds, particularly in the Hunter Valley vineyards and McWilliams was chief among wineries to do so. I presented my card at their winery offices in Sydney and the representatives pretended to be duly impressed. They invited me to a private tasting at their VIP tasting bar saying: "Come back about 4 p.m," which I did. Several officers of the company proceeded to open their best stuff including champagne with which, I believe, we started. My Staten Island days of "propriety" barely kept me on the bar stool— maybe they were testing my tolerance! At any rate, I managed to convey to them that I was most interested in reds, that I cellared reds, etc. By the end of the tasting, one of the officers suggested that I accompany him to the Hunter Valley and visit their facilities, spend the night, etc. There could be no better way to visit Australia's red wine capital than by private car and with an officer of a winery.

It was about a three hour drive to the country and by mid-afternoon we arrived at an old-fashioned hotel whose proprietor knew the official well. We had a fine roast lamb dinner—always the best choice in either New Zealand or Australia if you want to accompany it with red wine. The experience reminded me of my days spent touring for National School assemblies when I would stop at funky old hotels that served fine food. Except I didn't have fine local red wine with the meals in those former days. The next morning we visited the company vineyards as well as neighboring vineyards and wineries, stopping for lunch at Polkobin for another fabulous steak, complimented by a 1955 McWilliams Hermitage. In the afternoon we visited the boutique winery of Max Lake who happened to be a surgeon in Sydney, but was very interested in developing the Cabernet Sauvignon grape in Australia (the main ingredient of Bordeaux) and who had written a book on Australian wine making. He called his little winery "Lake's Folly" where he autographed a bottle of his Bordeaux-style wine for me and told me to stop by his office when back in Sydney to pick up an autographed copy of his book. When I did, upon my return to Sydney, he extended an invitation to dinner at his home. My little business card was working wonders.

His residence was across the beautiful bridge past the Opera House and thence northward up into the nooks and crannies of the extensive Sydney harbor. Max Lake met me at the door barefoot, while I was dressed, I believe, in coat and tie. He immediately produced a lovely French white wine which, I soon learned, I consumed too fast: "Oh you Californians drink wine as if it were water!" he remarked. Regulating myself as best as I could, we eventually went to "table" where the guests—including Wally from McWilliams who had taken me to the Hunter Valley—were about ten people in number. Max Lake's wife, also a doctor, was equally gracious and casually costumed. Their dinner (each took turn in preparing and presenting the courses) was in the form of a guessing game as to where the wines served came from. There was hardly any other conversation, only: "what is it and where do you think it came from?"

There was plenty of wine—that is, one bottle per course and there were innumerable courses. Each item was served separately accompanied by a different wine. I can't recall all the courses, but following the meat course I remember that we were served haricot verts (green beans), a bit stringy and undercooked, to my taste, but, oh yes: a fresh bottle of wine to accompany it. As I was placed at the host's left side (place of honor at a proper dinner affair) he repeatedly quizzed me first as to the origin of the wine. Being a neophyte at this kind of game, I could only exclaim, at best: "Its French!" Many of the company named the origins of the various wines more accurately than I, but I think they had been entertained before by Max Lake.

Manly Beach, as well as others up and down the coast, stage "Surf Carnivals"throughout the summer which pit teams of life guards competitively in the various life-saving techniques they are required to perform. The life-saving clubs each have their particular team color, in spite of the fact that the bathing costume is very brief. But they wear tight-fitting caps as well as jackets all displaying their team colors, making for a very colorful display on the beach. They march onto the beach in formations, carrying life-boats, surf-boards and pennants describing their home beach. The races take place under the careful watch of referees who are out-riding in motor-boats, often in very rough seas. I took quite a lot of slides over several week-ends of these carnivals and produced a cover-story for THE ADVOCATE which was published March 13, 1974 (I airmailed slides and story from Sydney.) When I was in France for that season in 1950-51, we went to England for the Easter holiday where we saw that Londoners, as soon as the sun emerges a tiny bit, rip off their clothes to catch a few rays on their otherwise pale skin. I had the distinct impression, after viewing these Surf Carnivals, that Australians are Englishmen who had come out from "under their rock" in England, and after catching plenty of fresh air and sunshine, turned into muscular giants.

After my one month in the "efficiency-apartment" was up, I spent my last two weeks in Australia on Cougee Beach in an old Greek revival hotel which faced the park and ocean directly across from the Cougee Beach life guard station. I had the use of a portion of a refrigerator and gas stove down in the basement so that, once again, it was not necessary to take all meals in restaurants. I was managing, for the most part, to live on "$5 & $10 A Day." Ah: life on the Lido!

OPUS SIXTEEN

$\mathcal{U}$p, up and away...to Bali! Now the truly "foreign" experiences were about to begin. Arriving at the airport for Denpasar, I immediately headed for the tourist desk, a tactic that I followed for the rest of the journey. Before I could get there, I was deluged by young men holding placards advertising their particular accommodation. I believe I got to the desk to inquire about modest accommodations; but it may have been one of the more persistent "guides" who convinced me that he would take me to a very reasonable hotel. In any case, after verifying with the desk that it was OK to go with this guy and that there was such a hotel, we took off in a hail of dust by taxi which he had already arranged for. The airport, as it often is, was a long way from the town, and the hotel we were heading for was beyond Denpasar. All I could think of was how exorbitant the fare would be. It turned out to be not too much...long taxi rides are the norm in such places. The "hotel" was a compound of low buildings, sort of like a court-centered motel would be in the '30's in America, not architectural speaking, but as to grouping. We were greeted by several youths garbed in batik sarongs, bowing, offering flowers, drinks, etc. I said that I'd be there for a week. They put me into a small dark room which, after the expansiveness of Australia, gave me claustrophobia. "Don't you have anything else?" I asked. All the rooms were on the ground floor (motel court style) save one which was sided on three sides by glass windows in the style of the old-fashioned school room. It was reached by a single flight of stairs with a turn at the top into the room which contained three single beds— dormitory style. But they said I could have it for the price of a single. I took it and basked in my view of the entire little villa which overlooked the gardens below, the family shrine and many palm trees. All family compounds in Bali contain a family shrine which must be attended to several times a day. The girls of the house-hold create a small offering basket made from a single palm-frond and filled with Fragapani blossoms and a little cooked rice or cake as offering to the Gods which acts as protection for the compound. The offerings are placed in altar-like stupas and are intended to ward off evil spirits of all sorts. I was told that the turn at the top of the staircase to my room was built especially with evil spirits in mind, because, while they might follow me up the stairs, they cannot turn into the room and therefore they plunge over the edge of the landing!

Along with warding off of evil spirits, I was serenaded by roosters crowing each morning, amused by watching tame pigs wander in the muddy streets below, and continually wafted with the scent of coconut shell smoke which came from the cooking fires in use throughout the neighborhood. Everything they say about Bali—at least in 1974—is right: lovely people, beautiful temples everywhere, marvelous artisans. Each town is famous for one or another craft; woodcarving in one, jewelry in another, stone sculpture, "opera" productions, dancing or the gamelan in others. Every town has a gamelan orchestra, but some towns are more famous for them than others. The orchestra consists primarily of struck instruments: low wooden-framed sets of metal bars which are struck by mallets by the player from a seated position. They are all dressed alike and wear a sort of military cap indicative of their particular community. Although the gamelan can be listened to for its own sake, it is used primarily to accompany the many story-dances which permeate Balinese life, the most famous being THE BARONG. As its most prized possession, every village has its head-piece for the Barong Dance, and every village performs this dance as it is a rite of passage for the young boys of the village.

As all Balinese life revolves around religion, which is a mix of Hindu and ethnic beliefs that has led to a unique version called "Bali Hinduism", the conflict of good and evil is central to the belief system. In the BARONG DANCE these forces are embodied by the mythical creature—half boar, half lion—called the Barong. It takes two men beneath the costume to perform the highly coordinated steps. Evil is portrayed by Rangda, the Witch. The "dance-play" is a series of interchanges between the Barong and Rangda in association with their minions. The great purification aspect of this spectacle is that the village boys (early teen-agers) are the Kris "dancers". The Kris is a dagger and as these dancers are "good" and in the service of the Barong, they try to annihilate Rangda with their daggers. But Rangda bewitches the Kris dancers causing them to turn their daggers onto themselves. The climax of the drama arrives when, amidst this frenzy of attempting to pierce their own bodies, their faith in the goodness of the Barong saves them, for no dagger penetrates their bodies. During this climactic event, the clanging of the gamelan is fortissimo. No blood is shed, Rangda withdraws, having once again been defeated in her endeavor to overcome the Barong by bewitching the Kris dancers. A Balinese priest arrives and sacrifices a baby chicken which releases the dancers from their spell...end of dance.

I have seen this performed several times, and being slightly curious, peeked in "backstage", prior to a performance, to observe a priest administering to the boy dancers prior to the spectacle. By prayers and incense, he places them into a trance-like state in order to prepare them for their encounter with evil Rangda. The boys believe it and it is a believable spectacle. Every village boy, at some point, becomes a Kris dancer, similar to the Thai tradition that every male must spend some time during his life as a monk.

The town of Ubud is the center for painting in Bali. I spent a few days there to see the art and to attend a dance production presented by the most famous Balinese group whose dancers had made at least two international tours prior to 1974. I stayed at what was really private grounds which had one or two cottages for rent. My water for bathing and toilet was hand poured into a cistern in an opening in the wall by one of the attendant boys. In order to bathe, you hand-poured the tepid water by tin cup over yourself.But fragapani blossoms everywhere helped you to survive.

It was in Ubud where a Dutch artist Smit came to Bali following WWII and, intrigued by the talent of the local artists who meticulously reproduced the age-old Hindu myths on fabric (over and over again), taught them to use brighter colors and to paint the look of their life-style instead of slavishly reproducing myth pictures. The "Young Artist" movement in Bali thereby commenced. Ubud became the center and that is where one goes if he wants to see and buy the New Art of Bali. I trekked by foot through rice fields to get to Penestanan, the most famous residence of the "young artists" where I purchased two oils. One depicts the Barong dance in vivid colors complete with gamelan players and audience watching, in other words a depiction of real Balinese life. The other picture was a colorful, primitivo picture of the bird-God Garuda carrying on his back the monkey king Hanuman as he goes to the rescue of Rama and his consort, Sita. All of that comes from Hindu mythology, but presented in a modern, colorful manner. The artists were an uncle and his very young nephew (perhaps only twelve years of age), busily painting away when I arrived. I bought one from each. Back in Ubud I found a gallery stuffed with paintings, but one, hung haphazardly over a doorway, intrigued me the most. It was an Impressionistic rendering of rice fields and palm trees—the landscape that I was seeing daily. It was small, but a very beautiful little painting and quite unlike the others as it was almost like a photograph of the landscape. Although atypical, it did follow the Dutchman Smit's dictum: "Paint what you see!" I bought it for $15.00! Finally, in another gallery, I encountered a large (3' by 5') oil depicting the Barong in all his vibrant motion: mythical head-piece of Boar and Lion in vivid red; glowering eyes; a frenzy of movement of its tassels of green and yellow creating the essence of the motion of the dance carried onto canvas: a Picasso-Matisse-like frenzy of color and movement. The picture captured the quality of the most important dance in Bali, THE BARONG! $20.00 purchased it!

One heard that Singapore didn't like long hair on men. So before leaving Bali, I had to have my locks shorn...I did retain my mustache, however. Upon arriving in Singapore I managed to find a "Y" where each morning one could see a whole field of people doing morning ritual of Tai Chi appearing quite like an army maneuver. Singapore was a little too purile for my taste, although I did enjoy some of the finger-food from the night stalls that do a big business in the evening from the roving crowds "grazing". As my film supply had been great-ly reduced by now, I was able to purchase about thirty rolls of film for about the same price as one can purchase them in the U.S., since Singapore is famous as a "duty-free port".

The most exotic thing I encountered in Singapore was going to an orchestral concert and observing their "symphony" whose string sec-tion contained long-necked instruments which are played with a bow between the strings and the wooden "sound-box", rather than in front of the strings as violins are played. The sound is also strange: a sort of out-of-tune whine in a mixture of Western and Eastern "tonal-ities". I wrote in my diary: "the one cymbal and drum drowned them out frequently. Chinese love noise for some reason—they cover up the refined and quite beautiful string sounds with banging!" But it was definitely "World Music", and would certainly be a plus for my obligatory Sabbatical report.

Malaysia is just above Singapore; in fact Singapore used to be a part of Malay during the legendary Raffles Hotel days. The flight to Penang was by Singapore Airlines and just as they advertise, the treatment for everyone is "first class". The flight was all too brief. I arrived in Penang at the end of the day but was able to find a central-ly located hotel right down town following three attempts. The next morning I awoke to find that I had arrived not only for Chinese New

Year celebrations, but during important Hindu penitential ceremonies as well. Again the dairy records: "for the Chinese parade it
was the first time in 48 years the Tua Peh Kong idol was taken in the
Chingay procession." The streets were so crowded, I went, instead,
onto the roof of my eight story hotel where I could see all the action
as well as take photographs. Although there were many colorful
floats, the more fascinating thing were the whole divisions of men
dressed alike (wearing white pants and distinctive tee shirts) whose
objective was to carry a huge bamboo pole, festooned with streamers, and balanced by a single participant. When he could no longer
balance the immense pole, the others would rush forward to catch it
and then pass it on to another "contestant". There were more than
one of these kinds of groups; in fact, each float was separated by such
a band of men, and just as in Australia's surf festivals, each team had
its own colors and distinctive tee shirt. It may be that the men-teams
were related to each float by club, for only women adorned the floats.
Being a foreigner and high up on a building's roof, I could only con-
jecture.

Off in the distance I became aware that something else was transpiring. Either coincidentally—or politically—on the same day that
Chinese New Year's was being celebrated, the Hindu population was
having an important annual event, this one more powerful in its
effect. This was a day of atonement when Hindus, mostly men, called
Kavadi, pierced themselves with needles or put swords through one
side of the mouth to the other, and wore head pieces of knives pointed into their flesh, all as penance or to propitiate for a year's worth of
good fortune. Thusly pierced, they then walked through the streets
accompanied by family and friends beating drums. From my roof
location watching the Chinese parade, the sound of far off drumming
was how I first became aware of this new activity.Leaving my roof top,
I went in the direction of the drumming until I came upon a staging
area where the penitents were getting their bodies prepared for the
ordeal. I witnessed (and photographed) a teenage boy being hypno-
tized by prayers and incense wafting into his face prior to his body
being pierced. The ritual requires that no blood will be drawn
because their faith is so strong. In fact, the administer of the piercing
uses copious amounts of alum as the objects are placed into the skin.
Indeed, when the penitent starts his march, his body looks ashen
from all of the alum that has been rubbed on him, creating a rather
ghostly appearance. I followed these penitents all the way up into the

hills above Penang to the Hindu temple. Through the open portals I was able to view the priests who awaited them to conclude the ordeal. The whole effect was quite different from the Chinese celebration , and I assume, intentionally so. From the diary: "a Hindu businessman yesterday broke 1200 coconuts because his business was good and he had vowed to do so. A Chinaman, fat and prosperous looking, was running around with great handfuls of incense, heaving them about all the statues of the Pagoda temple today! What does it all mean?"

Chinese New Years and a Hindu holy day is a lot to take in one eight hour stretch. It called for a leisurely Chinese dinner on an open-air second floor balcony restaurant where one could enjoy a San Miguel beer and oyster dumplings while viewing the crowd below...as the sun set into the Strait of Malacca and thence far off into the Andaman Sea...

OPUS SEVENTEEN

During my sojourn in Australia, new acquaintances told me where to stay in Bangkok, so for a change, I had only to tell the cab driver where to go when arriving by air. Throughout the Vietnam war Thailand was the favored R &R spot for American serviceman, but by the time I was there, that conflict had been settled, leaving the many charms of the Thai to be extended to tourists! As a matter of fact, one had to fight them off!

Other than the personal charm of the "Siamese", the most striking thing is the sudden and unexpected appearance of a splendid temple or Buddhist stupa haphazardly sprouting amidst hotels and houses. They abound. And they are beautiful. They all look as if they had just been built, glistening with gold leaf and exquisite filigree. Even the lorry trucks are colorfully decorated and "detailed" in an individual way for each vehicle.

The King's Royal temple (The Emerald Buddha Temple) is, of course, the most extravagantly beautiful and guarded everywhere by the sculptured dogs that keep continual vigil over the Buddhas and stupas, each seeming more radiant in gold that the last. One of the ritual venerations is to purchase gold leaf and adhere it to the base of a Buddha while also presenting flowers and incense. One must never sniff the flowers before making the presentation, otherwise the prayer and offering is not accepted!

Thai dancing is considerably more refined that Balinese dancing and demands extensive training at an early age in order for muscles to learn to bend hands backwards, as well as head and neck. The various positions of torso, hands and feet all have specific meaning and is only truly understood by a Thai. For the foreigner, it is enough to enjoy the consummate grace and dignity of the dance. I enjoyed this spectacle at a Thai feast which is made commercially available by certain hotels and restaurants. The natural spontaneity of the Ubud dancers was missing, but then we are speaking of two quite different cultures.

I journeyed to Chiang Mai by bus which requires a long day of travel from Bangkok, but one is rewarded with such sights as elephants doing road work much like bull dozers do elsewhere. The Northern Thai peasants wear very colorful wool costumes during all seasons of the year and are very much in evidence surrounding the temples either begging or selling there wares.More incense, flowers and gold leaf...one must continually be prepared to make offerings.

My ultimate "offer" was to Montree Suksusin who had acted as my guide during my last week spent in Bangkok and who had escorted me to the southern beaches of Thailand, currently made fashionable by the film "THE BEACH." His reward was spending two years in California under my sponsorship as a student in an English-as-a-second language program produced by the San Jose school system for the many foreign students that find there way to Silicon Valley.

India is an appalling place! Appalling in its squalor. Appalling in its magnificence. Appalling in its diet of curried food: breakfast, lunch and dinner, it all tastes the same. One thinks if for only one meal you could change the flavor then maybe the next regular meal of curried this and that could be endured. But no, it is a relentless taste that never lets up. By the time I had spent about ten days in New Delhi and then ventured to Benares on the Ganges I was beginning to feel really sick to my stomach. The sweet man who ran the little hotel where I stayed (as the only guest) said he'd have a supper fixed to soothe me following my complaint of feeling queasy. Following a rest in my room, I was called to dinner (alone). A turbaned attendant served me a meal replete with curry and tasting just like all the rest. That's how they cook in India; there is never a variance in flavor. The curry, along with the continuous breathing of dung-dust, contributes to a special ambiance that is unique to India. The religious veneration of free roaming cattle, with their concomitant defecation everywhere and anywhere, produces a pulverized powder which permeates every breath of air. On the way to Agra to view the Taj Mahal, one travels by overnight train. As we swept through the remote fields, the out-caste people, living like animals, were squatting naked in the fields making their morning defecations! During my flight from Thailand I sat next to a charming, educated Indian with whom Î had a pleasant conversation. When I asked about the "untouchables" (which I was yet to encounter), he said: "We don't see them ...they don't exist!" For a foreigner, having to move carefully between "untouchables" rolled up in old carpets and laying about on the steps of public buildings, one, indeed, "sees" them.

In my quest to use public transportation whenever possible, I boarded a municipal bus one morning. The press of humanity (packed like sardines would be an understatement) was overwhelming—over smelling! I had to elude a woman's breast near my face as if

I'd been her lover. From then on I took the Harley Davidson three wheeled motor cycle jitneys which take one or two persons along more or less prescribed routes. The train to Benares, however, was the ultimate local travel experience. As a foreigner one had to go seek a special officer at the railway station, show passport, etc. and then request a sleeping birth. I didn't realize that at the time of booking, if one wants a pillow and a blanket one needs to reserve them at that time. There were no regular "bunks" available as they had already been booked. I was placed in a compartment that was the magistrate's compartment as well as used for "spill over" when all the rest of the bunks had been taken. The magistrate was an official government judge whose job was meting out immediate punishment for violators of any railroad rules. The majority of the train was in open seating crammed with people, some even hanging onto the roof of the train. Obviously, there were frequent brawls and thefts with so much humanity crammed together. The judge was a delightful man and most eager to hear my thoughts on Richard Nixon who was yet to resign. When it was time to go to bed, his man-servant brought forth sleeping paraphernalia and laid it out for the judge's night's rest. When the judge realized I had not provided for bedding, he ordered his servant to lay on an extra blanket for me, saying that he always carried extra bedding. He was most gracious and when I complained of the sameness in the taste of the food, he invited me to his country residence on my return from Benares for a proper Indian meal. I would have done so, but by the time I was ready to leave Benares, I couldn't imagine that train ride in reverse. For, following the night journey, the reasonably adequate compartment was uncoupled from the train and the rest of an all-day journey had to be made in "coach class." Awaiting me at the small hotel in Benares was yet another curried meal!

Benares is a sacred city for Hindus, many of whom wish to be cremated there and have their ashes pushed into the Ganges River. To view this, one rises before dawn and is taken by small boat to witness the morning rituals as well as the cremations. As the sun rises, devotees are seen bathing in the river while wearing only thong-like scarves for covering.Holy men sit cross legged on little individual piers facing the river and the rising sun, some of whom are nearly naked while others are swathed in saffron robes. We were requested to not photograph the cremations. Following the boat trip, I made my way by land to where the cremations were taking place as I wanted to understand how a body could be burned up apparently so easily. The "funeral director" (essentially a wood salesman) was negotiating with a client whose deceased was already wrapped in white linen and laying on a litter. Their negotiations regarded how many pieces of wood would be received for such and such a price. Once established, (it wasn't very much wood) the body was placed on some rocks while the scant amount of wood was distributed around the head and a little down the side of the body...by no means a funeral pyre as we've seen in National Geographic pictures when some notable has been cremated. Once arranged, the relative is given a small vial of oil or ghee and is told to walk around the deceased anointing the body. This fellow didn't go in the prescribed direction and had to be turned around by the funeral director in order to complete the ceremony properly.The relative was then given a torch with which to ignite the pyre. My camera was in its case and I barely moved, being amazed that no one questioned or even seemed to notice my presence. It was amazing to see how easily the human body burns. Other pyres had already been ignited and as the "material" became more spread-out, the director would rake in the remaining parts just as one would rake a pile of burning leaves. When the pyre is consumed, attendants rake the debris into the Ganges and there, like vultures, await the scavengers who scrounge through the wet ashes seeking any bits of gold teeth or jewelry possibly left on the decedent. Meanwhile, carcasses of dead animals float by in the "cleansing" waters of the Ganges and another day in the endless cycle of birth and death in India ensues.

The Taj Mahal is everything its touted to be and is the people's national treasure. They come to play games on its great terraces and parks, and to picnic and bask in its beauty. The inlay of semi-precious stones in intricate flower patterns adorn the portals of the great empty mausoleum. Following lunch in a local restaurant, tourists are taken to a marble factory store where artisans descended from the original Taj builders continue the tradition of inlaid marble work. There one sees examples of this artistry in varying sizes of coffee and end tables as well as pottery and jewelry. I was intrigued by a soft pink marble end table top that had beautiful inlay design in the same manner as that seen at the Taj Mahal. For only $100 I purchased it and arranged for its shipment back to California. They had me sign the back of the table with a crayon so that I would know that I had received the one I had selected upon its arrival. It was promised to be delivered in six months time and they guaranteed that it would be replaced if it broke in transit. When it did arrive six months later I found that it had been wrapped tightly in heavy twine over every inch of the marble as one would make a mandalay and then placed in a wooden crate. I unpacked it at the post office just in case the "guarantee" would have to be exercised. Fortunately it was in perfect condition and today serves in the living room at Shelter Cove along side the Balinese paintings.

I feel fortunate to have visited Iran while the Shah was still in power because Americans were welcomed in their country at that time. It had only been the previous year or so when the Shah had hosted a huge celebration for world leaders in his elaborate tent city at the foot of the remains of Darius' palace in Persepolis. Spiro Agnew represented the United States and from the pictures we were privileged to see in our national magazines, he received the best tent, after the Shah's, of course; (oh, the vanquished "greats" even as Darius had been vanquished by Alexander the Great aeons before!) The clerk at the tourist desk at Theran's airport suggested that I stay at a hotel called America Hotel which happened to be directly across from the American Embassy whose fate was yet to unfold as the protracted hostage site during the transformation of Persian life several years later.

As is often the case in Islamic societies, men do the public chores in public places: my hotel was exclusively staffed by men—in suits and ties—as they made beds, waited on tables in the restaurant, and I'm sure, cooked in the kitchen. Everyone was very attentive and discreet. A bountiful breakfast was included in the price of the room and for dinner, I found an excellent French restaurant within walking distance of the hotel. I walked everywhere in Tehran, even up into their hills above the city on their New Years Day which is the first day of spring sometime in March. The tradition is to walk into the hills and pluck a branch which is just starting to sprout leaves or blossoms and bring it back into the city.I didn't pluck any branches, but I enjoyed the walk and seeing the many attractive, slender and well dressed young women in groups or with their boy friends. There were beautiful shops full of fashionable Western style clothing, so it was very hard for me to believe what happened to all those people's lives following the "Islamic Revolution" and the overthrow of the Shah.

On the overnight trip to Shiraz, the actual New Year's proclamation was made by the Shah over the radio at about 2:30 a.m. and was broadcast live on the bus. Nearly all the occupants were men and they were very attentive to his New Year's greetings. The Shah's son (of early teen age years) also spoke. There was much applause in the bus. It was very difficult for me to imagine the consequent happenings in that country following my very pleasant personal experiences there.

Two other vivid memories arise: one was seeing the bejeweled Peacock Throne which supposedly had been stolen from India centuries before when Islam conquered that country, and the great collection of jewels held for viewing in the basement of the Central Bank. There one saw mounds of loose gems: emeralds, diamonds, rubies, sapphires, as well as the tiaras, encrusted ceremonial swords, daggers, etc., all kept under surveillance by men wearing Western style dark suits and ties. It felt as if I were going into a Mafia den.

The other spectacle is to browse through the Bazaar which is a series of tunnel-like buildings filled with every conceivable item to buy, but especially exotic brass lanterns, platters, bowls, rugs, fabric, cushions, silks, velvets, all being hawked vigorously by vendors. Amongst this sea of activity, boys glide about balancing trays of tea to be delivered to pre-arranged customers.

On the bus to Isfahan following the Shah's New year's greeting, we arrived at dawn for a breakfast stop. My gruff-looking but gently kind seat-mate advised me what to do as they went off for brief ablutions and their morning prayer. The prayers finished, the entire bus load of men sat down at long tables and, as advised by my seat-mate, I ordered fried eggs and bread and coffee just as if it were in America. These experiences made it all the more difficult for me to comprehend the revolution that was to come and to compare my treatment as an American to those who followed me, only a little while later, to Tehran.

Postcards of "Cocteau chapel"

William J. Bryan on roof-top in
Villefranche-sur Mer, France

Clockwise: WJB in front of:
Sphinx, Eqypt
Hindu Temple, India
and Taj Mahal, India

Clockwise:
WJB in Bellomy St. Wine Cellar
Top of wine rack creating display
and
With Kim Ramsey in Wine Cellar

Clockwise:
Montree with WJB in
Bellomy St. Wine Cellar

Enjoying pool in Los Gatos

Newly earth-covered wine cellar,
Healdsburg

Gazebo at Bellomy Street

GLOBAL TELEVISION

Main Studio: 280 S. "I" Street, San Bernadino, CA
Auxiliary Studio: 1950 Cotner Avenue, Los Angeles, CA

Recording of three programs for Transcendental Meditation station ("SCI"
means Science of Creative Intelligence, a course offered by TM)

Follow-up discussion of programs
with Soboba Springs Center Director

Top left: Emptying bottles for sculpture!

Top right: Bottle Sculpture

Lower: Dining room built on back deck (Healdsburg)

From top:
"Wall" and fountian, Healdsburg
"Bryan Wine" on wall
Bottle Sculpture, Healdsburg

Clockwise:
Bruce and Isabelle Adams, WJB
Bottle sculpture in arbor
Arbor in full wisteria bloom

OPUS EIGHTEEN

In 1974, if one had visited Israel before entering Egypt he was denied entry! I wanted very much to visit the land of the Pharaohs so I had to forgo Israel. A colleague at Foothill College, Gordon Holler, had spent two years in Egypt as photographer for an official dig.When he knew that I would be spending time in Egypt, he hand-drew a map of Cairo indicating things that I must see...including one of the famous baths!When I did venture out at night to that venue, after acquiring handwritten indications of the bath's name and address, the cab driver was very nervous about taking me into "that part of the city". Nevertheless, following my visit to the baths, I blithely walked the several miles back to my hotel, stopping along the way at an orange juice stand which was busily preparing fresh juice for the new day, and I never felt uncomfortable in the least bit. Either times have changed or I have (had) the luck of the Irish!

Again, upon arriving at the airport outside of Cairo, the tourist desk referred me to a reasonable hotel right in the center of Cairo, within walking distance of the famous Hilton Hotel on the Nile and around the corner, almost, of the National museums. In this hotel, although all the attendants were male, instead of being dressed in coat and tie, as in Tehran, they wore "nightgown" type of costumes as they glided about the hotel like ghosts in soft slippers or barefooted while showing you to your room, waiting on you at table, etc.

I'm afraid that when you've seen one mummy you've seen them all. They all look pretty much alike. The uniqueness appears in the coffin paintings and decorations as well as the tomb objects that were placed within the sarcophagus. The obligatory trip to the Pyramids was made complete with the terrifying experience of crawling up a wooden ladder within the great pyramid in pitch darkness until one finally emerges into an empty inner chamber! It's not worth the fright just to say you've been inside. I don't recommend it for anyone, like myself, who has claustrophobia. Rather, enjoy the incredible sight from the outside and then take lunch, as I did, within view of the Sphinx.

Luxor was an overnight train ride from Cairo and, in spite of recent terrorist activities, is worth visiting. The great temple with its series of immense columns is even more impressive to me that the pyramids. There is a sound and light show offered in several languages which is well worth attending (which I have enjoyed on a more recent visit.)

And if you have the chance for a sunset sailing in a felucca on the Nile, take it. It can be one of the most romantic things you'll ever do. Choose your boat boy by intuition and inspiration...take some wine with you and then relax and enjoy the sunset over the Nile (no beer, this time...the Nile deserves a fine wine or cognac.)

Europeans visit Egypt like Americans go to the Caribbean: an easy trip from cold Northern climates during the winter where one finds very attractive resorts for sunning and swimming. I lunched in one outside Cairo and wished I had stayed longer in Egypt when I arrived to a cold Greece in April.

Greece, the cradle of Western civilization. When I was there in April of 1974 one could still walk around the "cradle", the Acropolis. Today its closed off and one can only view it from afar. But it is a wondrous spectacle sitting atop the hill overlooking centuries of history, including Roman history. Hadrian's Gate was just a few steps from my little room in what we would call a "rooming house." I was staying there before I belatedly discovered a "teacher's tour" exploring Classic sights through the whole of Greece which had already left for its first stop in Delphi. The tour agent put me on a regular commuter bus and I joined up with the group by nightfall. The group of about 20 people included three seminarians from America who were studying in Rome but were spending their Easter break exploring Greece. One feels the mysteries of ancient Greece, with its oracular pronouncements and legendary thinkers, at every step and stone: a pile of rocks takes on profound meanings when one is in Greece, and amidst little grottoes and swaying pines, one imagines he hears the oracle speaking. Arriving in Corinth, our very pleasant guide had one of the Novitiates read from an Epistle of Paul to the Corinthians while we stood about in the very ruins that Paul had spent time in himself (again the "oracle" speaking?)

My most treasured moment of that trip was viewing the incredibly beautiful statue of Hermes by Praxiteles, sculpted during the Golden Age of Greece. It is in Olympia, birthplace of the Olympics. In the museum, one enters the large room to see Hermes standing in the center of a large sandbox which, in case of an earthquake, would cushion his fall. In its original state it was painted with colors and gold leaf. Today it stands in all its naked alabaster glow simply staring out at you with blind eyes, as that is part of what was painted in earlier days. The baby God Dioniossius (god of Wine) is reaching out to catch hold of imaginary grapes as the arm and hand holding them has long been broken off. I've had only one other such moving experience while viewing a statue and that is when I saw (later) David in the Academia in Florence. He, likewise, stood alone in a room, incredible to behold, beholden to no other statue in the world more renowned than he. Upon seeing such originals one realizes the importance of viewing the original. I saw my first "David", in a copy made probably of cement, in the garden of the Ringling Museum in Sarasota, Florida. It's a lovely garden full of reproductions of various famous sculptures with David standing at the very end of the garden, well placed, effective, but not the thrill of the original. In visiting Florence, one sees David everywhere: in front of the Palazzo Signoria; high on a hill above the city on the other side of the river Arno, (Piazzale Michelangelo), there stands an oversized metal rendering of David, effective because one sees all of Florence lying below. But none of these compare to the original. That thought, perhaps, is the best reason for travel: seeing the original of anything, be it an artistic masterpiece or the authentic setting of a people or civilization. To see the original playing field in Olympia, with its earth shaped side banks where viewers stood in ancient times to observe the Games, is to recall one's own school football field, with its tiered bleachers raised on each side of a similar length of action. Then antiquity becomes less ancient.

Back in Athens, following our antiquities tour, in the National Museum, I could view the artifacts retrieved from the various sites we had visited and to appreciate them with a greater understanding. To get to the refinement of a Praxiteles, earlier sculptors, with less sharpened tools or techniques, created more massive renderings of the male figure called Kouroi, where face and figure were less defined, but where the legs, torso, and buttock were massively carved in an exaggeration (as in a football player)that seems to say: "This is MAN!" There are whole rooms of Kouroi, which is sort of like being in a locker room following football practice!

Several journeys were taken by ferry to various Greek Islands where I spent several days in Crete (where the Minoan palace and relics are) and Rhodes, which is very close to Turkey.Following a short ferry trip to Marmaris on the Turkish mainland, I went by bus to Izmir where I stayed almost a week. It was there that I discovered moussaka even though I'd already eaten it in Athens. But it was at a little suburban island cafe across the bay from Izmir where I saw moussaka sitting in the store-front window of a small cafe. Pans of the food prepared for that day's lunch were displayed, as if it were merchandise like any other, and although it was not quite lunch time, I found the food too tempting to pass up having had only coffee and rolls for breakfast anyway. The Turkish young men (as before, Islamic customs require that men work in public places, not women) looked inquisitively at the American peering in their shop window and motioned me to enter. It was not a tourist place at all and no one spoke English. So I went back outside with one of the men and pointed at what I wanted. There, in a large rectangular pan oozing with olive oil and tomato sauce and topped with what seemed like a thin layer of mashed potatoes was moussaka.It is a concoction of eggplant, ground lamb, sauteed onions, crushed tomatoes and seasoning (I use herb de Provence). Each item is sauteed before being mixed together in a baking dish. I've never followed a recipe, but created my own from the memory of that Turkish moment. The cooks and waiters all hovered about me while I ate—it was too early for their regular lunch crowd—eager to know how I liked it. Well, I liked it, all right. It was probably one of the most memorable dining experience of my life regardless of price or setting.I've since tasted moussaka where strips of eggplant and sliced potatoes are layered along with ground lamb, but I prefer my "tossed" approach of sauteed chunks of eggplant along with the other ingredients for I believe the flavors blend better. There is also a discrepancy in the topping of some recipes: a sort of Bechamel and/or meringue (without sugar) is covered over the entire contents and then baked. I prefer to place slices of cheddar cheese on top and leave it at that. I've tried a Bechamel sauce at times, but it seals the top too much—the moussaka should be able to lose some of its moisture while baking. Mashed potatoes may also be used as a topping, but this also seals in moisture. I prefer to serve freshly baked potatoes on the side which, incidentally, can be baked in the oven at the same time as the moussaka.

In Izmir, thick, heavily sweetened Turkish coffee may be taken following lunch at any of the cafes lining the harbor. There you will see men smoking water pipes while fondling prayer or worry beads,a sight that will make you feel far from home!

Wending further north, the buses are individually owned by their drivers and are decorated to their personal taste replete with radio station tuned to their favorite music—mine liked a sort of Islamic rock and roll. Finally arriving in Istanbul after a full day's journey, one sees that the city straddles the Bosperous as it symbolically straddles Europe and Asia. It is a city teaming with people—one is swept along as one is on Fifth Avenue in New York City: humanity moving in all directions. The mosques are beautiful. The bazaar is awesome. The fabrics are as colorful as the people. But for a very special reason I wanted to get back to Athens and hoped to be able to get on the overnight train, but it was full. I ended up taking steerage class on a steamship back to Athens. Was this what it was like for "Jack Dawson" in Titanic? We were herded (men) into a "dormitory" filled with double bunks where one had to hoard his possessions on top of the bed along with his body. It was the only accommodation I could get—all first and second class tickets had been sold. Since I was a foreigner and could afford to, I was allowed to eat in the 2nd class restaurant and order some wine for an additional fee, which I was happy to pay and spend some time out of the "hold" (hole?).

By the time I arrived back in Athens, it was Orthodox Easter week. While wandering about during the day not far from my hotel, I saw that a special platform was being erected outside the Cathedral in what was essentially an open square. There was to be a ceremony for Easter eve preceeding the candlelight procession that ascends the hill outside of Athens in anticipation of Easter sunrise. Following dinner in one of my favorite tavernas beneath the Acropolis (where the retzina is drained from barrels set high up on racks above the tables) I returned to the Cathedral square to observe what was going to happen. By then there were a great many people—and soldiers—gathering. I managed to find a slightly elevated position inside a shop doorway which also screened me slightly from scrutiny. The "President", in full military regalia, arrived, and along with the Arch Bishop and other priests and acolytes, proceeded to symbolically bang on the Cathedral door, seeking admission.Upon return, they carried out various icons to the platform for a public ceremony of speeches and blessings. I marveled even then that I had been as close to the "government" without being challenged. In November, 1999, I read, via the Associated Press, that President Clinton's visit to Greece had been greatly reduced due to the fact that "the United States is unhappy about Greece's failure to crack down on the terrorist group 'November 17'...the name refers to a November 17, 1973 crackdown on young democracy activists by the then-ruling military regime. Traditionally there are big demonstrations to denounce the United States, which many Greeks believe supported the seven-year junta that collapsed in 1974". Like Forrest Gump, I was there witnessing the dictator of the junta make religious (political) hay out of Easter ceremonies, Spring, 1974. He was deposed weeks later!

In Rome, Arthur Frommer's book "Europe on $5 & $10 a Day" really came in handy, not only in finding me a hotel, but in good descriptive suggestions for sight-seeing. One of his hotel finds was the Hotel Fontane, directly in front of the Trevi Fountain. The tourist desk at the railroad station helped me in reserving a room as well as getting me there by bus. Each morning I began the day at the corner cafe standing up, along with the rest of the locals, to consume a roll and a steaming cup of Cappuccino before commencing another day of walking and exploring. Rome is a wonderful city to walk in, but by noon the unevenness of the cobblestone streets brings on great fatigue and no matter how much one wants to press on, the body gives out. Many noons I took lunch at a government run "cafeteria" which was also one of the gems found in Frommer's book. Government office workers dined there but foreigners were welcomed. (Ministry of Agriculture building, Mensa Del Corpo Frestale; Monday through Saturday.) A good plate of food with wine was always available at a very reasonable price. After lunch I usually took my tired feet back to my little hotel for a nap, waiting to start out again only in the evening.

One of the pleasant excursions outside of Rome was a day trip to Tivoli to view the reflecting pools and statues at Hadrian's Villa Adriana and the beautiful water gardens at the Villa d'Este. In my walk about I stumbled onto a small restaurant on the outskirts of Tivoli where, again, no other patrons were present. I was served a delicious three course luncheon with wine, outdoors amongst the trees savoring what the Italians call dining *al frescoe*.

No musician should visit Rome without visiting the Church of Sant' Andrea della Valle where Tosca first act is set, nor the Castle Sant' Angelo from whose roof top she leaps to her death following the execution of Mario. Puccini has Tosca cry out: "Mario, Mario," repeatedly as she tries to raise him until she finally realizes he's dead. When Leonard Bernstein has Jose sing : "Maria,—I've just met a girl named Maria...Maria..." there are echoes of Puccini by the repetition of a beautiful name, not musically speaking, but psychologically.

Psychologically Roma IS history—one feels it with every cobblestone step, from catacomb graves to Sistine ceilings; from Colosseum ruins to the unruined columns of St. Peter's square. It is an immense city and immensely rewarding.

I've already spoken of David in Florence where I stayed in a *pen-*

sione which relieved me from having to worry about where to eat. A memorable musical event took place while I was there: a performance of Verdi's REQUIEM performed in the famous church San Lorenzo, where the Michelangelo sepulchers for various members of the Medici's are housed. There was to be only a single performance which was sold out, but the night before there was to be a full dress rehearsal inside the church for family members of the performers who likewise were not able to acquire tickets. I found the office for the event and in fractured French informed them that I was a visiting Professor of Music and could I possible get into the dress rehearsal?For some reason Italians like California (there are great similarities topographical as well as psychological between the two) and a ticket was found for me.

The REQUIEM is Verdi at his very best and dramatically very moving. It is an operatic version of the funeral Mass and was never intended to be sung in conjunction with an actual Mass service. However, to hear it performed within such an historic religious structure, by Italian soloists, chorus and orchestra , was more than just a "musical experience"! Due to the fact that the performance was sold out, loud speakers were set up outside the church the next night for anyone still interested in hearing the performance. So I was able to hear it a second time in succession while envisioning what I had seen and heard the night before.

The proprietors of the Florence *pensione* sent me to friends who had a pensione on the Lido across the bay from Venice, the setting for the famous "Death in Venice" of Thomas Mann. Although it was necessary to take a ferry whenever one wanted to visit Venice, it was great fun experiencing the true water traffic of Venice. The famous gondolas are confined to the canals. If one is really in need to get somewhere, he goes by water taxi which are sleek, polished speedboats that dart about hither and yon. Regular ferry service from the Lido is a scheduled affair with pier stops just like a subway or commuter train stop would be. There are ferries to the island that contain the famous glass works of San Marino, and one of the stops along the way is the cemetery island where Stravinsky, Diagliev and other notable artists are buried, and to which I made pilgrimage.

In Milan I was able to visit the fabled La Scala opera house, but opera season wasn't on at the moment. I settled for a performance of the Vienna Philharmonic playing Mahler, which put me at least inside the famous theater. As soon as I arrived in Milan I went to La

Scala to see what I could buy in the way of a ticket and purchased one of the last ones available for that night's performance. It still being early, I strolled past the nearby Cathedral and Capanella into a shopping mall where I took an early dinner in order to be ready for the concert. It was a second floor "cafeteria" overlooking the arcade below. It was just dusk when suddenly a group of police, garbed in riot gear, appeared at one end of the arcade and let loose with a barrage of bazooka-like fire: I think it was tear gas canisters. It produced a tremendous noise and certainly startled everyone around. Beneath me were several sidewalk cafes which I had briefly considered stopping at before deciding on the second floor cafe. Below me, the waiters were hurriedly bringing their tables back inside and slamming the doors shut. Had I chosen to eat there, I would not only have forfeited my meal but maybe been gassed as well. Presumably, the strike, which had been going on with the railway all month long, had now erupted into industrial Milan.

The "strike" continued throughout the next day as well. No public busses were moving, and so I took a taxi to the airport in hopes of getting out of Milan. That took the whole day, a day of considerable uncertainty before I was able to board a plane for the few miles across the lip of the Ligurian Sea to Nice, France.

MOUSSAKA

Two large eggplants, (trimmed, but unpeeled
and cut into cubes one inch square)
Two large onions (chopped)
Two pounds of ground lamb (or 1 lb. of ground turkey
in exchange for l lb. lamb)
Handful of Herbs de Provence
Cheese slices (optional): cheddar or swiss
One can of stewed tomatoes

Saute each of the above separately using generous amounts of olive oil for eggplant...brown lamb well continually chopping while cooking so that the meat is separated. Add a clove or two of chopped garlic near end of browning (to prevent scorching.) Place all the above in a heavy baking dish, stir in herbs and one can of crushed tomatoes. Lay over cheese slices and bake uncovered in 325 oven for one hour and a half. Serve with baked potatoes.

OPUS NINETEEN

$\mathcal{D}$uring my piano teacher's tour several years before, I had stayed a few days in Villefranche sur Mer which is half way between Nice and Monaco. I was so enchanted by that village that I was determined to stay there longer and also to stay in the hotel that seemed so much more attractive across the street from where I stayed before. As is often the case with resort hotels in Europe, full or half pensione is included in the weekly price. One could take his breakfast where he wished, either in the restaurant, in his room or outdoors in the patio. I chose the latter due to the fine weather, which was by now, in June. Villefranche is fully booked during the summer, especially in August which is the traditional French fermeture annuelle.Fortunately in early June, I was able to book into Hotel Provencal for a week. It is a charming yellow stucco building with rounded balconies from many of its rooms which overlook the narrow bay of Villefranche. It was originally a fishing town, but was discovered by Jean Cocteau during the thirty's and forty's and then, later, by Richard Burton and Elizabeth Taylor during one of their several engagements. Cocteau eventually persuaded the Catholic authorities to let him decorate a tiny chapel at the edge of the harbor where formerly fisherman would say prayers or attend Mass prior to going out to sea. It was no longer in use as a church, and Cocteau, wanting to compete with Matisse's decorations for a new, modernistic church in the hills above in Vence, managed to completely re-paint and decorate both the inside and the outside of Chapel St. Pierre. It is now open to the public as a museum. I wrote extensive descriptions of the chapel for the ADVOCATE following my first trip to Villefranche which was published November 21, 1971 (see Appendix E).

Hotel Provencal was a delight. I had a single room without bath (older hotel) but it did contain a sink and a bidet: French requisites. The bath was right outside my door, so for all intents and purposes I had a private bath. The price included either half or full pension and since I wanted to be out and about during the day, I opted for half pension and took my dinner at the hotel at night, even though, in France, the main meal is prepared for noon. But I was more interested in traveling about than only dining well. Also the beach, although pebbly, was very inviting as the water was clear and clean, fresh from the Mediterranean. The coast is not called Cote d'Azur for nothing! I often spent the day swimming and sunning and having only a sandwich and beer for lunch.

One day the excursion was to Antibes to visit the castle on the ramparts of the sea that Picasso had lived in during the German occupation of Paris. It portended the estate which he later purchased called *La California* in the western region of South France. In both large-roomed locations, he would roam from room to room painting on several huge canvases at once. Above Antibes is the hill town of St. Paul de Vence where many artists would congregate for stays and meals at La Colombe d'Or, often paying for their stay by leaving signed paintings. The Colombe is still very much in vogue but one commentator in a recent Conde Nast Traveler suggested the food was not up to a painting's worth today and advised eating at nearby places. That is exactly what I did. One of the most interesting paintings displayed is the little painting by Braque about BACH in which he paints that name centered large on the canvas and decorated with instruments from the Baroque era. For years I had used a slide of that painting when introducing my lecture on Bach, so it was thrilling to see the original.

Besides the art at the Colombe, there is a very modern museum full of sculpture and paintings sponsored by the Maeght Foundation. In their literature they state to be: "Neither art gallery nor museum, (but) a collective creation born of the collaboration of artists with the architect Jose Luis Sert, and dedicated to the love and understanding of modern art." There is a reflecting pool with especially designed ceramic tiles made by Matisse and the largest collection of Giacometti sculptures in the world. The overall museum design was incorporated later by the designers of the Kimbell for Fort Worth, Texas. But the most fun piece of "sculpture" seen in St. Paul is one made from used wine bottles which sits in a niche of a nearby hotel to the Colombe. I promised myself that one day I would make one of those creations...and that came later after I had moved to the wine country of California.

One of the amusing aspects of resort towns in France, at least along the Cote d'Azur, are the many sidewalk cafes and restaurants where one dines al frescoe while being entertained by various street performers. A memorable one was a bicyclist who could make his cycle dance, hop, twirl, while all the while he was riding backwards, upside down and the like. It certainly takes care of the time while waiting for your meal.

"Have you had your MEAL?" is one of the memorable remarks put to me by a hostess. My dancer friend and I were driving to Seattle to attend the Wagnerian Ring Cycle and on the first overnight stop on the way north, we stayed at the historic Hartsook Inn at the southern edge of the redwood country. The inn was a pretty lodge with a huge dining room. Cottages across the road contained the accommodations and after our usual "happy hour" in the cabin, we proceeded to the dining room for a full course prime rib dinner, beginning with soup, then salad and eventually the prime rib. We ordered a bottle of red wine and enjoyed our soup and started on our salad. But no bread or rolls had yet been provided. We asked the waitress (a college student working during the summer) if she might bring us some bread. That apparently upset the routine of the dining room, for in a moment the "head lady" appeared to demand what had been our request. When we suggested that we would like some bread, she asked: "Have you had your MEAL?" Well, no, we thought we'd like it with the salad. "Well, bread comes with the main course!" was her retort. Although the prime rib was delicious, as was the rest of the meal, the episode was poisoned by the disagreeable "hostess." We had one or two other restaurant discomfortures along the way and so by the time we got to Oregon we found accommodations with kitchens and henceforth, I cooked in. This became particularly useful once in Seattle as the operas either started in the late afternoon for one act with a dinner intermission, or we ate later after the evening's performance. Seattle is a fine place to shop for food as they have a wonderful waterfront market where fresh fish, bountiful vegetables and lettuces are plentiful and handsomely displayed.

We did enjoy some luncheons around town (the only time we ventured into restaurants) and Sunday brunch on the pier was lovely as we also benefited with a perfect view of snow-covered Mt. Rainier off in the distance. In fact the weather for the entire time in Seattle was clear and beautiful. Not one drop of rain! But "Have you had your MEAL?" rings on forever.

The Sabbatical was completed in England before flying back to America. After having visited many historical sights in Greece, it was something of a shock to see that the English have all the pediments from the Acropolis exhibited in their National Museum—the so-called Elgin Marbles. It was a professor Elgin in the 19th Century, who convinced the Greeks that the invaluable frontal pieces that adorned the ancient ruin would be better protected by the English than the

Greeks. Perhaps that was so. But Greece has been trying to get them back ever since. At least one sees them in England up close which would not be the case had they been left in Athens.

OPUS TWENTY

*U*pon my return to the fold of Foothill College, my mandatory report was given at the first staff meeting of the Fine Arts department. Later I would organize a full presentation open to the college of a specific topic which turned out to be a lecture and slide presentation on Bali. My paintings, which I had framed upon my return, were exhibited in the library to coincide with the presentation. But for the first meeting of our department, I arranged a brief overview of the entire trip shown in slides and entitled "AROUND THE WORLD IN 80 SLIDES". Obviously, finding 80 slides out of hundreds took some organizing, but it helped me to get things in order in a hurry.

Meanwhile, Montree Suksusin joined me from Thailand, and his language classes began immediately. Attempting to re-start piano practice(after 10 months away from the instrument), re-start teaching, and re-start a household with an added person in my life was a daunting task. In addition to the above, I was eager to get the storm cellar in Santa Clara, where the wine had been stored, transformed into a proper wine cellar. The model of what I wanted it to look like was the San Martin Wine shop in Morgan Hill, California. They had taken an old stone and brick building (unusual for California's earthquake country) and transformed a portion of the interior with vertical racks made from rough-sawn redwood fencing material. Each rack contained a case of wine vertically while the top was covered by a half-slant shelf that could hold one bottle for display, indicating the kind of wine below. Since Morgan Hill was only 45 minutes away, I requested my artist-tenant (who was to construct the cellar) to visit the winery so he could see what I had in mind. At Bellomy Street, there were water pipes across the center of the cellar, as well as the water heater for the house above, all of which had to be removed and re-routed. When the room was clear, I purchased a load of six foot by eight inch fence board which Michael then cut into the appropriate pieces for the racks. He made a mistake by not taking into account the different width of some of the bottles. "Burgundy" type bottles are fatter than "Bordeaux" bottles and I believe Michael only used the Bordeaux shape for measurement. When it came time to load up the racks, there were some tight squeezes in places! But over all the cellar was very satisfactory and everyone that has ever seen it has oohed and ahhed and wished they had a cellar like that too! I dedicated the cellar with a dinner for about 25 people. We dined in the Italianate gazebo which was adjacent to the cellar door and connected the main house to the cottage behind. After having spent time in Italy, France and Greece, the whole event, coupled with lots of wine, seemed very European indeed: dining again *al frescoe*!

During that first winter of Montree's American stay, I helped inaugurate the sister campus' beautiful new auditorium named for the Chancellor of the district who had interviewed me those many years before, Calvin Flint. The first event to take place was a performance by the Nova Vista Symphony which my department chairman, John Mortarotti, conducted. I performed with the orchestra, "Nights in the Gardens of Spain" by De Falla.De Anza College had just purchased a brand new Steinway concert grand and had even sent their resident pianist to New York to pick it out. But at the dress rehearsal I found the piano to be muffled in tone and thought the action to be unresponsive. Our piano technician worked on the action anointing the hammers with a solution to harden them right up to the moment people were admitted into the hall. It was an excruciating experience, particularly when one expects the best from Steinway. I believe the instrument was eventually exchanged for another from New York. But that didn't help me then!

Following the first school year for "Montree in America", we drove across the country to visit my father and aunt in Florida. Montree was very excited whenever we entered a new state and fresh pictures were taken by each announcement-sign at the borders. He had a particular fondness for bridges and those had to be photographed with him standing by the entrance. A Thai custom is to be very deferential to older people and he was particularly gracious to both Dad and Aunt Anne. We always had bamboo growing in the back yard as I grew up...it's one of those organisms which you can't get rid of once started. So Montree decreed that he would make a healthful soup from young bamboo shoots, and that Dad and Aunt Anne would eat it: "Bamboo shoots are always reserved for the elderly in Thailand" he proclaimed. So off we went to dig up some shoots and Montree, with his typical swash-buckling way, proceeded to chop up and prepare the soup. Dad was a good sport and managed to down some of it. I don't think Aunt Anne ate very much of it and I tasted it just in order to know what it was like. Montree swore that it prolonged life, etc. We all watched Dad carefully as he ate his soup, probably expecting instant changes to occur. I'm reminded that the favorite food for Pandas is bamboo, and I'm afraid they don't live very long lives.

Following our visit in Florida, we drove north to visit my brother and his family with a trunk load of fresh bamboo where Montree's kitchen expertise came into play once again. I think the shoots had faded a bit by then as I don't recall there being much to do about the elixir-soup this time. Upon returning to the West coast, we drove through Iowa and saw great fields of corn being harvested. I couldn't figure out how the machines separated the ears from the stalks as it appeared that everything was being chewed up and conveyed into trucks. I simply had to stop and find out. Pulling off the road, I was able to spot a farmer watching his field being harvested and I asked how the ears were separated from the stalk. He informed me that this was feed-corn for cattle and hogs and that the entire stalk along with the ears was mulched for feed. So when you read that something is "corn fed", you'll know that they're not talking just about yellow kernels!

Later, when I had my own vegetable garden in Healdsburg which included corn, I always thought that there was a great effort expended by the plant in growing a thick stalk only to produce a few ears of corn. I'm pleased to know that some creatures are able to eat the whole thing. I wonder if Montree could have made a healthful soup from cornstalks?

After two years, Montree decided he didn't want to stay on a student visa any longer. The visa required that he move on after two years of English language study, and, although I had arranged for him to enter as a foreign exchange student in the community college district serving Los Gatos, (West Valley College) he didn't want to try that. So with fond farewells, I put him on one of the last Pacific flights of Pam Am before airlines de-regulated. I believe he crossed the Pacific in a nearly empty plane which would be unheard of today....and once again I was alone...and as the sun set over Los Gatos....I had another glass of wine!

My "school year" started: Music 101, three classes of beginning — BEGINNING—piano students! How much can one endure year in and year out? I know how to teach beginning piano—my students were the best. But the best of what? I recall the elementary supervisor from practice teaching days (when I suggested that maybe I didn't always want to teach elementary ages) saying: "But you'll never receive musical satisfaction from whom you teach. You'll have to achieve that separately." She was right, even at the college level: I was always teaching beginners.

One of the hardest things for me, as a teacher, was not the return in the Fall to teaching, but in January, following the Christmas break. Now that Foothill was on the quarter system, it meant that a new quarter began immediately following the vacation. For me the return to teaching in January was always the worse time. Following summer, one is "refreshed" and ready to go again, but not after only two weeks at Christmas time. January 3, 1976 I started and by the end of that week I thought: "I just can't keep on doing this!"

In the local newspaper was a small ad announcing that Maharishi Mahesh Yogi was going to be on the Merv Griffith show. I had heard of MMY for years, perhaps ten years. My first T.A. at Foothill had exclaimed how he had been initiated into TM at U.C. Berkeley for only $25.00 I asked what it was about and he answered: "They give you a 'tone' to meditate on." "A TONE?", I yelled! "I know all about tones—how can they give me a tone upon which to meditate?" Of course the T.A. (Stephen Satterlee) used the wrong term to describe what was to be given and therefore prevented me from experiencing this beneficial activity.

Ten years later, January, 1976, alone and in a repetitious rut, I thought: "What the hell, it's either suicide or give it a try." I wasn't suicidal in the clinical sense (I don't think). I was just bored by the repetition of the process of teaching. I believe that today they call it "burn out!".

So I watched the Merv Griffith show, which I had never seen before. There came this Indian Guru wearing a flowing white robe, dangling long, graying hair, and proceeded to sit cross-legged on a throne-like chair. (Maharishi had become well-known as guru to the Beatles; Merv Griffin had become a meditator as well as the magician, Doug Henning). Merv asked: "What's happening in the movement now?" Maharishi laughed and said: "Our advanced meditators are flying now!" It wasn't the concept of levitation that intrigued me in his presentation. It was his delightful, joyful, hopeful presence. I thought: "There IS a Santa Claus and I've just seen him!" The newspaper advertisement for the telecast gave a local TM center's address and phone number. I phoned and was told that there would be an introductory lecture on Thursday. I said I'd be there.

OPUS TWENTY-ONE

*T*ranscendental Meditation - TM - is not a set of beliefs as in a religious allegiance. It is a practice requesting that you meditate on the word or phrase that is given to you at the time of your initiation. It's as simple as that. Maharishi always says: "It's simple!" and he's right. But the discipline that is required is in doing it every morning and evening for twenty minutes. In the prefatory lecture, we were told that once practiced: "New, imaginative ways of doing what you have already been doing would spontaneously occur." If that constitutes a core belief, then so be it. But I can attest to the fact that within the first week of meditation, I suddenly had new insights into and inspirations for presenting the same material I had been presenting for years! The most important change that took place within me was that I no longer saw the student as an adversary to whom I had to constantly prove that I was worth listening to. I no longer felt in competition with students, but instead, master of my material. This change didn't come about because of a "belief"; it came about as a result of the technique of Transcendental Meditation.

Oddly, I had seen a picture of Maharishi on a billboard at the University in Auckland when I was on sabbatical and thought about going to the lecture. Of course he wasn't there, but I didn't know it at the time. Seeing him on the Merv Griffith show is what finally propelled me into finding out what TM was all about. (Seeing is believing?)

Maharishi and/or his American advisors, were astute about property purchases. They came upon defunct resort properties and bought them cheaply and then turned them into meditation retreat centers. The first one I attended was in the former Hoberg Resort on Cobb Mountain in California. Formerly it had been a swinging summer resort during the thirties and forties where famous dance bands performed at the outdoor dance floor. San Franciscans came up for the mountain air and a week of dancing for their vacations. When air travel became more frequent following World War II, nearby resorts to large cities lost their appeal. The same thing happened to the Russian River resorts in Gurneville. Also declining were the resorts in the Catskills in upper New York state. Maharishi acquired two hotel resorts in the Catskills, turning one into a ladies-only retreat and the other into a men's-only retreat. Outside of Riverside, California, he found another defunct resort at Soboba Springs and turned that into a TM retreat which became my favorite. To these centers, meditators would go for a week or two of intensive meditation. When we were not in our private cottage meditating—as at Cobb Mountain—we met as a group where, among other things, we viewed video tapes of Maharishi explaining what happens in meditation and where we, as meditators, were heading in our progress along "the path"—the path to enlightenment. Many of these videos had been assembled from his first summer assembly of the then new movement held on the campus of Humboldt State College near Eureka, California. This was shortly after his stay at 433 Harvard Blvd. in Los Angeles, which has been referred to earlier in this book.

These tapes were made at the height of the rebellious and marijuana-ridden anti-Vietnam era. Maharishi's movement, TM, recruited "converts" from these ranks of generally bright, young people and turned their lives around. It was a requirement that an inductee into TM be drug-free. Maharishi offered, in exchange for their giving up drugs, an infinitely higher "high" through TM. The core of early meditators came from these potentially bright young people, many of whom later became teachers of TM. All the while Maharishi was working with scientists and physicians to verify the effects and effectiveness of the TM technique. (Today, physicians routinely recommend some form of meditation for stress reduction and lowering of blood pressure.)

Personally, I can attest to the positive results I obtained from the practice of TM. From a "what's the use anymore?" attitude, I was experiencing a resurgence of excitement for my teaching as well as in my piano performance. Instead of being nervous before a performance, I was now approaching piano playing as another chance to demonstrate the beauty of the music. I was less focused on myself and more focused on the music—which is always what one wants to do, but not always what one can do. TM changed that for me.

By that summer of 1976 I had already attended a retreat on Cobb Mountain and a two week workshop for school teachers (not TM teachers) at the Maharishi International University in Fairfield, Iowa. Again, Maharishi had found a decaying institution that could be bought cheaply. It was the former Parsons College that had been a noted party school and diploma factory until its accreditation had been removed. Maharishi transformed the college by a revolutionary form of advanced education as well as making it the seat for his ongoing scientific verifications of the TM technique. The novel approach to "learning" was to entertain a single subject all day long for six weeks along with morning and evening meditation. At the end of six weeks, a two to four week "retreat" of prolonged meditation would take place, followed by the immersion into a new subject matter. After several years of this regime, M.I.U. was granted full accreditation based on the exceptional test results of its students.

This memoir is not meant to proselytize for TM. It is meant to indicate TM's importance in my life—at least as important as my going around the world, to which I have devoted many pages. TM saved my life—it's as simple as that!

Following my "initiation" into TM, my first retreat was close to home at the former Jesuit Seminary in the hills above Los Gatos. At that time, the Jesuits were still making wine which they labeled "Noviate Wine". Their best was a sacramental wine which had been their mainstay product all during Prohibition. I had been there for tasting before and the idea of actually staying at the monastery intrigued me equally as much as experiencing a TM retreat. Although only a mile drive from my home, it seemed many miles away in atmosphere. It was as if one had been suddenly transported to Tuscany: grape vines covered the hills behind the former seminary which was now used as a Jesuit retirement center for the entire Pacific Rim. Our meals were taken in their spacious dining hall at specially set tables for us which contained no wine bottles or glasses, while the nearby Jesuit tables were set with glasses and both red and white wine bottles.

Although the TM movement only serves vegetarian meals at their own facilities, as we were at a Catholic institution and eating their meals, we were served fish on Friday night and chicken on Saturday.I loved it, but the stricter TM'ers only ate the vegetables and salads. On the other hand, I not only enjoyed the fish and chicken, but would have loved to sneak a glass or two of wine from the neighboring tables.

Los Gatos never looked so picturesque as from the Jesuit seminary. At night, the city of San Jose twinkled in the distance like the mural of my childhood castle..all this and TM too! Maharishi and the Catholic Church have always managed to buy good properties...I wonder how they do it? On the other side of the canyon from the seminary, above the famous old restaurant "The Cats", was the summer property of the Yehudi Menuhin family, where, as a child, he spent many summers. Like Cobb Mountain and Guerneville on the

Russian River, the hills of Los Gatos were a favorite vacation place for San Franciscans (where Menuhin was born). Maharishi says that when we retire, we should stay home quietly and meditate, which would produce greater coherence in universal consciousness.In the days of the Hoberg resorts, the Guerneville river inns and the family retreat of the Menuhin family above Los Gatos, I'm sure there was a tranquility of being that somehow escapes us today. I haven't taken Maharishi's advice yet about staying home since retiring and maybe I've contributed to the current restlessness within universal consciousness. But I am slowing down.

Between Christmas and New Year's, 1977, I went on retreat to Soboba Springs, near Hemet, California. Like the others I've described, it was a former resort for Los Angelenos, but now a defunct resort. So Maharishi bought it! Nestled against a hill, it contained igloo-type cement structures replete with Indian names for each cottage. The dining hall was a marvelous "turn of the century" edifice where one picked up his vegetarian meal cafeteria-style and enjoyed the company of his fellow meditators while dining. Mealtime was essentially the only recreational event out of a full day of viewing tapes made by Maharishi and practicing meditation. For the final "banquet" at the end of the retreat, we were served a Kool-Aid type beverage and I, in my inimitable outrageous style rather loudly proclaimed: "Prost! Here's to Jim Jones!" The Jonestown suicide had only recently taken place in Guyana, and I was still a little bit of my former outrageous mode prior to taking up TM. Soboba Springs was located on traditional Indian territory and for this banquet, a guest Indian speaker told of his heritage and of "knowing secrets" of life that the white man was yet to learn. Again, I interrupted: "But we're catching up!"

Soboba Springs appealed to me so much that I planned to return during the Easter break for another retreat. During those three months time, so inspired was I by the TM movement, that I developed three thirty-minute TV scripts describing certain pieces of music as comprehended through Transcendental Meditation. They were the second movements of the 4th and 5th piano concertos of Beethoven and "Jesu, Joy of Man's Desiring" by Bach. (see Appendix F) The TM movement had a TV studio in nearby San Bernardino, where broadcasts went throughout the Los Angeles area. Tapes were also sent to other studios in the rest of the country. One of the directors of that studio resided at Soboba. It was arranged that my three programs be taped the day before the Easter retreat was to begin. I wanted the tapes to act as an audition for a music position that was to be made available at MIU. The taping went very well and they were broadcast over several Sunday afternoons in the L.A. area. At least one of my friends saw them! Maharishi had not settled in his mind the relevance of Western music to the movement, preferring Indian music and chant. So nothing "opened up" at MIU at that time. But the satisfaction of creating the concept and performing the tapes was reward enough.

During that Spring I attended at my local center in San Jose the twice-weekly class entitled "Science of Creative Intelligence." It was very stimulating and the more I got into it the more I could feel the alacrity of my brain. There was a final exam at the end of the six week course and I "burned" it as in "a piece of cake". I saw how the approach that was used at MIU, of total immersion in a subject for a period of time, really gets results. By now I was ready to become a Sidha. At both Soboba Springs and Cobb Mountain (where TM teachers were undergoing Sidha training) we novitiates were aware of the unusual things that were taking place, most noticeably (through gossip) that they were learning how to "fly."! That summer there was to be a huge new class of Sidhas to receive their final training on the campus of the University of Massachusetts at Amherst. Maharishi wanted five thousand meditators to become Sidhas to help purify world consciousness. Prior to going to Amherst, we received initial instruction at local centers, a little bit at a time, from Maharishi himself via country-wide conference call. His instructions were never emitted into the room. It was all transferred by earphone directly to the novitiate who was, in essence, one on one with Maharishi. One needed to listen closely as nothing was repeated and you didn't ask a TM teacher what was said. "Don't ask, don't tell!" When one receives his mantra at the very beginning of learning to meditate, the usual doubt is whether you've got the mantra right. I experienced that early on, and after requesting a private interview with a TM teacher and telling him of my uncertainties, he asked what my mantra was and after I offered it, he only nodded his head. A word to the wise: "Listen up!"

I'm not at liberty to say what went on at Amherst due to my "oath" to TM. I will tell you that about 400 men (the largest group ever assembled for Sidha training) were placed in a large padded-by-foam room to practice the sutras we were taught by Maharishi. I was, at age

52, the oldest person there, but even then I never felt anything else but "young." Our actual levitation is referred to as "hopping". It is a spontaneous, non-muscular event which is induced purely through meditation. It's like the knee jerk one experiences when a physician hits that certain place below the knee cap, except that the entire body moves up and often some distance forward. The bedlam of 400 novices at various stages of awakening to this phenomenon (while frequently uttering unusual sounds: one is tempted to compare it to evangelical "speaking in tongues") makes the entire experience mind-boggling. During the night the body tends to do a great deal of jerking; I attribute this to the stress which the body—mind, sub-conscious—is releasing. One soon understands how Rolfing, Primal Scream and the like got started, but they are not grounded in Vedic knowledge which has come down from time immemorial. It is important to realize that all mantras are from Sanskrit, the world's first language, and that in Sanskrit the sound of the word is its meaning. The therapeutic value of the mantra is in the sound which is also its meaning. Hence, Stephen Satterlee's statement, those many years ago, that I would be "given a tone!" was probably right after all!

After the two week period of initiation, I extended four more weeks in order to experience the benefits of Sidha meditation along with the rest of the five thousand Sidhas. The college cafeterias—accustomed to "meat and potato" menus, didn't prepare very interesting vegetarian fare. But we weren't there for gourmet meals. We were there for mental ambrosia.

OPUS TWENTY-TWO

*U*pon returning from Amherst to Los Gatos, I had this strange hankering to move to the country. I wanted to start a private retreat for meditators of a certain persuasion. That brought a lot of house hunting including an overnite trip up to Lassen County to view a six room, 6 bath lodge adjacent to a lumber mill. Although it was cheap enough, it seemed too far away from my work and a little bit too rugged without the privacy I was seeking. At that time, United Farm Reality had a wish book filled with country property throughout America. In many parts of the country the inflation, which had already begun in California, had not yet started. There were 60 acre farms with house, barns, etc. in up state New York for sixty thousand dollars. In Arizona and New Mexico there were whole ranches for under l00 K. There was a mansion on Lake Champlain that by today's prices was free! But feeling the need for proximity to Foothill College, I limited my horizon to the West Coast. I had a train reservation on Amtrak to visit a seaside, three story house on the Oregon coast when my dancer friend talked me out of going: "It rains all the time up there!" he said. Finally I made arrangements to visit a site in Healdsburg in Sonoma County that contained a spring, and a small house on 20 acres of pine and redwood trees. The property had great potential for privacy and improvement. But not being a craftsman myself, I felt unable to cope with the improvements to be made, nor to envision a new structure. Twenty acres in the hills adjacent to Dry Creek Valley would be worth over a million dollars today. Then it was available for 100 K!

After showing me other properties without buildings, I told the realtor that I wanted something ready to live in. He took me to lunch in Healdsburg, and after one or two glasses of wine, he said: "I have one more property to show you." He drove me out Dry Creek Road, past Gallo vineyards and winery, past Lambert Bridge all the way up to Yoakim Bridge Road. I thought: "Papy and Mammy Yoakim and Lil Abner?!" Crossing over to West Dry Creek road and turning back south through the vineyards, there stood a two story, redwood barn-style home looking very new. In fact it turned out to be only two years old having been custom built by the owner's brother. Divorce required a sale of the property and, as the realtor said: "One man's misfortune is another man's opportunity." After having searched for country property for an entire year, I decided: "This is it!"

The living room was on the second floor which afforded an un-obstructed view of the vineyards beyond the one acre lot. At the rear of the lot was a thick retaining wall which was once the back of a pre-prohibition winery. It was anchored at one end by a concrete build-ing which had been the still. All wineries prior to prohibition made their own grappe distilled from the pulp and pips of the fermentation pumice. It was used to fortify dessert and sacramental wines or drunk straight if you could stand it. I realized immediately that the former still building could be earth covered and turned into a wine cellar. The old grey wall reminded me of Europe. The bells and whistles went off to tell me that I could make this place into my ultimate retreat.

Once purchased, I spent the next few weekends re-painting the bedrooms and sanding out the crayon marks left on all the woodwork drawn at a two-year old's height level. The entire kitchen, stairwell and living room was paneled in diagonally cut lap-board and all had crayon marks to be removed. By Thanksgiving—the weekend all teachers look forward to as the first respite of the school year—the house was ready for the big move. Included: the 7 foot 4 inch Yamaha grand piano; boxes upon boxes of books, china, glass ware; furniture, clothes, heirloom Chinese rug inherited from Staten island, and dozens of framed pictures all carefully wrapped and/or boxed by me. The precious Cocteau Candelabra, from the coffeehouse days in Santa Monica, was hand carried in my campy Renault station wagon which was filled with the potted palms and plants I was not going to leave in Los Gatos. Even the ornate Greek-style urn which graced one end of the pool, found its way to Healdsburg to become a focal point against my European wall of weathered, pebbly cement.

The mover was a Sidha friend who recruited an Olympic shot put trainee to help in all the lifting and carrying. His remark: "I didn't know you had so much stuff in your closets!" predicted that we would arrive in Healdsburg late in the day and exhausted. They chose to sleep on the carpet floor rather than attempting to unload anything that night. The next morning, with only the three of us to unload everything including the piano, there was a drizzling rain. The piano got only as far as the downstairs dining area. There wasn't a chance that it was going to get to its desired location—the second floor living room.

On the north side of the house was an unfinished, single large room—the size of an oversized two-car garage—with a half-cathedral ceiling. Having already collected a lot of art—there having been a lot of display space in Los Gatos—I realized that the main house didn't have adequate display space and that this building could be turned into a gallery. Although electricity had been brought to the building from the house, the room had not yet been wired. On the electric panel the former owners referred to the building as a "playroom"—so they never intended it to be a garage either. For the lower side of the room I envisioned custom-built book cases atop large storage cabinets below. But for now the many boxes of books and paintings had simply to be stored in that room. Its transformation would take another year.

The property was exactly an acre in size and fit at the top of a vineyard like a postage stamp to an envelope. I had the pleasure of uninterrupted vineyard views without the upkeep. The vineyard owner's house was twenty acres away and invisible when the vines were in full foliage. On the Eastern horizon was a small mountain separating Dry Creek Valley from the Alexander Valley, both of which are now distinctive wine appellations. There is a legend that during the Mexican land-grant days of early California, General Vallejo took one of his successful lieutenants atop a hill and said: "Everything you see in all directions is yours and I will so deed it to you!" Sounds great until you have to take care of it all. I had sweeping views from the second floor plate glass windows "in all directions" without worrying about the upkeep of all I surveyed. My little acre was bereft of trees or shrubbery which gave me a clean palette from which I could "paint" my garden.

Fall of 1979: gold was soaring in price—hundreds of dollars an ounce; land and housing were inflating in price by the minute; interest was 17% on second mortgages—if you could get one. Howard Ruff was screaming in his *Ruff Times* (in every interview he would be asked: "just how rough are the times?): "Buy gold, buy silver, buy dehydrated food and, if possible, plant a vegetable garden."

Part of my reason for moving to the country was in order to become more self-sufficient. I forgot to mention that there were two wells on the property, one electric and the other a forty foot hand dug well good for an emergency. I planted the vegetable garden in the "front yard" facing the vineyard. There was a lone peach tree right in the middle of the plot which I transplanted to one end adding another peach and two plum trees thereby creating a little orchard. Then I began cultivating the ground for the following spring planting. I had already made feeble attempts at growing vegetables in the hard soil in Los Gatos, learning thereby, that the most important thing in having a successful garden is properly preparing the soil. Over the next ten years I developed my knowledge of soil-preparation and it became almost more pleasurable than growing the crops themselves. One can see soil being made: cover the ground with chicken manure; cover that over with pumice from the neighboring wine presses; bury all garbage from the kitchen (never use the disposal in the kitchen) and as you shovel that in each time that you have vegetable peels or grass trimmings, you can see the worms working the soil. That's how new soil is made: the worms make it for you!

During the early summer of 1980 my first garden produced such huge beets that when I took some to Florida while visiting my father, he couldn't believe their size nor sweetness and tenderness. A good summer recipe for beets is to slow boil them with their skins intact and when cooked and cooled, peel off the skins, slice thin , add slices of red onions and sprinkle with oil and vinegar. Its delicious as a side dish or as a luncheon salad. Chilled Sauvignon Blanc goes nicely with cold beets and compliments their redness.

Although West Dry Creek Road is winding and twisting, it straightens out for a direct run of a quarter of a mile westward to the edge of my lot where it abruptly turns south again. A private road continues westward from the main road and then turns back at the top of my property above the wall. Since no trees existed around this perimeter, I purchased redwoods and other pines and planted a "forest" of three trees deep along the side. A huge California oak tree anchored the far end of the wall overlooking what was to become the wine cellar and providing the much needed shade for the wine. I envisioned a redwood arbor in the center of the field against the pebbly wall which would then be covered with the wisteria that I had fallen in love with in New Zealand. During the past few years, great purple clusters of blossoms hang like huge grape bunches during the Spring, but it takes a few years for wisteria to develop...do not be discouraged.

That first summer, the removal of the collapsed peaked roof of the "still" building was completed and old railroad ties, laid tightly together and covered with layers of mineralized roofing, formed its new roof. There was a large pile of dirt in my neighbors vineyard which he didn't want. After my handy-man built an extruded front and retaining wall to the "cellar", I contracted with a backhoe operator to move my neighbor's dirt onto the roof of the cellar. It had the shape of a pyramid when completed and I immediately planted junipers and ivy to form more insulation as well as to retain the soil. Handyman Dave built redwood fencing shelves for the wine but this time—unlike the elaborate shelving of Bellomy Street—they were made in large criss-cross triangles capable of holding several cases of wine each. Dave found and re-engineered two metal cooler doors which were hollow on the inside but which, after hanging, we filled with cement resulting in very heavy, temperature-resisting entry doors. There was a three foot space between the front and interior door which increased the insulation factor. Then I hasped both doors with the biggest hinges and locks I could find!

Two more projects completed the first summer's activity. A former Foothill student of mine had become an industrial arts instructor at the specialty school of the San Jose School district, where he taught carpentry. He used as his principal project in teaching construction and design, the building of small utility buildings suitable for garden tools and the like. At the conclusion of the school term, whatever had been built was put up for sale. I purchased one of these buildings and brought it to Healdsburg. It required several trips to transport the sides and roof of the little building. It was re-assembled at the opposite end of the wall from the cellar. Along with that construction, the arbor was built at the middlepoint of the wall which was now anchored by a wine cellar at one end and a utility building at the other. Although nothing had yet grown to complete the picture, I was satisfied with the results and, as in Genesis, we rested on the "seventh day"—that is, we went back to work for the winter at Foothill College.

OPUS TWENTY-THREE

The next Spring I went back to the Industrial Arts school to commission specially built book cases and cabinets to line one wall of the "gallery"—the next major project for Healdsburg. The building had never been finished—it was just an empty shell. Dave returned to wire and sheet-rock the interior as well as to lay a teak paneled floor which I had been hoarding for sometime in hopes of transforming the Bellomy Street barn into a residence...that would come later. Down the center of the ceiling we ran a series of track lights so that individual paintings could be pin-pointed with light. Once more the trusty Toyota pick-up was used to transport the book cases which required at least two trips: they were very heavy and awkward. I disappeared to Florida during the transformation of the "shell" into a gallery.

Upon my return, I was not disappointed. Everything had been completed: cabinet placement, tile surrounding the wood burning stove, inlaid flooring, sheet rock, taping and texturing as well as everything painted. All I had to do was to hang my pictures and lay the beautiful Chinese rug inherited from the Staten Island house of Auntie Mae. It fit the gallery perfectly, with enough teak flooring around its edges to frame it as if it were a painting, which, indeed, it almost was as it contained medallions of exotic creatures dispersed amongst the Chinese blue. I believe there is no better way to value heirlooms than to use them, enjoy them, and never fail to say where they came from. In this way the objects are not merely objects of beauty themselves but represent an ongoing experience, which, in the case of the rug, started before I was born. A Federalist cherry wood dining table likewise had come down to me from Staten Island and has been in all my homes from Los Gatos to Texas currently. The two half-moon end portions are used as console tables in Texas and the square center part is the dining table for Shelter Cove. When I was in Michigan during those early days of school assemblies, my brother's family and I went to see the Ford Museum in Dearborn. In addition to the multitude of tools and vehicles, there is a fine display of American furnishings. In the center of the Federalist room was an exact copy of the cherry wood table. I wish I knew our family history of the table; all I know is that it came from the home on Staten Island. I used its full size when I added the dining area onto the kitchen in

Los Gatos, and again for the house-warming party in Healdsburg, but it is really too big for most houses unless you own a mansion. I don't recall seeing it in Staten Island. Uncle Will had custom-built wooden table and chairs made in a solid, square style reminiscent of Frank Lloyd Wright's furniture, but that would have been prior to FLW's time. I liked the massiveness of the chairs and would have liked to have inherited them also...but they went elsewhere.

My concept of creating a special retreat for gay Sidhas soon faded. Following a weekend retreat at the Cobb Mountain TM center where I met a San Francisco couple, I invited them for a weekend in Healdsburg. We decided to spend the week between Christmas and New Year's in Mexico, dividing time between Cancun and Merida ...three to a room. I soon realized that just because someone is gay and a Sidha doesn't automatically make them good friends! Friendship is probably as difficult as a marriage and with about the same "divorce" rate. Never mind the Sidha retreat: I had my retreat complete with two wells, a vegetable garden, a mini fruit orchard, a "wall", an art gallery and the beginnings of a forest-border, while all the while viewing endless vineyards and low mountains on the horizon....and as the sun sets, another glass of wine, please.

I started saving used wine bottles, even gathering extras from the local tasting rooms. I had photographed a wine bottle "sculpture" in St. Paul de Vence during those final days of the Sabbatical. When in New Zealand I had seen a wall made from wine bottles and had used that concept of laying them horizontally and placed in cement when filling up the small basement windows for the Bellomy Street wine cellar. But now, with my empty acre, I decided to place (build) a bottle sculpture centered in front of the arbor. I spent restless nights trying to engineer in my mind what was needed in order to achieve the desired effect.I concluded that a foundation and center pole would have to be built and encircled with chicken wire so that the neck of each bottle could be supported.My original tenant from Bellomy Street, Mike Cooper, had also moved out to the country to nearby Sebastopol, and I enlisted him to help.I dug a way-too-big foundation pit which required more cement and rocks than were needed, but we certainly achieved a "firm foundation." A discarded piece of well-pipe became the center pole.Mike and I placed the pole along with the foundation cement and chicken wire on a Thursday.Friday evening saw my weekend guests arrive for their bottle sculpture party Saturday morning. Following too much feasting and drinking the night before, the many hands were conscripted to place and hold bottles while I feverishly mixed cement. Mike oversaw the construction. We soon discovered that the chicken wire was insufficient to hold everything up while the cement hardened. Mike called for duct tape and as each new row of bottles was installed, each bottle was taped from its bottom and then secured to a higher rung of chicken wire. We found that only about three rows could be installed before we had to wait for the cement to harden. I was placing a quick-setting additive into the cement mix, but even then we were only half way up the pole when daylight was over.

After more feasting, we were able to finish the project the next day. A neighbor came by and pronounced it one of the ugliest things he'd ever seen. I went indoors to retrieve my photo album from France and showed him what our model looked like as it sat in chic St. Paul de Vence whereupon he softened his objections slightly. I softened the effect by planting climbing English Ivy which, when it grew, regrettably covered up all the bottles. It is now an English Ivy sculpture rather than a bottle sculpture! So much for listening to neighbors. For years I collected more wine bottles hoping to replicate the sculpture. That never happened and eventually all the bottles went for recycling.

There was a bad spot in the wall which had me worried from the beginning. I filled in most of it with quick setting cement but there was still an indentation. Later, on a three week stay in Portugal during my first year of semi-retirement, I had fallen in love with Portuguese tile pictures (every building and home in Portugal contains at least one.) I found a set of tile approximating the size of the troubled spot. It depicted a satyr, his female companion and a child. The satyr was holding a goblet of wine. I thought it more appropriate for my residence than a religious picture which are the prevalent pictures in Portugal. The application of the tiles, one at a time, against a perpendicular wall again required a party of many hands. As I made the magic quick-setting cement, various members of the group held the tile in place until it became stuck. When finished, my wall looked even more European. On the opposite side of the arbor, we embedded tiles that read BRYAN WINE topped with a tile of a Renaissance-looking Portuguese gentleman. This was balanced, again on the opposite side, by terra-cotta angels and a large lion head. I had already placed sitting and kneeling lions atop the wall on either side of the arbor and now all that was left to do was plant roses....80 of them!

About this time, as Jim Lydon was present for one of my many projects, we were checking on the lighting of the arbor just at dusk when a big Shepherd wolf-like dog appeared. He was shy but docile and I noticed that he was without a collar. I'd been told by my vine-yardist neighbors that Yoakim bridge area was a frequent dumping spot for unwanted pets. I hadn't had a dog since I was a child in Florida, when my constant companion had been Colonel, a collie with a "Smith College stare" as proclaimed by our neighbor...more neighbors saying things! That was his little dig at my mother who was very proud of her Smith College degree, a rarity in those first decades of the 20th Century. Most "girls"(if they went to college at all) settled for a two-year teacher's diploma as my Aunt Anne had done. I had cats in Los Gatos (the Cats) but one can leave them all day without any worry, but not so with a dog. Now that I was semi-retired, it was perhaps possible to once again "have" a dog. I found the stray some left-over cat food and placed it along with a blanket and some water on the covered stoop, wondering if he would still be around the next day.

Next morning he was still there. I had again spent a near-sleepless night worrying about him and thinking that if he was still there, I would buy dog food and collar, etc. for him. Off we went for our pur-chases in the pickup where I found he enjoyed riding in the back and barking joyously as we proceeded down the road. I named him Wolfie and he seemed to respond to his new name without hesitation. In fact, he responded fine to me altogether and the realization took place for me that dogs respond to love and genuine caring. This is something that cannot be faked. There is either a positive feeling or there isn't. Fakery doesn't cut it. That is one of the treasures of "hav-ing" an animal in your life: there is a genuine bond that exists with-out any legalism involved.

Wolfie was an older dog. I knew that. When I took him to the vet to be vaccinated and examined, the vet drew blood and informed me that Wolfie had an advanced case of heart worms. Also, that he had "flea teeth" ground down by excessive chomping at them. Obviously he had been woefully neglected by whomever previously "owned" him. Wolfie had to be tethered so that he wouldn't run after anything which would disgorge the worms too quickly into his lungs causing imminent death.

We got through that and Wolfie's cough (one of the signs of heart worms) ceased and we enjoyed some tranquil months. I went on a cruise with Robert while Bruce and Isabelle house-dog-sat for me. A rare thunder and lightning storm ensued. Petaluma, down the road forty miles, proclaimed it the worst storm they had ever experienced. Only Wolfie was aware of the distant thunder and in his desperation to get into the house, cracked a window and pierced its metal frame with his "flea teeth". The commotion awakened the Adamses who finally brought the poor dog inside. It was then that I learned that Shepherd dogs and any of their mixes are mortally afraid of thunder and lightening. My current part-Shepherd spends any thunder storm huddled by my head (in bed) trembling. My Vet tells me that two tablets of Benadryl will help calm them if taken four hours in advance of a storm. But who has four hours notice of a lightning storm?

Wolfie developed hip displaysia, a typical Shepherd affliction. Hating to see him struggling to his feet, I gave him a half dosage of my arthritis medicine. He perked up immediately. Then I would go on a trip while the Adams cared for him without telling them about the arthritis medicine. Upon my return, Wolfie would be struggling once again to get up on his legs, so I would resume the arthritis medication. One day I found him prostrate in the garden and, after a considerable struggle lifting him up into the pick-up cab, rushed him to the vet. I could see he was dying before my eyes. The vet asked: "are you giving him any medication I don't know about?" When I told him about his lameness and of my giving him the arthritis medication, he replied: "dogs can't take human medication! He's got a ruptured stomach—his veins are so depleted of blood I can't even euthanize him via the veins. You'll have to leave the room so I can...." I was devastated...but also realized I had to find another dog with whom to enter my retirement years.

This segment is all about Olga. I met her on the trans-Atlantic maiden voyage of the CROWN JEWEL which had just finished serving as a floating hotel for the Barcelona Olympics of 1992. As there were few ports of call, the cruise offered a variety of lectures to keep the passengers entertained. The ship was incapable of the knot-speed of a QE2 so that more amusements were necessary to while away the long days at sea. One of these lecturers was Olga Czyrkowski, a psychic from Australia, born in Norway and married to a Pole, hence the exotic last name which sounds almost like Tchaikowsky!

Olga's first lecture—on the first full day at sea—was held in a corner of one of the bars at 2 p.m. with only about 30 folks in attendance. As I am a little hard-of-hearing (as they say) I like to sit on the front row, especially if I'm intrigued. Olga's first lecture was a potpourri of some of her abilities: she handed out a few flowers (about three or four) asking the selected person to hold them for awhile and then took them up, one at a time and made a "reading" of at least some aspects of the person's life. The same thing was done with a few cups of tea handed around and from which she "read" the leaves. Jewelry worn was also read from a few individuals. In all instances, as Olga made her remarks to specific people, you could see their jaws begin to drop in total amazement at the apparent accuracies of points in their lives that Olga was revealing.

While this only involved a portion of the relatively small audience, her final trick for the day—as she handed out half sheets of paper and pencils with the help of her daughter Krystyne—was asking us to draw a picture of five items which she enumerated slowly, giving us time to draw each item before going on to the next. The items were: 1, a house; 2, a river; 3, a tree; 4, a sun; 5, a snake. I draw very poorly and my picture resembled a kindergartner's effort for the five items requested. But Olga assured us that "art" was not required. When we had all finished, she took up about three to "read." I had not been chosen for any of the previous readings and I was most anxious by now to have a "reading" of my picture, childish as it was.

In the few readings we did hear aloud, we discovered that placement of the house on the page meant things either in the past or future or now, as the final request was that we fold the paper into four quarters and then on the back of each quarter write "past, present, future and near future." Of importance was how people placed the river in relation to the house: its length, for instance. If it was treated as a side issue or central to the picture indicated the amount of emotion that a person brought into his life. The way the windows and doors opened on to the world indicated one's readiness to be open to others, etc. I'm not going to attempt to re-create the readings, but they were most fascinating. How one's tree looked pertained to one's interest in intellectual pursuits; the sun represents spirituality and the snake—sex (of course!).

After "reading" several, Olga asked that we carry our pictures with us at all times and if we saw her anytime on the ship, except during meals or shows, she would read our picture. It took several days for me to catch up with her for my picture-reading. Olga decided that my home was very important to me (it is—all of them!). It was centered on the page. My river (emotion) went from one side of the page to the other in front of the house. My tree indicated continued intellectual curiosity and my sun indicated advanced spirituality. She even said that I was a "purple"—the most advanced state of spirituality! The snake? Well I've always had a horror of them but I grudgingly placed a little one on the path directly leading to my front door! You figure it out!

After reading my picture, Olga and I became great friends. She was convinced we had known each other in a previous life. We dined together several nights and I became a devoted attendee of all her lectures, which by now had to be moved to larger quarters as word of her remarkable ability spread like wild-fire around the ship. She had SRO audiences after her first meager 30 participants. Of course, those that came later never knew about the picture and could only request a private seance for which they paid.

Robert and I have since visited Olga in Sydney and she to Healdsburg with daughter Krystyne. I divulged the Hindu astrologer's comment about my not reaching the 21st Century. Her answer: the stars indicate directions, but the ultimate determination of one's life is in one's own hands.

The variety of Olga's lectures was obtained by her speaking one day on numerology, another on astrology, another on palm reading, colors, etc. She concluded each lecture with a "thought for the day," which was always very uplifting. At the conclusion of the voyage, she had printed and handed out the collection of the "thoughts". One day her voice gave out and she had Krystyne read the thought for the day. It was not the same. Only a Delphic oracle can make oracular statements. Olga was and is Delphic.

OPUS TWENTY-FOUR

*T*he trouble with dogs, especially big ones, is that they don't live long enough! Wolfie had ears that stood straight up. So did his bushy tail which didn't just dangle. Following his death, I was determined to find a similar dog as a replacement. The search took about four months: visits to animal shelters, answering advertisements; I even attended a gathering of wolf devotees where I viewed domesticated "half-breeds"—part wolf, part dog. I don't recommend acquiring such an animal. Since my search I have read considerably regarding this matter . All authorities discourage such ownership as being a very unpredictable and potentially dangerous situation.

In my visits to the shelters, I saw how sweet black Labradors could be and although they have droopy ears and sticks for tails, I thought I might be able to settle for a lab. Upon seeing an advertisement in the Santa Rosa paper for a Lab-Husky mix, I made arrangements to meet the dog who was residing in Sebastopol. "Charcoal" was only nine months old, extremely active, but beautiful. He was all over me during the visit. I had brought little dog biscuits which I gave him one at a time and a long, yellow rope that I had used when walking Wolfie during his arsenic treatment. I wanted to see how Charcoal behaved outside and to be alone with him for awhile. Because he was part Husky, his tail was bushy with hair. He held it curled up over his back instead of it sticking out straight like a Lab. Although his ears drooped like a Lab's, he had lots of hair instead of the linoleum finish of a Lab. After about a twenty minute walk we returned to the house and I said I'd try him. The deal was that he was free to a good home and was returnable if it didn't work out. They gave me his collar, leash and heart worm medicine and off we went in the Toyota, and as I have often said: "He never looked back!" Before reaching home, I stopped at the vet to have him looked at and the first thing they asked was: "what's his name?" I had resisted the name Charcoal from the moment I first heard it and so when they asked for a name I replied "Alfie...Alfie-Charcoal". The euphonious sound to "Wolfie" must have entered my head because I hadn't considered what I'd call him except I wasn't about to call him Charcoal: ("Here Charcoal; here Charcoal...." please!)

I've always liked big dogs: little dogs bore me for the most part; besides they tend to be yappy. My childhood collie, Colonel, was my constant companion out in the sticks from St. Petersburg. Clam Bayou was within walking distance of "2616" and we often went there to swim and hang out together.For a Collie, he was a great swimmer and as he splashed his front paws in front of himself , he would bite at the splash-up that ensued. One day we went skinny dipping together—I couldn't have been more than ten or twelve— and I had an erection while swimming about with Colonel. A fishing boat (real netting mullet fisherman) came down the channel and I pulled Colonel over me to hide my "problem." The cracker fishermen seemed to know what was happening and gave a hearty laugh as they passed by. Oh youth! Where art thou?

Dogs: what wonderful creatures they are. I've often thought of the millenniums of domestication that has taken place and how subtle the changes have been to eventually arrive to where we are today with the myriad varieties of dogs which authorities say all derive from the wolf. How can the sleeve-dog of Imperial China and the guard dog of the Royal Palaces of Thailand come from the same source? Incredible!

No sleeve-dog for me. I want one that, when stretched out on the bed, is almost human in size. Sublimation? I guess so—which reminds me of the story that took place during Fleet Week in San Francisco when the Navy makes its entrance under the Golden Gate. One of the best places to view it is on the hill of Fort Mason. A very attractive young San Franciscan came by with a beautiful collie-type mix attached to him. I spoke of the beauty of his dog and his reply: "Yes, he's much more satisfactory than a lover!", and I hadn't even asked. Man's "best friend" is indeed a gay man's best friend: no quarrels, no clandestine behind-the-back activities, no "break-ups" except by their nearly always untimely deaths compared to we humans. That's the hard part. But their fidelity is unquestioned.

I retired from full-time teaching in 1983, but I still taught the adult "music appreciation" lectures at the Palo Alto Senior center twice each week. Since so many of the "students" were repeaters, I could no longer repeat the course I had developed for Foothill. As many of the class members went to the Thursday matinee of the San Francisco Symphony, I produced new lectures each week based on the programs of that orchestra or of the San Jose Symphony. These lectures were not thirty minute "previews" (as often given these days prior to a concert), but an in depth look at the chief work being offered, usually a symphony or concerto. This required extensive listening on my part as well as research, for often the pieces were new to me as well. While listening, I often heard comparisons to other pieces by the same composer (or another) which are not usually noted in book sources. I have kept all my "lesson plans" for these lectures and they might make for an interesting publication someday. I give a single example (briefly) herein.

The famous Sixth Symphony of Tchaikowsky (the Pathetique) has many unique features of symphonic construction. The classically molded first movement, in Sonata-form, contains the well-known melodious second theme in D major (it was even made into a popular song at one time). It follows the tumultuously writhing activity of the first theme (in b minor). Note that the keys of the two exposition themes are never in the same key; they should always be opposing "personalties" and they usually are in speed and direction. Tchaikowsky follows this scheme precisely. The fulfillment inherent in Sonata-form is that in the recapitulation, the themes all re-appear in the same key, hence resolving, so to speak, their oppositeness of the beginning section. If a first theme is in a minor key, the consequent resolution of "oppositeness" can only be reconciled by using the same key-note—in this case the tone of B. The melodious second theme, first heard in the key of D major, now appears in the key of B major. Since there is no need for a modulation from one key to another in the recapitulation, Tchaikowsky uses his "pretty" second theme as a powerful redemptive force to counter the self-destructive first theme without need for transition material. It creates a powerful psychological effect out of what, for some, is only a "pretty" melody.

In the second movement, most annotators will note the use of 5/4 meter in what passes at first "glance" to be a waltz (3/4 meter). But they will fail to indicate that, by so doing, Tchaikowsky has created a lop-sided "waltz": the effect is that there is one measure of three followed by a measure of two which creates an off-balanced, or "pathetic" waltz.

The third movement is a blazing march which frequently elicits applause upon its conclusion. But, of course, there is more to come: the downward spiral of the fourth movement. Besides the fact that both themes are downward in direction, there is something more mesmerizing about the first theme. It is a crying, desolate utterance. But where does it come from? It comes from the tenor aria from his opera "Eugene Onegin" which Tchaikowsky had composed in 1879 during which Lensky mournfully recalls his youth just before being killed in a duel with Onegin. This tenor aria is one of the great laments in operatic literature and Tchaikowsky uses a version of it to conclude his own personal lament as he faced his own duel...the duel of life! The sixth symphony was not composed until 1893—fourteen years after the composition of the opera, which he actually began composing in 1877. Recall that only a few days after the first performance of this symphony, Tchaikowsky more or less died by his own hand. In "Letters to His Family" translated by the granddaughter of Nadezhda von Meck, (Tchaikowsky's near life-long patroness), Galina von Meck writes in an Epilogue to the letters: "'I am prouder of this symphony than any other of my compositions,' wrote Tchaikowsky to P.O. Yurgenson on 18 October, 1893. Three days later (following premiere) the composer came back home seemingly very upset by something—we shall never really know what—and not feeling very well. He asked his brother (Modest) for a glass of water. When told that he would have to wait for the water to be boiled, he ignored his brother's protests, went into the kitchen, filled a glass of water from the tap and drank it, saying something like: 'who cares anyway!'" Diagnosed with cholera, he died three days later in great agony.

Lensky "died" in 1879 to the melody to which Tchaikowsky died in 1893, dejected by rejection, not so much of his music, but of his person. I can imagine what happened in some cafe in Petersburg that day he drank the water: somebody was, once more, rude to Tchaikowsky in regards to his person. Yes, Galina, "we'll never know"...but we can envision it!

Addendum: when I was a snotty-nose music student in St. Louis (end of 40-'s) Toscanini was bringing to town "his" NBC orchestra to perform in what turned out to be his last concert tour. The major work was to be Tchikowsky's Sixth symphony. My lover and I decided we didn't want to hear Tchaikowsky. We later learned that last minute tickets were available cheaply for the front rows. I could have heard one of the most legendary conductors of the 20th century perform one of the great masterworks of music from the 19th century, but didn't because Tchaikowsky (at that time) was beneath my "dignity"! There's something about "you can lead a horse to water, but you can't make him drink!" So ever since then I've been "eating crow" realizing what I missed yet destined to "teach" the wonders of Tchaikowsky's Sixth Symphony for the rest of my life.

Top down:
Wisteria and Wall, Healdsburg
Terrace of Bellomy Street Carriage House
Alfie atop Wisteria, Healdsburg

Top: Alfie looking through picture-
window, Healdsburg
Right: Alfie in Cadillac with WJB

Left: WJB in Puerto Vallarta airport
Below: WJB horsing around in France

Shelter Cove and Northern California Coastline

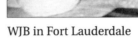

WJB in Fort Lauderdale

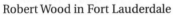

Robert Wood in Fort Lauderdale

Robert and Bill drinking margaritas in Cozumel

OPUS TWENTY-FIVE

$\mathcal{S}$omething strange happened during the Spring of 1983. It had been ten years since I had applied for the first Sabbatical and I was eligible to apply again...which I did. There was a policy that following a Sabbatical the recipient was required to teach for twice the amount of time of the leave upon return. I figured that if I asked for a Spring Sabbatical over two years time, I could continue my two quarters of teaching (Fall and Winter) and then retire. The plan was accepted by the college—I didn't tell them I planned to retire immediately following the completion of my obligation. But for some reason, after the Sabbatical had been granted, I changed my mind and retired all together instead! I regret that now (I guess), but like the snotty-nosed music student of St. Louis days, mistakes are made in life! I had already set up a Greek historical journey for about a dozen of my "senior" students and a first cousin and her friends from North Carolina. That was to have been the first of the two Spring sabbaticals. Instead, it turned out to be my "graduation" present from teaching.All together we were fifteen explorers. The very informative Swann's Helenic Cruises was our implementor but the ship was a disaster compared to modern cruise ships. Swann's is an English company providing at least three specialists in history, religion and geology-botany on each of their cruises. Our cruise featured the assistant to the Archbishop of Canterbury as well as published historians and lecturers from Oxford. All tours were included at a very reasonable price. It was an extremely enlightening trip which started from Naples and went along the coastline of Italy as we heard the heroic tales from World War I and II, and then the more ancient tales of Troy as we approached Turkey. The lectures were fascinating and made the visits to a pile of stones much more interesting!Arriving back in Athens near the end of our journey, one dog-faced Englishwoman, while taking coffee following dinner, asked me where we were from and I exclaimed "California". In a marble-filled voice she replied: "Oh, you Americans have to come so far for your CULTURE!"

Our trip concluded with a three day stay in Venice following the departure from the "tub". Arrangements had been made by my agent in California for the hotel as well as getting us there by water taxis. We were met by a local agent only to find out there was to be one water taxi for all fifteen of us including our luggage. I was considerably upset as I had charge of several elderly travelers as well as my very overweight cousin. The "taxi" kept bobbing up and down as we precariously attempted to board. Everyone was getting quite nervous, especially me. After placing all the luggage on the bow of the speed boat, the agent attempted to help us aboard as the taxi continued to move up and down beside the dock. He kept saying: "PIANO, PIANO", which amused me very much because that is such an important word in music and of course, is Italian for softly. Here was an Italian using the term in its primary non-musical meaning: tread "softly!"

Piano, piano, indeed. The desire to return to practicing resulted in my preparing a program based on poetry of Walt Whitman that I had previously treated photographically. The first half consisted entirely of American composers beginning with Aaron Copland's fan-fares from Appalachian Spring to musically illustrate "I Hear America Singing". The original version of Copland's score, composed for Martha Graham's dance company and originally called "For Martha", features the piano considerably more than the usual orchestral version. The second half of the program utilized Preludes of Chopin, concluding with the last one in d minor which is demonic, ferocious music to interpret Whitman's poem: "I dream'd in a dream I saw a city invincible to the attacks of the whole of the rest of the earth, I dream'd that was the new city of Friends..."(See appendix G for the program contents.)

The program was first presented by the ONE Institute in Los Angeles, and subsequent performances were given in Glendale and San Francisco, including a memorial performance at the Swedenborgian Church on Sunday, October 24, 1993. There is a video of the ONE performance.

Beethoven wrote a Rondo a capriccio for piano entitled "Rage over a lost Groschen (penny)". It is not one of his significant compositions, but I'm intrigued by its title.

To be in a rage over a lost penny seems a bit absurd. But rage plays an important part in music. One needs only to think of the last pages of every major composition by Chopin: all four Scherzi, the four Ballades, the F minor fantasy and many of the Etudes, (including the aforementioned D minor prelude) to realize that true rage can be expressed sonically. It is a far cry to envision the "Poet of the Piano" dripping blood on the keyboard—a la Cornell Wilde—and then to hear these demonic outpourings. Likewise, the olive shaped face of George Sand portrayed aside Chopin in Delacroix's famous portrait in no way conveys the rage she felt within herself over the plight of the unemancipated women she wrote about. The musical rage continues in the Etude Tableaux of Rachmaninoff and the outpourings of Scriabin. Where does all this rage come from? Where does the rage of Messr's Klybold and Harris come from in their shooting up of their high school? In their video tapes left as messages to us, we see they had a great sense of being denied: denied friendliness and understanding, denied a sense of belonging.

The rage of humanity seems to be this sense of being denied... denied Eden?...a primeval sense that we can't have something that belongs to us? Various religions attempt to offer an ultimate reward if only we would do this or that. The rage of wars continue to this day because there is no convergence of belief systems. Tchaikowsky felt compelled to say, as he drank his glass of "hemlock": "who cares anyway!" But as his Sixth Symphony dies down in fury to the lowest and most hushed levels—as the Rage burns itself out—it is only to re-emerge in yet another greater or lesser soul.

Speaking of "so far for one's culture", brings me to the reasons for moving to the desert. Having made a "Jack and the Bean Stalk" of growth in Healdsburg, I yearned to be in warmer climes for the winter with less caring for all the vegetation. Although the desert may be culturally dead, at least in an English sense of the meaning of culture, I did learn to make Boeuf Bourguignon from an Alsatian chef who had his own restaurant in Borrego Springs, Bernard's, which I've already given (see page 37).

But one of my early self-invented recipes was a favorite of Paul and Linda Mayo for whom I served as best man for their wedding years ago. They wanted the recipe so I wrote it down.

TURKEY LEGS

4 turkey legs, fresh or frozen
several cloves of garlic
cream sherry
soy sauce
poultry seasoning

Peal and sliver garlic. Pierce turkey legs with a small, sharp knife on both sides in several (4 or 5) places and insert slivers of garlic. Place in a covered baking dish into which the legs just fit (not a big roasting pan). Pour about a half-cup of sherry over legs; sprinkle generously with soy sauce and poultry seasoning. Bake in slow oven for at least two hours, until meat at the skinny end begins to pull away from the bone. Serve with a hearty rice like brown, wild, or saffron.

Besides learning the European version of "pot-roast" from an Alsatian chef, I enjoyed the real desert experience (not Palm Springs) including watching the comet "Hale-Bopp" while some neighbors in San Diego county decided to commit suicide in order to join the moving comet. My greatest unhappiness with that event was that the leader was a "musician" and having been discovered to be "queer" while working as a successful choral director at a college, was fired. He then changed his name several times, organized the "Heaven's Gate" cult with another person and finally settled on the titles of "Ti" for her and "Do" for himself. In the music alphabet of solfeggio (Do, re, mi, etc.) the seventh and eighth steps of the scale are Ti and Do. We also call the seventh-step the leading tone because it leads up to Do. Whatever rhyme or reason was in their heads for such titles, the mystery remains that some "bright" people can become addicted to a guru that rules their lives even to the point of taking it away. Do people really need to lean on the beliefs of others in order to fill in the essence of their lives?

I watched "Hale-Bopp" nightly from my desert home in Borrego Springs and thought again and again what could be within the heads of the Heaven Gate adherents to pretend (with a quarter in their pocket in case they needed to phone home) that they were going anywhere else but to their cultist deaths. "Phone home, E.T.!" No answer.

OPUS TWENTY-SIX

I have suggested that I moved to the desert during the winter in order to avoid the Northern California rainy season. I should point out that my reasoning included the concern about wiping up a muddy, wet dog every three or four hours! The clean, sandy soil of the desert, with very little rain, provided a swipe-clean life for Alfie and me. Besides, he loved chasing the rabbits and coyotes that abound in the desert. Fortunately he never caught any, and only once was I a bit fearful when a pack of coyotes, which he started to chase, began to back-track some members in order to surround him. Fortunately my yelling alerted him to the danger and he returned home safely.

When the temperature began to reach the 100's everyday, it was time to go back up to Northern California. It was also time to think about gardening or not to garden. The latter prevailed. My long time house sitters, Bruce and Isabelle Adams, who resided in San Francisco, but loved coming to the country, wanted to make a permanent decision about country living and felt that they had invested considerable time into the Healdsburg property which "entitled" them first consideration of buying my property. We worked out a plan of half-ownership for them with a ten year right-to-buy for the remaining half. Since I was wintering in the desert and spending a good portion of the summer by the ocean (more about that later) it seemed a sensible solution for the care and upkeep of a highly vegetated property. Furthermore, they had two children who they preferred being educated outside the city environment. Isabelle, besides being an excellent mother, was an energetic gardener and food preparer, having grown up in France with a mother and father who lived in a 250 year old Normandy farm house and who were avid providers for their own table.

So I converted the Gallery into private quarters for myself and installed an office trailer adjacent to the building. This was remodeled into a normal-sized bath and kitchen with a deck built to connect it to the Gallery. The arrangement ended up being something like "having your cake and eating it too," for I was able to enjoy the fruits of my labor in planting all the roses, wisterias, grape vines, forest-of evergreens, and not having to "water and weed" them anymore.

What I did instead was to sneak off to Shelter Cove for three or four days at a time where I had already built a cedar-log house 1200 feet above the Pacific Ocean with a magnificent view of the King's Range mountains as they cascade into the sea on what is known as "The Lost Coast."

All my life I had wanted to have a residence with a view of the sea. (My Grandmother's home where my Mother grew up was in Avon-by-the-Sea, New Jersey, and my favorite town in France was Villefranche-sur-mer—somehow "by-the-sea" was in my blood.) I grew up two blocks from Boca Ciega Bay in Gulfport, Florida and my grammar school days were spent at the gulf-side school on Pass-a-Grille—my father used to refer to it as a country club rather than a school! My dancer-friend, who also grew up in Florida, frequently talked of having a property that went directly to the edge of the sea. He even designed what the house should look like and we often went hunting for such property in the Pinellas Point area of St. Petersburg (then largely undeveloped), as well as in Sarasota, home of the Ringling Brother's Circus. During the 20's, John Ringling had built a villa at the edge of Sarasota Bay in imitation of a Venetian Palazzo along with his fore-mentioned Museum where I saw my first David. Ringling even had a pier festooned with "barber poles" where gondolas could land and discharge guests for his lavish parties.

Having given up such fantasies for myself, I discovered the Lost Coast through the mailing of an auction pamphlet. I receive frequent real estate mailings due to the fact that I'm an inveterate "looker".My father, years ago, wrote to say: "Stop looking at and buying property!" Property is the only thing that I've ever made any money at in regards to investments...but that is not why I buy anything in the first place....I just like houses and "location, location, location".

Shelter Cove is 160 miles north of Healdsburg and requires a strenuous trip over some primitive pavement for the final 22 miles, due west from Garberville to the Pacific ocean. There is a flat area close to the coast which was paved for an airstrip and around which the majority of houses have been built. I chose to go up the hillside about 1200 feet to build the cedar log house that I had secretly coveted for a long time. My oasis, facing as it does the North Coast line of forests reaching down to the sea, lends itself to listening to Sibelius and other Romantic composers who attempted to express the grandeur of nature in music. Since I didn't install any TV satellite system, I depend on either my own piano playing (an electric Yamaha full-size keyboard) or my many cassettes for sound. There are two large speakers sitting on either side of the picture window (set facing the

North coast) which provide much intoxicating sound to go along with my intoxicating drinks...retirement with a glass!

It was during one of these moments, while listening to Liszt's B Minor Piano Sonata, that I had this vision of what that complicated piece of music meant. I wrote out a descriptive scenario right then and there and vowed to produce a performance of the piece with my lecture as preamble. I realized that Liszt was a very religious person.

Robert Wood, who had been my practice teaching mentor at the high school level those many years ago, and I both retired from teaching about the same time. We had maintained a friendship throughout the years; he often stopped in Los Gatos on his way to Oregon or Northern California during summer vacation and then later in Healdsburg. When we both had the freedom from a "job", we began going on cruises together, sometimes as often as five or six cruises a year! As we were both pianists, we kept saying that instead of a cruise, we should attend the Van Cliburn Piano competition some year—they only occur every four years. After letting two of them go by (8 year time-frame) we decided, in 1997, that we had better go instead of just making promises to go. They are always held in Fort Worth, Texas as that is where a group of piano teachers originally started the competition and named it for their favorite-son pianist, Van Cliburn. He himself did not institute the competition, but he does lend his support and is, I think, honorary chairman of the foundation named for him which puts on the competition. Robert's longtime colleague from Westchester high School, Esther, had a niece in Texas who welcomed us to her guest house in Granbury, a few miles southwest of Fort Worth, for the duration of the competition. We attended only the semi-finals which take place over a five day period. The twelve semi-finalists from various countries had only a single American representative, Jon Nakamatsu. Each pianist performs a 90 minute solo recital and on another day, performs an entire quintet with a professional string quartet group. Cliburn himself introduced that requirement as he is a strong believer that solo pianists should be competent in chamber music performance.

The performances began at 1 p.m. in the afternoon with a solo recital. That is followed by one of the quintet performances and then the afternoon concludes with another solo recital. In the evening, the reverse takes place: starting with a chamber performance and then a single, solo recital and concluding with another chamber performance. Jon Nakamatsu appeared as the second solo program on the first day of the semi-finals. I knew nothing about him...neither Robert nor I had yet purchased the $25. catalog which gave pictures of each performer, their repertoire for the competition and background information. By that evening we had done so. The first afternoon we didn't know anything about anyone performing. The first performer was a 19 year old Russian "boy" with an extraordinary technical ability who played his difficult choices of compositions like a whirlwind. The second solo performer was Jon Nakamatsu and half way through his program, I nudged Robert and said: "If I were Bill Gates, I'd pay that young man a million dollars a year to play the piano while I took bubble baths!" It was meant as a compliment in that Jon had such a comfortable, relaxed stage presence without "smash or dash", yet played the piano beautifully and elegantly. The thought entered my head that if I were the richest man in the world (Bill Gates) I would subsidize this lovely pianist, (to go along with the 75 million dollar mansion that was under construction—and much in the news—at that moment). The effect of Jon's playing—masterful but relaxed—was a calming sensation following the extraordinary display of the young Russian.

All the contestants had admirable ability and talent. The contest days were Thursday and Friday with Saturday free. Then the remaining performances occurred on Sunday and Monday. The Fort Worth Star Telegram featured the Cliburn competition on several full pages each day and for Sunday's edition—due to there not being any Saturday performances—devoted the pages to some special articles on some of the contestants...all being treated equal at this point in time. One of these specials was a feature on Jon Nakamatsu due to several unusual facts: he was the only contestant who had never studied at a conservatory; he was the only contestant who had studied since the age of six with the same teacher; in fact the teacher was there with him at the contest. Her name was Marina Derryberry and Jon Nakatmatsu had studied with her in Sunnyvale, California all his musical life! With a name like Derryberry, it is not easy to forget. Marina had sat in on my lectures all during those early years at Foothill whenever I was playing the piano, and those were exactly the years when she began teaching Jon. Sunday evening was Jon's time to perform with the Tokoyo Quartet, for which he had chosen the difficult but musically interesting Dvorak A major quintet. Following his performance, I attempted to go "back stage" to see if I could meet Marina Derryberry. AT TCU's Landreth Hall, the entire side hallway to the auditorium was considered "back stage" and due to the number of performers involved, no one was allowed beyond a certain point. Following the tumultuous autograph period with Jon, where I told him I knew his teacher, he said: "Go on back, she's there." Well, the guard wouldn't let me pass but he took my name and went back to speak to Marina. In a few moments, she appeared, looking exactly as I remembered her from almost twenty years before. When she recognized me, she turned to the guard and said: "Oh, he's a very good pianist!"

She had taught this young genius from the beginning and he was on the threshold of at least being one of the six finalists to perform concertos with the Fort Worth Symphony which was the final round of the competition. Robert and I had planned only to stay for the semi-finals, but on the morning of our departure back to California, we sought out a newspaper to find out who of the 12 semi-finalists had made it to the finals—and Jon's name was among the six chosen.

Each of the finalists performed two concertos—not consecutively. Jon performed the Beethoven 2nd concerto (which is really the first composed by Beethoven, but published later) and then, on Saturday evening, the huge Rachmaninoff Third, by now made famous by the movie Shine. Back in California, we eagerly awaited the outcome of the competition. Sure enough, the boy from Sunnyvale, California had won the Tenth Van Cliburn International Piano Competition, the first American to win the gold since 1981. The prize was two years under management with guaranteed performances in Carnegie Hall and other important music venues through out the world. Amongst those early engagements, Jon returned to Landreth Hall in Fort Worth (Bass Hall was not yet finished) and the local critic, Wayne Lee Gay, headlined his review: "Nakamatsu shows his Cliburn win was no fluke", but in a feature article prior to the concert, Mr. Gay sub-titled his "Golden Boy" headline with: "Van Cliburn winner Jon Nakamatsu returns to the scene of his unlikely triumph" (!) So much for keeping everyone happy. In fairness to Mr. Gay, it might be pointed out that in the Dallas Morning News following Jon's gold medal win, critic Nancy Kruh wrote: "No one seemed more stunned by the results (gold medal) than the recipient."

Following the excitement of hearing so many fine young pianists performing all of the music I had spent my life trying to master, I realized that I was wasting my retirement time watching the desert-scape of Borrego Springs age—beautiful as it is—while I aged along with it. After three winters of listening to the coyotes and fearfully watching Alife chasing them, I decided I was wasting valuable time.

At the Cliburn, Saturday was a free day. Our hostess, Carolyn Robinson, drove us about Granbury and environs. We entered the gated community called Pecan Plantation which is nestled amidst the largest pecan grove in the world. She owned a lot which gave her membership there in the Country Club, but she was also interested in looking at a builder's house that was just about to be finished. We stopped and went through the still-open house, although cabinets were in, molding, etc, already installed. The living room had twelve foot ceilings, recessed lighting, attractive half-round topped windows, and ten foot French doors opening out to a rear patio area. The rest of the rooms were ten feet high and all had attractive beveled moldings all around the ceiling. There were four bed-rooms, or three and a den, and two and a half baths. The master bath contained a glass-sided shower, and a large jet-tub besides the "his and her" basin area. The exterior was covered by attractive pale bricks. Altogether it looked like it would cost a million dollars in California. I wondered what the price was and Carolyn opined that it would be about $160,000. I couldn't believe it. She said she'd find out. The next morning there was a note on our cottage door saying the house was priced at 162 K. We went back to California and I phoned the contractor within a couple of days to say I wanted to buy the house. I put the Boreggo Springs house up for sale and the rest of summer was spent preparing for the move to Granbury, Texas.

I feel compelled to make some explanation for leaving the various and intriguing residences I have had during my life. I'm frequently asked: "why did you give them up?!" The answer is: each venue was a step on my evolutionary path of "existence." Los Gatos was my first house and a "show-case" to a certain extent. Although attractive, it had a swimming pool difficult to maintain and the house was built prior to when insulation was required. Although there was central heating, I was always chilly during the winter in that house.

Healdsburg provided the "back to nature" episode in my life, and in fact, represents the longest period of time of ownership of any of my properties—twenty years. Bellomy Street was always a "work in progress" and eventually I didn't want to keep at the "work." Also there were complications regarding my adopted son's divorce, etc., as they were the occupants of the restored barn for about 12 years. Yes, I finally realized my dream of remodeling the barn from an artist's studio (with holes in the roof) to a bona fide "carriage house." Meanwhile, I had developed two properties in the desert at Boreggo

Springs and now have settled in my "estate" in Texas where I can come for the "season" of musical events in Fort worth and go back to California for the summer.

During those last few years in Healdsburg, I had begun to learn how to make wine. Beginning with left over grapes from neighbor vineyards, I learned the process of home wine-making from my dear friends, Joan and Larry Franceschina who had, for awhile, lived diagonally across from me on West Dry Creek Road. They had about 20 acres there and were avid home wine-makers. They tutored me through my first attempt at wine making and from then on, each fall I was able to proceed on my own, eventually buying a used Italian-made press which is more useful than owning one's own crusher. All of these pieces of equipment can be rented, but it's nice to have some of the main items for one's self.

The most important thing about wine making is cleanliness. The washing of all containers, the constant care to keep wineflies and gnats from entering containers of wine, etc, is crucial. If you ever take a trip into one of California's wineries, you will see that the cask rooms and fermentation tanks are medicinally clean and that special lamps to zap flies are always on. A good winery is as clean as a hospital...or more so.

Eventually, not enjoying the little left-over clusters of grapes (called second-growth), I planted a few rows of my own grapes so that I could have big, luscious clusters of my own. The plantings were muscat (out of which I make a dry table wine), malvasia and zinfandel from which I attempt to produce a late-harvest, port-style wine. Some years have been more successful than others in regard to the late harvest style wine. In order to achieve the desired level of alcohol as well as sweetness, I've stopped the fermentation with the use of brandy or 90 proof vodka on several occasions. Into all of my late harvest wines, I've added Elderberrys hand-picked from along the roadside just as my wine-making friends in New Zealand taught me.

Beginning with the lil' ol' Italian winemaker in Yonkers, to learning to make wine myself from my San Francisco Italian-restaurant-heritage friends, Larry and Joan, I've come full circle in wine-making knowledge and appreciation. (A life-time achievement award, please!)

Olga and Krystyne on board Crown Jewel

Granbury, Texas
Upper: Dining Room
Right: Main Salon
Lower: Family Room

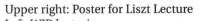

Upper right: Poster for Liszt Lecture
Left: WJB lecturing
Lower right: Budginas receiving applause

Sixty-ninth Birthday Festivities

Robert and Bill—S.F. before Cruise, in background Crystal Symphony in port

Robert in a Norwegian pub

Robert and Bill "cruising" the Captain

Upper: Sunset over Shelter Cove

Right:
"Wall" and fountain in Healdsburg;
Portugese Tile on Wall

Lower: "WJB and Smokey"

OPUS TWENTY-SEVEN

*D*uring my first season of residency in Texas (never mind the difficulties of moving—that's a whole other story!) I became acquainted with an Arts Council that sponsored programs throughout a seven county area. I had already fallen in love with a tiny concert hall straddling one corner of a block in Granbury that a former piano teacher had bequeathed to Tarleton State college of Stephenville for use as a cultural center for off-campus courses and events. It contained a near concert-size Yamaha grand piano (7', 8") in this restored Presbyterian church, which had actually been the first church built in old Granbury. The ceiling was open to its peaked rafters of wood making for a vibrant sound box in itself. It held about 125 people and was exactly the sort of venue that I wanted to perform in. A young Lithuanian pianist, who was studying at U.S.C. for his doctorate of music degree, had already won the Los Angeles Liszt competition with special commendation for his performance of the b minor sonata. I had heard him in a preview concert at Robert's house in Manhattan Beach. Rudolfas Budginas' prize was a performance in Budapest at the Liszt Museum and the Manhattan Beach performance was a warm-up for that concert-trip.

During that first winter in Texas I researched my lecture from biographies of Liszt, Chopin and George Sand. I wanted my lecture rooted in facts, not just "inspiration". The Cross Timbers Fine Arts Council agreed to sponsor the program and pay Rudolfas a good fee. I did not want any money for myself, and in fact, paid for Rudolfas' air-fare to Texas from California and hosted him in my home at the "Plantation"...which was my pleasure to do so. The date set was for January 22, 1999. I was to present my lecture at the beginning of the program, followed by my specific listening points which I would illustrate at the piano. I began the whole program by performing the lovely melodic section from Liszt's Funerailles which concludes in very dramatic harmonies after which I quote Liszt in regards to his own estimation of his talent in which he muses that he will at least be remembered for his harmonies! I had learned the Funerailles under the tutelage of Leo Sirota those many years ago who said then of my endeavor: "With that piece I pushed you through the door of MUSIC!" Well I do remember his pushing me on my back while performing the massive chords in the piece during those lessons.

One month to the day before the scheduled concert, I slipped on the icy sidewalk in front of my own house and crushed my right femur beneath the weight of my entire body. It required two steel plates and 15 screws to pull it back together. Not only was it a great shock to my system, but also a great shock to my plans! Fortunately the lecture was all but completed and for the most part typed. Three weeks were spent in hospitals, spending several hours each day in physical therapy. There was a single hour set aside for "recreation" during which time I attempted to keep my fingers active by playing on a tiny, battery-operated keyboard of about three octaves. I could only do some exercises and some Bach Inventions. Nothing else would fit; certainly not any Liszt!

There was but one week back at home before the recital-lecture to re-practice the themes from the b minor sonata and the section from Funerailles. My niece, Beverly Ann Bryan, came from Michigan to retrieve me from the hospital and care for me during my first week home. On the drive from the Southwest Fort Worth rehab hospital—about 35 miles—we managed to buy everything I needed to start life over again: a used wheel-chair, an arm-chair for the bedroom and one for the dining table, a shower seat for the stall-shower, and a rolling high-stool with five casters (a must according to the therapist) for the kitchen. The Cadillac was crammed full and the trunk lid had to be tied down, but we got it all home and all on one trip!

The concert was to take place on the first weekend following my return from the hospital. I practiced each day and rehearsed the reading of my lecture. My adopted son Kim arrived about the same time as Rudolfas on Saturday before the Sunday afternoon concert. Kim wheeled me onto the stage of Langdon Cultural Center the next day and the only deviation from what I had planned was simply to say: "I'm a victim of the pre-Christmas ice storm". After being helped onto the piano bench, I turned to the keyboard and began to play. Everything went precisely as I had envisioned it (except for a broken leg!).Rudolfas played magnificently, including encores, and everyone said that Granbury had never experienced such a cultural event. And I'm sure they hadn't! (see Appendix H for text of lecture and copy of program.)

About forty years ago my "dancer-friend" was having a hard time in his relationship, and sought astrological help from an English astrologer and a Hindu astrologer. I decided that I would have my "charts" done as well. The Indian charged $25.00 for about a five or six page, single space typed report and for an additional $10, would answer any questions the report raised in the mind of the customer. For some reason, in my friends report, a time-frame was given regarding his death-date, which in his case was to happen after the dawning of the 21st century. In my chart there was no such reference. So I wrote back questioning whether I was to see the "New Millennium" and he replied that I wasn't! Well, forty years ago that didn't bother me very much. But as the years have gone by and the approach of the "next millennium" drew closer, I began to give more thought to his prediction. You may well imagine that I gave very careful attention to my travels, my driving, my everything, as we approached December 31, 1999. "New Year's Eve" day began with CNN's Millennium celebrations starting in New Zealand, then on to Sydney where the most magnificent fire-works were put on over all that beautiful bay where I had spent so much time during my Sabbatical. As the day proceeded from one time zone to the next I watched it all. When it was finally mid-night Central Standard Time in Texas (and I had spent nearly 24 hours watching TV) I felt that I had made it into the next century....and several months later I'm still here!

Opus 27 is the volume of works by Beethoven that contains the famous "Moonlight Sonata," which he entitled " sonata quasi una fantasia": sonata, but like a phantasy—sort of like a Fairy Pudding! And as the moon sets in the west, let's have a toast of champagne....

RECIPE FOR FAIRY PUDDING

A batch of music lessons.
One dose of ballet lessons
Several distinguished teachers
Lots of world travel
Lots of good friends
Lots of good food
Lots of good wine
Mix well
ENJOY

APPENDIX A: MUSIC
The Hermaphroditic Art
by Brian Jennings

Notes from a Lecture-Recital given in ONE Institute Assembly Hall, April 5, 1964 (Published in ONE INSTITUTE QUARTERLY, Spring, 1964)

Homophilia cannot lay claim to the giants of Music: Bach, Beethoven and Brahms, as it can to the giants of art, Leonardo da Vinci and Michelangelo. But it may be that when the dust of this century settles, a few more "B's" with lives extra interesting to us, will have been added to the list of great composers.

Bach may be said to have been the most ordinary of the three giants in that he did marry and have children—20 to be exact—and so, perhaps, wasn't so ordinary either! Beethoven, on the other hand, never married and seems to have led a miserable life, as far as romance goes, constantly falling in love with some unattainable lady of rank but finding only rebuff: something, after all, that happens to even the best of us, if only occasionally!

Bachelor Brahms moved into the household of the Robert Schumann's as a fledgling composer and, while his host quietly went mad, offered solace to Robert's wife, Clara, the gifted pianist, who almost preferred playing the music of Brahms to her husband's notable piano compositions. It was not until after her husband's death that Clara, rather remorsefully, devoted her pianistic energies exclusively to Schumann's compositions.

Debussy preferred cats—and feline-like women. Berlioz was a Bohemian in an exaggerated Puccini manner. Liszt had illegitimate children that grew up to be famous. Wagner may well have flitted across the threshold of homophilia in the Court of Ludwig II.

So perhaps, after all, the several composers we are going to hear today may not turn out to be psychosomatically so different from their heterosexual brothers, when, if we viewed some aspect of their lives, we found that they preferred the intimate company of men to that of women.

Our program begins with the music of Jean Baptiste Lully. Born near Florence, Italy, in 1639, we know that an old shoemaker gave the gifted but mischievous child some elementary instruction, and taught him the guitar and the rudiments of music. Lully was in the midst of these studies when the Chevalier de Guise chanced to come across him, and to please his niece (who wanted a "joli petit Italien" to teach her his language!) brought this child, then about 10 or 12 years of age, to France. Thus, when quite young, fortune smiled upon the little Lully and further favors were probably in store for him at the Palais d'Orleans, when his mischievous habit of writing sarcastic verses and setting them to characteristic music brought him all at once into disgrace with the princess. Mademoiselle, having discovered that he had composed the air of a satirical song, full of gaiety and 'go' at her expense, promptly dismissed him from her service. However, that which seemed a loss was really a gain to Lully, for the young King Louis—then a youth of 15 or so—had previously taken a fancy to Baptiste, and perceiving his superior gifts, made him a member of his band of 24 violins. (1)

A born courtier, full of the resource and aplomb necessary to face an intriguing court, he knew, above all, how to please and amuse the king, and how to profit by this precious favor at the beginning of a reign full of youth, passion and art. He was soon chosen to compose the music for the court ballets, in which Louis XIV himself danced side by side with Lully.

Of the music still heard today by Lully, none is more famous than the music for the play Le Bourgeois Gentilhomme, still given in Paris as it was in the Court of Louis XIV. I play two Scenes de ballet from this work. They depict the young tailors dancing around the bourgeois gentilhomme as they measure him! (2) (Music)

And now to the art of music, The Hermaphroditic art. Erich Fromm tells us in his essay for happiness, The Art of Loving that "the awareness of human separation, without reunion by love—is the source of shame. It is at the same time the source of guilt and anxiety. The deepest need of man (he says) is the need to overcome his separateness, to leave the prison of his aloneness."(3)

Gertrude Stein on her death bed asked "what is the answer?" There was silence. "Well then what is the question" she asked and then died. (4)

Fromm says that man of all ages and cultures is confronted with the solution of one and the same question: the question of how to overcome separateness, how to achieve union, how to transcend one's own individual life and find at-onement. He goes on to say that the more the human race emerged from its primary bonds, the more it separated itself from the natural world and then the more intense became the need to find new ways of escaping separateness.

One way of achieving this aim lies in all kinds of orgiastic states. According to Fromm, all forms of orgiastic union have three characteristics: they are intense, even violent; they occur in the total personality—in mind and body; they are transitory and periodical. (3)

The most satisfactory way of escaping separateness is through love which Fromm describes as an activity, not a passive effect. The active character of love can be described by stating that love is primarily giving, not receiving. Giving is the highest expression of potency. In the very act of giving we experience our strength, our wealth, our power. This experience of heightened vitality and potency fills us with joy. We experience ourselves as overflowing, spending, alive, hence joyous. (3)

A contemporary composer, Ned Rorem, says that history has provided ten thousand solutions to Gertrude Stein's: "What is the answer," but that those responses only raise other questions. He feels that only the work of art satisfies, for its questions and answers are mutually inclusive and form the one "finished" thing that exists. (4)

The hermaphroditism inherent in this mutually inclusive asking and answering is in no art more apparent than in music.

I hope to show in the music I play today, the orgiastic analogy of intensity, even violence and the occupation of the total personality which most composers bring to their music. That this act of creation, for them, contains the three characteristics of an orgiastic state, I hope, will be apparent. In the act of their creation, giving is total and therefore becomes the highest expression of potency.

The repetition of creation throughout a life-time embodies the third orgiastic characteristic of transience and periodicity, yet each time contains that element of "finish", asked and answered, which is often lacking in human affairs. Through sound, a physical component of nature, the composer—for a time—relinquishes aloneness and separateness and joins nature in one of her dynamic mediums.

CHOPIN: ETUDE IN C MINOR

The publicly avowed pederast, Andre Gide, preferred the music of Bach and Chopin above all others. He was an accomplished amateur pianist and spent many days practicing instead of writing, to the chagrin of some of his colleagues. Of the Prelude No. 17 in A flat, Gide has written in his Journal: "the voice that sings can hardly be made out in the beginning; it remains profoundly involved and as if floating in the regular flow of the six quavers, where an impersonal heart beats. I like the melody to rise in a quite natural way, as if by a foreordained blossoming forth; at least in the beginning of the piece, for as soon as it has developed, the melody bursts forth and clearly dominates, to fade away and be reabsorbed only at the end. I like its seeming to melt again into the atmosphere. In the work of Chopin there are many more powerful passages, but there is none in which joy assumes a more tender, more confident, and purer accent. Everything is lost if in the modulation in E major, the accent becomes triumphant. I want to find there a vague rapture, full of astonishment and surprise ..." (5)

CHOPIN: PRELUDE NO 17

We have not spoken specifically of Chopin and homophilia. We can't. We can know his music, though, and we can know the swath he cut through Parisian life. Perhaps the most accurate picture we can have of him, other than through his music, is the one drawn by George Sand in her novel *Lucrezia Floriani,*which authorities say is based on her affair with Chopin. In the novel there is no doubt that in analyzing the principal male character she was analyzing Chopin. She wrote: "Prince Karol was sweet, sensitive, exquisite in everything. At 15 years of age he possessed all the graces of adolescence united to the grave demeanor of maturity. He was delicate in body as in spirit. But this absence of muscular development meant that he preserved a charming beauty, an exceptional physiognomy that had so to speak, not age nor sex. About him there was nothing of the male and hardy air of a descendant of that race of ancient magnates who knew nothing but to drink, to hunt, and to wrangle. Nor was there about him anything of the effeminate gentility of a rosy cherub. He resembled the ideal creatures used by the poetic spirit of the Middle Ages for ornamenting Christian temples; he was an angel, beautiful of face, resembling a great, sad woman, pure and svelte of body as a young Olympian god, and to crown this combination, he was at once tender and severe, chaste and passionate." (6)

CHOPIN: ETUDE IN E MAJOR

Writing to his patron and near-life-long friend Madame von Meck, Tchaikovsky wrote: "That yearning, that discontent, that aspiration toward some undefined ideal, that apartness from humanity, the admission that only in music—most ideal of the arts—can you discover any answer to these agitating problems, all proved to me that your self-made religion does not provide that complete peace of mind which is peculiar to people who have found in their religion a prepared answer to all the doubts that torture a meditative and sensitive nature. And, you know, it seems to me that you care so intensely for my music only because I am as full of such ideal longing as you are. Our sufferings are the same, your doubts are as strong as mine. We are both drifting in the unbounded sea of skepticism, seeking a harbour and not finding it. Aren't these the reasons my music touches you so intimately?" (7)

For Tchaikovsky, there can be no doubt that music provided the one satisfactory solution to the eternal quest, the one affirmation in his life that was guiltless as we realize the remorse and guilt he experienced because of his homosexuality. As the above letter so clearly shows, Tchaikovsky, like all thinking, sensitive creatures, loathes the separateness, the aloneness, that Fromm speaks of as the deepest need of man to solve.

Tchaikovsky poetically wrote: "seeking a harbour and not finding it." Here he is being rhetorical, for his harbour was composing and within his flights of composition he achieved his orgiastic oneness with humanity and probably even psychologically with those he loved in a way he could not experience sexually with them because of his overwhelming sense of sexual guilt.

For us his music is readily understood as he seeks us out, finds us, and speaks to us in our attempt to find harbour, oneness.

TCHAIKOVSKY: ROMANCE IN F MINOR

Tchaikovsky became a close friend of Camille Saint-Saens during his several trips to Paris.Saint-Saens honored this friendship by recalling Tchaikovsky's Dance of the Little Swans from Swan Lake for the closing theme in his Carnival of Animals. This finale is preceded by "The Swan" for cello and two pianos, the most famous melody composed by Saint-Saens. The Carnival of Animals was written as a private family piece. Although it was later orchestrated, Saint-Saens refused to publish or perform it in public save for "The Swan". This ban lasted as long as he lived (1921), and still contains some unexplained family jokes. This reticence in certain matters is apparently the reason that we don't know more about him, personally.George Painter in his biography of Marcel Proust writes that: "Proust quarreled with Reynaldo (Hahn, the composer) over his loyal attachment to his master Saint-Saens, who, as was notorious, was himself an invert." (8)

Principally, however, we can know Saint-Saens through his music. The Concerto No. Two in G minor for piano and orchestra contains all the elements of oneness gained through intensity, and total participation of mind and body as the composer, for a time, overcame separateness in a monumental musical work.

SAINT-SAENS: CONCERTO NO 2 IN G MINOR, First Movement!

Maurice Ravel has written of himself: "I am not a 'modern composer' in the strictest sense of the term, because my music, far from being 'revolution,' is rather 'evolution.' I have always felt that a composer should put on paper what he feels and how he feels it irrespective of what the current style of composition may be. Great music, I have always felt, must always come from the heart. Any music created by technique and brains alone is not worth the paper it is written on. Besides being cerebral, 'modern music' is, for the most part, very ugly. And music, I insist, must be, in spite of everything, be beautiful. I do not understand the arguments of those composers who tell me that the music of our time must be ugly because it gives expression to an ugly age. Why does an ugly age need expression? And what is left to music if it is denuded of beauty? What mission has it, then, as art? No. Theories are all very fine. But a composer should not compose his music to theories. He should create musical beauty directly from his heart, and he should feel intensely what he is composing." (9)

RAVEL: SONATINE, First Movement

The next group of pieces are dances, each unique. The first one, by Eric Satie, might be the most pleasant one to observe. Satie was born in the province of Calvados in 1866 and died in Paris in 1925. An incomplete musician, Satie, partly by chance, partly consciously, outstripped by 40 years contemporary polytonalists and atonalists. A humorist, literary rather than musical, he searched for unusual titles for his compositions. But the title for today's composition, Gymnopedie, is not merely fanciful, for Satie was an overt homo-sexual and a free thinker in more than musical ways. So it was natural for him to set to music such a beautiful fancy as the idea of dancing athletes. The Greek word gymnos translates as naked, and pedie, as dance. So our athletes are even more attractive than the Olympic gymnasts of today when they perform their balletic free exercise. This music is soft and languorous, as a gymnopedie should be!

SATIE: GYMNOPEDIE NO. 1

It may or may not be interesting that both Ravel and Gershwin died following unsuccessful operations on the brain. David Ewen, Gershwin's biographer, has written of him: "His music was the be-all and end-all of his existence. He loved to write it, play it, talk about it all the time. He was in love with his music and he had a lover's expressiveness in extolling the many attractions of his beloved." It is said that Gershwin often plagued his friends with questions as to whether or not it was wise for an artist to marry; whether marriage did not put a serious impediment in the way of an artist practicing his art. But he was not really seeking an answer and often did not wait for one. He was only looking for an excuse to avoid a permanent relationship. (10)

Recently there has been an unearthing of letters and diaries regarding the other life of George Gershwin. We are not yet able to report the contents definitively. His second prelude, while not necessarily meant to be a dance, is rather suggestive, to me, of a certain sort of dance—or performance—and likewise may also be suggestive to you.

GERSHWIN: PRELUDE NO. 2

One of the most interesting contemporary composers is Samuel Barber. This third dance comes from his ballet suite Souvenirs and is called Pas de deux, which literally means "step for two." Mr. Barber gives no programmatic description for this music and the interpretation which I give may or may not be close to Barber's mood or thoughts regarding this music.

I like to think of this piece as a dance for lovers, not casual acquaintances, but real lovers. When we dance with our beloved, our emotions tend to be heightened and the ecstatic feelings we experience are very often increased by the nearness of the loved one. At these moments of heightened sensuality, we shout within "I love you" not once, but many times, although we may only whisper it once, shyly, into the ear of our lover, betraying ever so slightly our inner excitement.

One of the supreme attributes of music is that it can audibly shout out the thrill of the montage of love as beautifully and as completely as does orgasm. And then, as it is only with one we truly love, the soft, warm feelings of contentment, uttered in strange keys, signifies the departure from the pinnacle of excitement to the sounds and feeling of bliss as we drift off into the sleep of happiness.

Samuel Barber wrote of his Souvenirs: "In 1952 I was writing some duets for one piano to play with a friend...(11)

BARBER: PAS DE DEUX FROM "SOUVENIRS"

Bibliography

(1) Grove's Dictionary of Music and Musicians; Eric Blom, editor, Fifth edition. New York: MacMillan & Co., Ltd. 1954, 9 volumes

(2) Daniel, Marc: "A Study of Homosexuality in France during the reigns of Louis XIII and Louis XIV". Translated from ARCADIE by Marcel Martin

in HOMOPHILE STUDIES, Vol. IV, No. 4, Los Angles, One Institute, Fall, 1961

(3)   Fromm, Erich, THE ART OF LOVING

(4)   Rorem, Ned: "Listening and Hearing" Music Journal, Dec. 1963

(5)   Gide, Andre. JOURNALS 3rd Vol., Alfred Knopf, New York

(6)   Weinstock, Herbert. CHOPIN, THE MAN AND HIS MUSIC ; Alfred Knopf, N.Y. 1949

(7)   Weinstock, Herbert. TCHAIKOVSKY Alfred Knopf, N.Y. 1943

(8)   Painter, George D.: PROUST, A BIOGRAPHY

(9)   Ravel, Maurice. "Personal Note" in THE NEW BOOK OF MODERN COMPOSERS. Edited by David Ewen, 3rd edition, Alfred Knopf, N.Y., 1961

(10) Ewen, David. "Personal Note" in THE NEW BOOK OF MODERN COMPOSERS. Edited by David Ewen, 3rd edition, Alfred Knopf, N.Y., 1961

(11) Barber, Samuel: SOUVENIRS, G. Schirmer, N.Y., 1954

APPENDIX B
"A Pianist's Requiem for J.F.K."
William Bryan, Pianist (Program notes by William Bryan)

"I have taken from the piano repertoire particular works that seemed most meaningful for this occasion and that, as programmed, make for a spiritual and emotional catharsis. It is a coming-to-terms, musically, so to speak, with the tragedy of President Kennedy's violent death and its aftermath: the immense reaction of a distraught nation." (W.J.B.)

MARCIA FUNEBRE SULLA MORTE D'UN EROE, Opus 26,

Ludwig van Beethoven

This Funeral March "on the death of a hero" comes from Beethoven's piano Sonata, Opus 26. The celebrated Third Symphony of Beethoven, "Erocia", (the second movement of which is the famous orchestral Marche Funebre) was to be composed 29 opus numbers later; but, already in this piano sonata, Beethoven copes with the starkness and finality of death. The broadness and strength of the main theme gives the movement its heroic proportions and fitness for accompanying the hero to his grave.

ADAGIO CANTABILE, from SONATA PATHETIQUE, Opus 13, Beethoven

As if composed specifically for this purpose, the most famous of Beethoven's beautiful themes is placed in "A Pianist Requiem for J.F.K." immediately after the death march as a musical plea for mitigation: the anguish and pain of death, modified by the knowledge that beyond the grave is eternal peace and repose. Could any musical sound say this more poignantly than this Adagio Cantabile?

INTERMEZZO, opus 117, No. 2, Johannes Brahms

Of all the romantic composers, none match as well the introspection that clarifies the emotions as does Brahms. The Intermezzo's moving, questing theme explores many tonal possibilities—as does life itself—only to conclude in its somber closing minor arpeggio that death, finally, is the result of the quest.

Pas de deux from SOUVENIRS, Samuel Barber

This adagio movement from SOUVENIRS was originally written for two pianos, but, as played here, it was transcribed for one piano by the composer. It is a piece that could evoke varying emotions, but, as placed here, it creates a yearning for answers to both life and death.

Three PRELUDES, Opus 28, Frederic Francois Chopin

No. 2, Lento. Each of Chopin's 24 preludes deal with a single mood and this somber piece is based upon the plainsong motif of the Dies

Irae or Day of Wrath. The Dies Irae is the second movement in the liturgical Requiem or "Mass for the Dead."

No. 4, Largo. Shifting chords continually modify the effect of this prelude's lovely melody even as death continually colors the mosaic of life.

No. 22, Molto agitato. Fierce octaves in the bass storm at the madness of brutality and at the sometimes futile efforts of man to ennoble mankind.

GYMNOPEDIE No. 1 (Lent et douloureux), Erik Satie

A bizarre composer, Satie occasionally wrote sounds of unsurpassed beauty. Such a piece is the Gymnopedie No. 1. Each tone of the long melodic phrase drops singly upon the sound spectrum as if measuring and savoring each nuance of life and death.

FUNERAILLES (October, 1849), Franz Liszt

Chopin died October 17, 1849, and within a few days Liszt had composed this piece. He did not specifically state that it was in honor of Chopin. No statement was necessary. The composition reveals its dedication by its Chopinesque themes and the monumental closing section based upon octave passages for the left hand reminiscent of Chopin's famous Polonaise in A flat. This work, as does a funeral, begins with a tolling bell announcing the tragic death. The bell is joined by rolling drums and the death-march then begins. There is a pause in the terrible duty of burying the fallen one to tell of his accomplishments and of his beautiful thoughts and hopes. Inevitably, the procession must continue. The reality of death can no longer be held away by remembrance. Beauty, or active good, has been silenced by death.

"A Pianist's Requiem for J.F.K."

By William Bryan

(Instructor of Piano Rosemead High School)

Music education has long been coping with the task of making music meaningful in the life and mind of the general student. Leaders in the general music field encourage music education majors in our colleges to become general music specialists in the hope that more of the general student population will come to find music important to them through the special efforts of these teachers. This is all to the good.

In my capacity as a teacher primarily teaching for performance, I had the opportunity this past fall to come into contact with the general student in a way that had considerable impact.

On Friday, November 20, I played a memorial piano concert in tribute to John Fitzgerald Kennedy for sixty classrooms on Rosemead High School's newly acquired closed-circuit television equipment. It has been my custom to play regularly on Fridays for my own three classes of piano students as a part of the course work in order to acquaint students with representative works from the history of piano literature. For this special occasion, however, I enlarged my audience on a classroom-request basis, so that more students might hear this musical tribute.

An announcement was sent to all English and Social Studies teachers describing the special event and giving the program and a few suggestions for classroom orientation prior to the telecast. In outlining the program I explained that I had taken from the piano repertoire particular works that seemed most meaningful for this occasion, and that, as programmed, made for a spiritual and emotional catharsis. It was to be a coming-to-terms musically, so to speak, with the tragedy of President Kennedy's violent death and its aftermath: the immense reaction of a distraught nation.

The works programmed were:

Marcia Funebre sulla morte d'un eroe, Opus 26, Beethoven

Adagio Cantabile from *Sonata Pathetique*, Opus 13, Beethoven

Intermezzo, Opus 117, No. 2, Johannes Brahms

Pas de deux from *Souvenirs*, Samuel Barber

Three Preludes, Chopin

Gymnopedie No. 1, Erik Satie

Funerailles, Franz Liszt

Due to the number of requests, the program, originally planned for three presentations for the piano classes, was beamed—and performed—six times. All receiving equipment was made available for the general student; music and drama classes heard the presentation live in the 105-seat choral room. Student operators manned two cameras as well as the switching room equipment. Drama instructor Lee Blattner deftly handled the third camera from which he called the shots via a head-telephone exchange between all technicians. He had previously taped my notes for the narration that took place between each number. Title cards and appropriate pictures were produced by the Art department whose chairman, John Montelongo, contributed a moving title cover drawing. The total effort was made possible by the complete cooperation and technical assistance of Assistant Principal David Berry, a long-time proponent of audio-visual education, who had taken up my idea of a musical tribute to Mr. Kennedy and had seen to its implementation.

With such splendid assistance, I was able to focus my attention upon the music and to the task of communicating with my listeners. I am happy to report that the impact upon the listeners was a deeply felt experience.

The crux of the matter then, is that in order to reach a member of the general audience who has not already expressed his interest in music by enrolling in a music course, the musician must create a reason for him to give his attention to music. Some general students apparently have not yet had a reason, so to say that it is right and good for him to listen to music and that all people respond "more or less" to music is not sufficient in making music meaningful to the general student.

In giving the program an extra-musical format, a serious attention was extracted from the general student and, as in the revered circumstances of some of the ceremonies of life, his heart and mind were fixed on the possibility of responding to the beauty of a Beethoven *Adagio*, a Brahms *Intermezzo* and the intensity and irrevocableness of a funeral piece of Chopin and Liszt.

We were all gratifyingly aware of the success of this audio-visual experiment in music appreciation.

The complete program, notes, the art cover by Mr. Montelongo, and an introduction by Alex H. Zimmerman on John F. Kennedy's contribution to the cultural life of America has now been made available on a high fidelity recording. In receiving a copy of the album, Mrs. John F. Kennedy expressed ". . . deep appreciation for the special album . . . made as a tribute to the late President. 'A Pianist's Requiem for JFK' will certainly be a valuable addition to the collection of the Kennedy Memorial Library."

A PIANIST'S TRIBUTE TO J. F. K.

On Friday, November 20, Mr. WILLIAM BRYAN, instructor in piano and choral music at Rosemead High School, will play a Memorial Concert in tribute to JOHN FITZGERALD KENNEDY for multiple classrooms on the newly acquired closed circuit television equipment. Mr. BRYAN regularly plays on Fridays for his piano students as a part of the course work in order to acquaint students with representative works from

MR. BRYAN at the piano.

history of piano literature. For this special occasion, however, he will enlarge his audience, on a classroom-request basis, so that more students may hear this musical tribute. In speaking of the program, Mr. BRYAN said: "I have taken from the piano repertoire particular works that seemed most meaningful for this occasion and that, as programmed, make for a spiritual and emotional expression. It is a coming-to-terms, musically, so to speak, with the tragedy of President Kennedy's violent death and its aftermath: the immense reaction of a distraught nation."

Works programmed:

Marcia Funebre sulla morte d'un eroe, Opus 26, Beethoven

Adagio Cantabile from Sonata Pathetique, Opus 13, Beethoven

Intermezzo, Opus 117, No. 2, Johannes Brahms

Pas de deux from *Souvenirs*, Samuel Barber

Gymnopedie No. 1, Erik Satie

Funerailles, Franz Liszt

This event will be produced and rehearsed with the assistance of Miss GERTRUDE KLEEKAMP, Music Department Head, Mr. LEE BLATTNER, TV/Drama Production, and Mr. JAY LYNCH, AV/TV Equipment.

APPENDIX C
Introductory Lecture for Music 101, Foothill College

The entire reason for education—for your being here on campus—is to help you realize yourselves...there is no other reason. Perhaps that is the reason we are here on Earth: to realize ourselves. How to realize one's self totally is a very complex matter. Man has been toying with this matter ever since he's been around.

Most of you feel that when you have the job or position you are now studying for; when you have found someone with whom you may share your life; when you have bought the kind of home that suits your personality—and pocketbook—that you will have realized yourself. Maybe you will have. Statistics indicate, however, that many people still feel a lack, a void; have a sense of incompleteness even with the realization of those just-mentioned acquisitions. They feel this lack to the point of frustration-caused migraines; nervous exhaustion; stress-induced heart disease, diabetes, and ulcers; painful-reality-induced alcoholism, insanity, suicide.

How to realize one's self totally is a very complex matter.

In your studies in psychology and biology, you have come into contact with the basic needs of man. We may generalize them quickly as the need for food, shelter and companionship. If you would let your minds think back to stone-age man, you can quickly realize how important the first two needs became. His third need, companionship, took various prescribed avenues due to immediate and geographic necessities. Today, we take food and shelter for granted. Most of you were born into a fairly affluent household: the shelter was there—so was the food. You've come to expect these items and take it for granted that, with a little effort, they will be met.

We know that in our contemporary society—with its high standards of living—with a certain amount of effort we can meet these first two needs. Generally, most of your formal education concerns itself with preparing you to meet these first two needs. They might not say just that in their statements of purposes of education, but that's what it amounts to.

However, it is my contention that because we are born into our contemporary "way of life", that these first two needs don't continue to ring out loud and clear in our psychic life...but that other one—the need for companionship—does. Those unpleasant states of existence

I enumerated above are primarily caused by a general lousing up of that third need: companionship.

Youth is pretty much a gregarious time. Perhaps that is why most of those stress states mentioned are not so evident in people of your age I should like you to reflect for a moment, though, that all those "oldies" that comprise the unpleasant statistics were once your age; that they were gregarious, like you, once. What happened? Doctors, psychiatrists, religious leaders, even some educators have been trying to figure out what happens. Many of those professionals only meet the people after something happened. Only the religious leaders and the educators are in a position to do something before it happens. Most educators help you to meet those first two needs, and we sometimes find only partial answers from our religious leaders for the third need.

Perhaps I have over-generalized in outlining the basic needs. Philosophers have discussed the already mentioned needs and some add also a religious need as being basic to man. My encyclopedia informs me that the word religion comes from the Latin, *religio* which in turn comes from religare meaning: "to bind fast." Somehow, this seems to me to have something to do with that third need: companionship...companionship in a multitude of depths arriving at, perhaps, a need for a companionship with the infinite.

I'm going to change the word companionship to the word communication. It may handle more easily. Once again, my encyclopedia defines that word thusly: "To make common; to cause to be common to others; to bestow; to confer, as a joint possession, and to share, participate, or enjoy in common with others." Religion and communication seem to end up having great similarities when we define them!

Erich Fromm tells us in his essay for happiness, "The Art of Loving", that "the awareness of human separation, without reunion by love...is the source of shame. It is at the same time the source of guilt and anxiety. The deepest need of man is the need to overcome his separateness, to leave the prison of his aloneness."

Gertrude Stein on her death-bed asked: "what is the answer?" There was silence. "well then, what is the question?" she asked and then died!

Fromm says that man of all ages and cultures is confronted with the solution of one and the same question : the question of how to overcome separateness, how to achieve union, how to transcend one's own individual life and find at-onement. He goes on to say that the more the human race emerged from its primary bonds, the more it separated itself from the natural world and then the more intense became the need to find new ways of escaping separateness.

Francoise Gilot, who became Pablo Picasso's mistress for ten years during and after the Second World War, speaks of her feeling of ease with him and when she spoke to Picasso about this, he exclaimed: "But that's exactly the way I feel. When I was young, even before I was your age (she was twenty then), I never found anybody that seemed like me. I felt I was living in complete solitude, and I never talked to anybody about what I really thought. I took refuge entirely in my painting. As I went along through life, gradually I met people with whom I could exchange a little bit and then a little bit more. And I had that same feeling with you—of speaking the same language. From the very first moment I knew we could communicate."

I believe the need to communicate is, after food and shelter, our most fundamental need. As I have tried to indicate, in this contemporary age of ours, when the first two needs are comparatively easily met, the need to communicate becomes uppermost in our psychic life.

May I restate that young people are a gregarious lot. They communicate fairly easily, but much of their communication is within a controlled family and school life. But as they age and they expect more from life, and are placed more on their own—" like a rolling stone,"— communication becomes more individualized, more subtle. As we age, we make greater demands on life, just as our palate makes greater demands on our table. This becomes a continual search for attainment. What is it that we keep trying to attain? We can think of it as "at onement" with the universe, a real sense of belonging to the center-flow of life. How we gain this sense of attainment—at onement—belongs to the sphere of communication.

Before I go further with the "communication need", let me suggest another need which I have observed in mankind. It is the need for perfection. We see it in the football player as he digs in day after day on the practice field; or the dancer after years of grueling preparation for the effortless pirouette; or the musician rehearsing endlessly for perfection.Can we account for any of these endeavors as a basic need for food and shelter? No, the need for perfection seems more apparently to be the reason for their tireless efforts. And what they are perfecting is a form of communication.

Now a lot of you will scoff and say: "but I don't practice long hours on the football field, or at the ballet bar, or on a musical instrument.

"If I could talk with each one of you, I would be able to tell you in a little while where you DO seek perfection.And I would also point out how thrilled you are by the perfection of others as you WATCH the football game, or watch Rudolph Nureyev, as I saw 20,000 people in a single night watch him at the Hollywood Bowl and then stood to cheer for thirty minutes following his performance. They had witnessed a degree of perfection and were moved by it and responded to it as if they had danced miraculously themselves.

We want it in everything we touch in life!

Nureyev had reached many individuals in his audience. He had communicated to them a sense of perfection in the art of movement—which is the plastic form of sculpture—that art-form which inspired Michelangelo to create human beauty from stone, and which generations have been moved to appreciate la form divine: the devine form, which really means the PERFECT human form.

Michelangelo released from granite images of great beauty. The stone was a mineral deposit of nature. He also took color pigments from natural sources and painted his conceptions of beauty upon walls and ceilings, as have generations of painters. One of man's first expressions, even prior to the establishment of a language, was through the picture that told a story, the picture that communicated

meaning to others through visual means. We know likewise that early man responded to the rhythms of his body and his environment and constrained these rhythms into specific patterns—in a sense, he made perfect, for a time at least, a specific aspect of rhythm as he beat out patterns on various woods and skins. He achieved an esthetic fulfillment by "creating" a rhythmic pattern himself even as the ultimate forces of nature apparently created rhythms of day and night, half-moon and full-moon, movement of stars across the heavens, the ebb and flow of the seas. Man recognized perfect patterns in the universe and endeavored to imitate them. His were artificial rhythms, artificial in the sense that he made them instead of the forces of nature making them. This artificial, man-made grouping of patterns of sound, of sight, of shape, became "art" as we think of it today. (Art, by the way, derives its name from artificial.) Perhaps the chief satisfaction of art is that it is a controlled moment of pattern and experience, having thereby a perfection, which, because it has balance and perfection, satisfies.

The need for perfection in our lives is basic and universal. Artists for centuries have sought perfection through their art. The onlooker gains a sense of perfection by perceiving what the artist has made. Both artist and perceiver are rewarded. And, for a moment, communication between the two has been established—and one of our fundamental needs has been met.

Making pictures, dancing rhythmic patterns, constructing images were the first arts. The addition of melody to the early rhythmic patterns and the constructing of music has been a later and more gradual development because it is more abstract than a picture or a dance. Because it is more abstract, some people are put-off by it. Some find that painting, for instance, has more immediate appeal for them. But for those of you who respond to that part of nature which we call sound, those that can be moved to a sense of attainment by the perception of the beauty of music, that can get in touch with—communicate and be communicated with—the artist who has made this artificial moment of perfection in sound—then you have added another dimension of satisfaction to your life, another manner of appeasing the continual need of the psychic life to be nurtured, to be spoken to.

Music has many answers. There are answers in all true communication. It is a combination of all the artifices than man has devised to explain and to satisfy life that will help us to attain real communication with the life-force and supply us with elements of perfection in our individual life.

College commencement addresses are often summations of some of the things I've been trying to say today. The graduate has achieved two or four years of higher education. He has added many specific disciplines to his abilities and then, at the end, after the struggle to learn, he hears a message of what it was all for, and in one hour or less, he is supposed to get it all in focus and go out into the world—adjusted and ready. I choose to tell you now what it is you are working for, so that, perhaps, greater perspective may come into your endeavors as you add specific dimensions to your life. I choose to tell you what the race is all about, instead of at the end when, perhaps, you're too tired to listen.

I would like to quote the closing paragraph from the commencement address of John Gardner at the University of Southern California recently. He is president of the Carnegie Corporation of New York and of the Carnegie Foundation for the Advancement of Teaching. He said: "The conventional thing for me to do in closing would be to wish you success. But success as the world measures it is too easy. I would like to wish you something that is harder to come by. I am going to wish you meaning in your life. And meaning is not something you stumble across, like the answer to a riddle or the prize in a treasure hunt. Meaning is something you build into your life, starting fairly early and working at it fairly hard. You build it out of your own past, out of your affections and loyalties, out of the experience of mankind as it is passed on to you, out of your own talent and understanding, out of the things you believe in, out of the things and people you love, out of the values for which you are willing to sacrifice something. The ingredients are there. You are the only one who can put them together into that unique pattern that will be your life. Let it be a life that has dignity and meaning for you. If it does, then the yardstick by which the world measures success will hardly be relevant."

This course is designed to help you to build meaning into your life. That is essentially the philosophy behind this college's fine arts requirement. It is the foremost reason for my being here with you in this classroom and is my uppermost thought as we proceed through this semester. How well I succeed is my personal challenge in the tremendous sphere of communication, and therefore to MY satisfaction of a basic need.

APPENDIX D
New Zealand

If you're like me and like to travel by boat, bus and train, then a circular trip of the South Island of New Zealand using public transport is just your cup of tea...and they'll serve you that too...frequently! When considering whether to rent a car and drive yourself or not, the first thing to consider is the English style of left-side driving. The first few days in Auckland kept me busy just trying to remember which way to look when crossing a street. I quickly decided I wanted to be free to look out the window rather that worrying about which side of the street was the right, I mean, correct, side.

After arranging some North Island trips on my own to the Bay of Islands, Rotorua, Lake Taupo and the wine country around Henderson, I decided to let the Government Tourist Bureau organize my trip to the South Island based on suggestions of what I wanted to see. One of those suggestions was that I wanted to return to Wellington by one of the day-light cruises of the Rangatira and that a portion of the trip be by the luxury train Southerner. Also I wanted to stay in economy hotels as my American dollar was only going two-thirds the distance it does in the states.

With considerable deliberation—I thought boredom at first—the fellow behind the counter plotted, scratched out, retraced words and letters, started anew on fresh sheets of itinerary paper, until he had organized the trip in order to meet up with the twice-weekly sailing of the Rangatira, yet still giving me sufficient time to take the launch up Milford Sound, walk the base of Mt. Cook, visit Walter's Peak Station across Lake Wakatipu from Queenstown and in general get the feel for much of the wonderful country-scapes of South Island.

In a day or two I returned to the bureau to pick up my packet of coupons arranged in the order of my tailor-made tour: all I had to do was present myself at the departure depot and start at the appointed hour as in a monopoly game but with the added satisfaction of knowing that everything but meals was already paid for.

South Island lies a little to the right and 12 nautical miles below North Island. One crosses to it either by sea or air. I took the N.Z. Railway Ferry to Picton which rests at the end of a long fiord. The Aranui hugged the tip of the coastline around the bottom of North Island. I was surprised that it didn't go directly across Cook Strait. But when we finally did I realized why we stayed near the coast for so long a time. Like the infamous English Channel, the strait can be very rough. My trip was accompanied by just enough rocking to inform me that we were truly at sea.

Picton exists mainly as the terminus for the ferry. Busses await your arrival and depart for both east and west sides of the island. Baggage had already been placed in a numbered trailer at Wellington indicating which side of the island you're going to. Miraculously, the luggage appears besides the appropriate bus (all part of the charm of public transportation in New Zealand!). The trip along the east side of the island to Christchurch passes more arid pasture land than I had seen on North Island. The grass was sparser and the slopes swooping down to the sea were less richly green. I had heard that rain fall in the South Island was plentiful but even in a land whose width averages only 200 miles, it is a land of great variation.

Lulled by the uphill, downhill, weaving in and out of pasture lands, I had just about dozed off when suddenly we were on the edge of a cliff high above the South Pacific. Rugged rocks jut out from the sea rather as they do along the Northern California and Oregon coasts. Fields of low-lying rocks are washed by waves beneath which crayfish seek refuge from the traps of fishermen. So rugged are the rocks and so precipitous the road that at several points the road comes smack into a giant rock that has been bored out for a single lane's worth of traffic. The first vehicle to the entrance of the tunnel at either end has the right of way, a clue to the lack of density of motor travel. So intent was I in watching the rocks and sea pass beneath me that when I turned my head momentarily from the sea on my left, I was completely surprised by the spectacular mountain to be seen on my right. Rising straight up from sea-level pastures stood the magnificent "Kaikoura" range, snow-capped and shining forth in brilliant sunlight. The Maoris discovered the fishing potential of this coast and settled in large numbers. They named the area Kaikoura from their words Kai, meaning food, and Soura, meaning crayfish. Evidence of Maori habitation remains in the Pa sites which are located on the most commanding promontories along the coast.

The University of Canterbury has built a marine laboratory here, realizing the wealth of sea life produced by the upwelling of cold mineral laden water from the South meeting a warm current from the North, resulting in prolific plankton growth and a vast variety of marine life. I thought "what a marvelous place to retire, with its combination of mountains and sea." Surprisingly, I later met a woman from Washington who had done just that. She was escorting visitors from Oregon on a sight-seeing tour when I met them on Milford Sound.

The pastures from Kaikoura south toward Christchurch become greener, reflecting the mountainous terrain by rising and falling in undulating waves. Vistas of pasture land are framed by occasional stands of poplars. Devoid of any billboards along the roadside, the landscape is reminiscent of the vast perspective distances seen in Renaissance paintings. It is as if one were returned to those uncluttered times, absorbing their openness and freshness.

Christchurch, the largest city of South island, was formed as an experiment in English life. Early in the colonization, a cross-section of classes and professions were brought from England to commence this most English of all towns in New Zealand. The town centers itself around the Anglican Cathedral, then branches out in all directions from this focal point. Town planners were careful to reserve ample open spaces. Being more level that either Wellington or Auckland, Christchurch was able to create beautiful parks, the largest being the Botanical gardens which are filled with trees, flowers, and shrubs of every variety. The Rose Garden is spectacular. Equally so are the rhododendrons that line many of the walks throughout the park.

Rivaling the Cathedral for center-stage nowadays, is the new Town

Hall, just a year old. Architects from all over the world were invited to submit plans for the building which was finally narrowed to one of Christchurch's own architects. The entire complex is revolutionary in concept as it is a magnificent combination of wood, cement , stone, and glass. The interior contains, along with city-hall functions, a lovely concert hall where viewing is easy from all seats. The acoustics are so fine that normal speech from the stage can be heard throughout the auditorium without amplification. With this edifice, Christchurch outshines the capital city of Wellington and more prosperous Auckland, still encumbered with their older buildings, to the perplextion of their citizenry. In a recent editorial on the need for such an edifice in Auckland, the article concluded with the question: "What about it, Auckland?" Meanwhile Christchurch can enjoy events in surroundings that can rival Sydney's fabled opera house.

One can profitably spend two or three days—or more— in this lovely city in order to savor the sights that are offered. I started out for the Southern Alps from there and returned there for the final leg of my South Island journey.

The route south from Christchurch by Mount Cook Landliner goes through the Canterbury Plains to Timaru.In the distance the Southern Alps can be seen for the first time. It reminded me of the stretch between Denver and Longview, Colorado: flat fertile plains, stretching for miles and framed on the right in the far distance by mountains. Since it is the principal wheat producing region for the country, the Canterbury is the breadbasket for New Zealand. Race horses are also reared here comprising a very important industry and sport for New Zealanders. All New Zealand papers devote several pages daily to racing and radio stations call the races from any point in New Zealand or Australia whenever they occur. During these broadcasts, all else stops in order to listen as nearly everyone in the country has placed a bet on their favorite horse via the nationally owned and operated TAB betting bureaus.

Following a luncheon stop at Timaru at the bottom of the plains, the Landliner turns westward and heads for the hills that form the approach to the Southern Alps. As the mountains near, the road boarders the lower end of Lake Takapo. It is here that huge new hydro-electric developments are underway. A canal is being built linking Lake Takapo with Lake Pulaki in order to raise the water level of the latter 150 feet. This increase will create water power sufficient for several more hydro-electric plants, part of the far-sighted development by New Zealand in meeting it's energy needs. An enlarged Lake Pulaki will then have even greater reflective powers as the mirror for Mount Cook, the highest peak in Australasia, some 12,349 feet high, perpetually snow-covered and always magnificent. This alpine region contains no fewer than 17 peaks over 10,000 feet high. Mount Cook, known by the Maoris as Aorangi ("the Cloud Piercer"), forms the centerpiece of the spectacular views seen from all windows of The Hermitage, the descendant of the oldest of the tourist Hotel Corporation of New Zealand's accommodations. There have been at least three other Hermitages, the most recent built after fire consumed the previous formidable wooden structure in 1957. Constructed along contemporary lines, the use of local stone, timber and wide expanses of glass makes the current Hermitage compatible with its beautiful surroundings. One of the advantages of this particular TMC hotel is, that in addition to the luxury rooms, economical rooms without private bath—in the tradition of B & B's—are available. While more modest, they offer full use of all the luxurious hotel facilities including the Panorma Room which offers Continental dining with an unsurpassed view of Mount Cook and the surrounding peaks.

The journey between The Hermitage and Queenstown is marked by rolling countryside. There are dramatic cliff-edge views of streams as they gather from various points and merge together to form powerful flowing rivers, their glacial waters crystal clear and tinged with blue. The Landliner, acting as a service to all significant points along the way, detours to Lake Wanaka, another summer holiday resort, for tea at Tarras. For 30 cents, one can have his fill of sandwiches and freshly made scones. Unrivaled for quality and quantity, the tiny shop has stacks of guest registers filled with grateful comments from all over the world attesting that Tarras is the best tea stop in New Zealand. Dutifully refreshed, we press on to Queenstown where the first glimpse of Lake Wakatipu is a startling luminous blue color. I was told by an officer from the Rangatira that this iridescent blue is caused by the kind of marine bacteria present in the water and caused by the water being totally from glaciers. Surrounding the lake on one side are The Remarkables, a jagged repetition of peaks jutting into the sky that indeed must have made early settlers catch their breath while exclaiming "remarkable!" Part of Queenstown's charm is its age, a truly mid-19th century town clustered about the lake and helped in its look by the sight of the coal steamer T.S. Earnslaw tied to the wharf. Built in 1912, the Earnslaw cruises the lake between

December 18 and Easter each season. When it is not running, just the sight of it lying at dock gives character to the waterfront. The Queenstown Mall is a narrow street running directly into the lake and is reserved for pedestrians only. 19th century style shops flank either side exhibiting a variety of offerings from sheepskin rugs to New Zealand wines. The wine is well displayed in a natural wood-finished shop whose host, Don Luzmoor, will offer you samples of N.Z. wine. If you're interested in talking N.Z. and Australian wines, Mr. Ryan, host of Melbourne House, is very knowledgeable and enjoys meeting and talking with wine aficionados. His small hotel is kept up very well and accommodations are most reasonable for such newness and cleanliness.

When gold was discovered in 1862, thousands of prospectors swarmed into the area where signs of their activities can still be seen. Such famous gold-mining towns as Lower Shotover, Arrowtown, Oawerau Gorge and Roaring Meg are all within easy reach of Queenstown. Arrowtown is being preserved by city ordinance forbidding the alteration of any building without borough approval. There you can see Simon Mullins spinning wool at his High Country Crafts shop where he sells only goods made by N.Z. artisans.

A stay in Queenstown—which should be at least two or three days—is not complete without one or more of the lake cruises. Two different sheep stations, Cecil's Peak and Walter's Peak (named for the mountains that are contained on their vast pasture lands) are destinations for the cruise launches and offer a personal tour of the stations complete with sheep dogs corralling sheep before your eyes. Walter's Peak station has turned the original residence into a charming museum. All the utensils of life in the 1800's are carefully kept in their appropriate places so that one feels that he has suddenly turned back the clock and returned to an age long past gone. Granny is even reading in bed all trussed up with pillows. (Life-size models costumed for the times is a feature of many N.Z. museums.) Before leaving either of the sheep stations, tea is served along with home-made scones and jam. If the weather is cool enough, as it was the day I visited, there will be a roaring fire in the fire place as well, making things even cozier.

Within walking distance from the Queenstown Mall is the gondola to Skyland Chateau. Purchase your luncheon ticket at the Information office in the center of the Mall and you'll receive a 50 cent discount on your luncheon. The view of Lake Wakatipu from the restaurant is spectacular and should not be missed. (It is here that I saw my first wine-bottle wall.)

A New Zealand Railway bus is the conveyor for the land traveler between Queenstown and Te Anau. We are now on our way to the high point of the journey—Milford Sound. A change of bus is required at Lumsden, a tiny crossroads town that is also the starting point for the Kingston Flyer, an antique train that operates twice daily during the holiday months. If you like old-fashioned carriages and a smoke-belching locomotive, then this is one of the few places left in the world where you can re-live such an experience.

The arrival in Te Anau comes late in the afternoon, but in time to see the majestic mountains surrounding New Zealand's largest lake. With a coast-line of some 300 miles and depths up to 1300 feet, Te Anau is the gateway to the fjords and headquarters for Fiordland National Park. The whole south-western portion of South Island— three million acres—make up this park, one of the largest national parks in the world. It is also one of the most inaccessible as there are no interior roads. Only the road from Te Anau to Milford exists and this is at the eastern edge of the park. Boats have the advantage as they can explore the sounds along the western coast whose names conjure up mysteries in themselves: Doubtful Sound; Dagg Sound; Five Fingers Peninsula; Desolation Island; Dusky Sound and Chalky Inlet. But the destination for most is Milford Sound which Kipling described as "the eighth wonder of the world." Prior to reaching the sound, one passes Glade House lying at the head of Lake Te Ana where the famous Milford Track hikers assemble for their five-day journey through mountain and forest to Milford. At one point in the bus ride, the road looks as if its going to end right at the side of a sheet of granite. That is the way it ended until 1935 when the first bore of Homer tunnel was made through the rock affording passageway. It was not until 1953 that the tunnel was made car-size. And not until 1958 that regular bus service began. Although the sound was made by glaciers aeons ago, few persons viewed its wonders until the last couple of decades.

The sound is dominated by Mitre Peak, named for its resemblance to a bishop's hat. At 5,560 feet, this mountain is the highest in the world to rise directly out of the sea. As the Sound averages 340 inches of rain annually, your chances of seeing it totally unobstructed are rare. Changes occur, however, rapidly and though a veil of clouds may be covering the peak at one moment, it may reveal itself in the next. Part of the Sound's beauty is its ever-changing quality. The most moving part of experiencing Milford Sound is to be quiet somewhere where you can watch it in silence...not moving about in a boat, or listening to geological explanations, or even walking on its headlands. It is awesome as a cathedral is awesome and, as in those edifices, the silent moments of contemplation are the most beautiful and meaningful.

As most people purchase their ticket at the Milford Hotel, which operates its own launches, I recommend that you pay the 30 cents extra and go on the launch Friendship . The hotel launches are so overcrowded that it is difficult to have the contemplative experience I've spoken of. While they move over the water bursting with passengers—each of whom are trying to see and photograph the multitude of waterfalls and geological formations—the Friendship passes more slowly and, because it is not the "official" launch, carries only a handful of passengers who can view in comfort the very same sights. If you have the time, stay a night or two at the TMC operated Milford Hotel and then you'll be able to experience daybreak and sunset as well as all that passes between in this cathedral of nature.

A word about Youth Hostels for the young and thrifty: they are present in each of the centers I've spoken of except Milford. However, there is a cabin site at the terminus of the Milford Track and some camping sites in the surrounding bush. Most of the young people who use the hostel at Te Anau take the bus to and from there as well as to Milford Sound. Hitch-hiking is unsatisfactory because of the few cars traveling the road. Bus drivers are very helpful by stopping for you if, after attempting to hitch a ride, and failing, you want to make the next stage by bus. Naturally, you'll have to pay but the ticket transaction can be handled by the driver and he'll let you off at convenient crossroads if you ask. Throughout New Zealand bus drivers point out places of interest en route over an amplification system. Between Te Anau and Milford Sound the bus stops often for picture-taking as if it were a private tour! Altogether it was a very personal trip made extra pleasurable by the graciousness and knowledge of the driver.

Upon return from Milford and a night's rest at Te Anau, my journey continued south to Dunedin by N.Z. Railway bus. The road passes the Hokonui Ranges which once harbored illicit liquor stills. In N.Z. the name "Hokonui" is synonymous with "moonshine" or illegal spirits. (The first legal whiskey produced in N.Z. will be uncorked during 1974). The plains one passes are relatively flat but very fertile producing—besides sheep—crops of wheat, barley and oats. Dunedin is reached by late afternoon, in time to settle in a hotel and still have daylight to explore New Zealand's fourth largest city. I stayed at the Leviathan Hotel which has the advantage of being across the street from both the N.Z. railway bus depot as well as the train station which I would use later. The Early Settler's Museum is also directly across the street from The Leviathan and is filled with the photographs of the early residents. Dunedinites are encouraged to hunt their ancestors amongst the portraits which cover the wall from floor to ceiling. Interesting old coaches and a cable car are in the transportation room while "The Cottage" is a replica of dining, sitting and bedrooms of the 1800's.

Mini tours are available for morning and afternoon trips but if you have only a little time or want to do it on your own, take a city bus from the Exchange out to St. Clair. This offers a lovely beach and, if you're willing to climb, there is a magnificent view of the beach, ocean and all of Dunedin from the hill. The cost: 20 cents bus fare each way. During the trip, you will also be amused at the prams young mothers bring along on the bus. Drivers dismount from behind the wheel and hang the prams on hooks at the front of the bus. When the mother alights, he repeats the task in reverse. Such service all for 20 cents! Of course, there is also no tipping for anything as it is not the custom anywhere in New Zealand.

If it's Sunday and you want to have wine with dinner (as I did) you'll want to go to The Checquers in the center of town. Red plush and elegant, it is nevertheless medium priced and very comfortable. To start your meal, try the cream of Toheros soup. Don't let its green color startle you. That's just what cooking does to this large shellfish peculiar to chilly South Pacific waters. Little shreds of white meat pierce the pea-green cream as a very delicious, mild shell-fish flavor greets your palate. You may want to add salt, as I did, to bring out the flavor even more. You'll find N.Z. chefs very wary of salt.

If you're staying a day or two in Dunedin, see Larmach Castle, a conglomeration of Italian marble, Aberdeen stone, and kauri blocks situated high on the Peninsula hilltop. The afternoon mini-tour will take you there along to other places of interest. By day or night, Signal Hill, above Opoho, (the site of a N.Z. centennial memorial) offers a splendid overall view of the city and harbor. It may be reached by a city bus conveniently marked "Signal Hill" and boarded at the Exchange. Another bus from the Exchange is marked "Maori Hill" and offers the rider not only a good view but relics of New Zealand's first people, the Maoris, as well.

Be sure to have tea or luncheon at the Savoy, a very handsome second floor restaurant on the corner of Princes Street and Moray Place. Lightly stained glass windows cast a rose-colored hue to your repas as you watch the busy street below.Moray Place is also the location of the First Church of Otago, probably the finest example of Gothic architecture in New Zealand. It is the Mother Church for Presbyterians who founded Dunedin. Catholic and Anglican Cathedrals also grace the city helping to make Dunedin architecturally interesting.

The luxury train "Southerner" leaves Dunedin for Christchurch daily at 12:20 p.m. except Sunday . This enables you to have another morning of either sight-seeing or resting. This might be a good time to see the Early Settlers Museum as it is next door to the station. Check your luggage early so you don't have to bother with it which they'll do for seven cents until you're ready to board—or you can leave it there for an entire week for the same price! The handsome, roomy passenger cars of the "Southerner" are former first-class cars that have been completely refurbished. Armchair-style seats offer the most leg-room I've every experienced on any public vehicle. If you like to drink, Hostesses in the style of airline stewardesses serve alcoholic beverages right at your seat. From Dunedin to Timaru the views are spectacular as the tracks follow the coastline north for 130 miles. Skirting the edge of cliffs above the sea, the Southerner offers dramatic views that the highway, further inland, can't provide. Looking more like sculpture are unusual rock formations easily seen from the wide train windows and close enough to offer good photo opportunities.

Leaving Timaru on my way back to Christchurch, the train retraces the route through the Canterbury Plains that I first experienced by bus. In a very comfortable chair, however, and sipping a sherry (for 20 cents) it seemed much more luxurious this time! My journey was scheduled so that I could take one of the twice-weekly daylight sailings of the Rangatira from Lyttelton back to Wellington. If you book one of the night sailings, the Southerner, after an hour's dinner-stop in Christchurch, takes you directly to the gangplank in time for departure. Comfortable sleeping cabins are plentiful on the Rangatira and most offer private toilet facilities. There is a movie theater, lounges and a pub on board. But for me, the actual feel of a ship is enough recreation. The daylight sailing takes nine and a half hours and is just long enough to generate the feeling of an ocean cruise. If you want to imagine you're far away to sea, look starboard and there will be nothing but open sea all the way to Antarctica. If you feel safer viewing shoreline, look to the port side as the ship hugs the South Island all the way up the coast.

Ships are a way of life for this island country. When New Zealanders return to ancestral lands, they more often travel by sea than by air. Watching the liner Britanis depart for London from Wellington, I was struck by the crowds on both ship and wharf. Greek music played from loud-speakers,(the ship is Greek registered), while paper streamers floated from port holes and deck rails. Some people were weeping, both on shore and on the ship. Finally the ominous long, low blast of the ship's horn signaled the departure and slowly, the tug pulled the ship away. I asked a boy nearby where it was going and he had to repeat twice before I understood, "Britain!", so choked-up was he by the emotion of the leave-taking. I realized that this old fashioned leave-taking—so prolonged due to the mode of operation—produces a much more emotional scene than today's jet transportation where frequently our loved ones are delivered to a curbside departure where swift goodbyes are exchanged. Today everything is so fast, so mechanical, our contemporary emotions respond similarly: there is no feeling of "departure." One simply steps from one speeding machine to another. But at shipside, the loved one is before us, weeping, waving, enduring the slow withdrawal to be matched by six long weeks at sea. Arms are waved, then kerchiefs as, slowly, the separation is increased porthole by porthole until, finally, the ship is past the dock and the water intrudes between traveler and those that remain behind. The arm-waving continues until identities are lost and become mere specks against a toy ship. A great exhaustion sets in, for this vigil has lasted four and a half hours—the time it takes to jet from San Francisco to Honolulu.

Yet it's appropriate that such ships ply between New Zealand and England, taking more time, yet creating more feeling of the togetherness and separations of humans. It's as if New Zealanders savored the nuances of life more than some other people do. With their life so closely associated with the soil, they seem to maintain a greater affinity to nature. And this naturalness is what I think you will find in abundance on a trip to New Zealand.

APPENDIX E
COCTEAU'S ANGELS SOAR AT VILLEFRANCHE
Sensuous, Erotic
by Brian Jennings, as it appeared in
THE ADVOCATE , November 24, 1971

Villefranche-sur-Mer nestles against the rocks and hills that form one of the beautiful bays of the French Riviera. It lies halfway between Nice and Monte Carlo. Across the sparkling bay is splendid and secluded Cap Ferrat where Somerset Maugham had a villa.

Villefranche, though, has simpler charm, less pretensions and more of the sea. For many years following the Second World War, the U. S. Navy kept a ship in the harbor and sailors were more the rule than the exception until recently when, in cutting back certain NATO forces, Villefranche lost the pleasure of its U.S. sailors.

Jean Cocteau had been a visitor to the Cote d'Azur all his life, but he was particularly fond of the water sports of Villefranche, not the least of which may have been its sailors.

Villefranche and la mer are inextricable. The tiny Chapel Saint Pierre had been built upon its very wharfside to afford the early-rising fishermen a nearby place for prayers for safety and success. In recent years it had fallen into disuse as a place of worship, a larger, more worldly church having been built higher up the hill.

It was to this remnant of a time when there was greater immediacy between one's work and one's worship that Cocteau brought his contemporary vision of church wall-painting. And it was this particular creation that brought me to this beautiful Mediterranean town. Sometime before, I had seen a booklet showing the various images Cocteau had drawn upon these old walls, and it became, for me, a pilgrimage to view them first-hand.

Jean Cocteau wrestled with angels all his life. From his first glimpse of Dargelos as a child (as told in his "White Paper") to the beau garcons of Villefranche in his maturity, Cocteau was always seeking—and finding—angels.

Surrounding the several picture-stories he painted on the walls of Chapel St. Pierre at Villefranche are the angels of his life. There is the childlike round-faced angel that is helping to hold up Saint Pierre as he attempts his unsuccessful walk upon water. He has a countenance of beatific innocence as he helps the older man. One thinks, perhaps, of Cocteau's one-time lover, Raymond Radiguet, at the age of 18 who, with childlike simplicity and exactness, gave direction to Cocteau's writing by the example of his own classic simplicity.

There is also the angel from Orphee , dressed in Cocteauesque space suit, gesturing to the reclining St. Pierre to arise from his sleepy watch. To one side of Pierre's half-risen figure is a study in satiation: a Roman soldier, nude except for loincloth and helmet, slumped down asleep by the side of St. Pierre.

The Roman appears to have been drinking and exposes a massive crotch. His nipples stand erect as if still intoxicated from recent excitation while his legs splay uncontrollably as if he were drained of energy from the waist down. St. Pierre creases the edge of the bed sheet in his hands as if drying his fingertips!

The angels that are the most significant are not those that are incorporated into the Biblical stories, but those that seem to have an existence holy (sic) unto themselves. The first panel on the left as one enters the Chapel depicts two fisherwomen with a basket of phallic-like fish. Cactus surround the fish in a most bizarre juxtaposition as if they were somehow keeping the fish fresh by their cool cylinders. Thusly, Cocteau makes a visual pun with a basket of pricks!

But above this scene, and totally unsuspected by the fisher-women below, are youthful angels dancing in a brightly sunlit sky, which can only suggest the brilliance of the Cote d'Azur itself with its thick population of earthly angels who always seem to have an exis-tence unnoticed by the ordinary mortal.

The exception here, however, is that two fisherboys—with beauti-ful fish eyes and elongated throats—stare into the skyful of youth-angels, their lips slightly apart as if thirsting for what they see.

The angels themselves are totally absorbed with one another. One has his hand directly in the crotch of another as they traverse the heavens together. Other angels gesticulate wildly as if calling for more ecstasy. Although the angels are faceless, patches of hair in their armpits identify them as pubescent.

It is the center ceiling that is the most removed from any partici-pation in the rest of the scenes. Dominating the ceiling is a very large angel kneeling back on his haunches while his left hand holds his massive crotch. Like the other angels, this one is merely wearing a wrap-around cloth similar to the small towel worn in our popular baths today.

Cocteau makes a lose fold to fall about the angel's waist giving the suggestion, by the pleating, of the outline of a cock. The center angel is holding the base of his fold as if having relieved himself of a massive discharge. Greater credence is given this speculation as, a little distance outward from the angel, there are two unique creatures: they have heads that are completely formed, containing facial features, but their bodies are nothing more than sperm-like shapes. Two of them frame the edge of the center ceiling and form a reverse 69 pattern. They somehow appear to have emerged from the loins of the center angel. The fact that they have identifiable faces but no bodies suggest an identity of personality within the sperm.

On either side of the massive fertility angel are other youthful angels. On one side, three are dancing together, their legs as well as their dancing arms getting mixed up with one another. Each gesticulate with one pointed finger which further heightens the erotic effect.

Two other angels, replete with mature wings, are shown walking with arms flung about each other's shoulder as they mount the sky. One of them has a pronounced bulge to his loincloth, and he seems to be gesturing toward the center "fertility angel" and beyond to the offspring sperm-angels.

On the other side of the ceiling, another angel appears to have just flown in as he points directly at a youthful angel below as if to say: "I've got you!" In response, the younger one points with one hand toward himself as if to say: "Who me?" while his other hand seems to be about to tear off the small covering from his loins.

Another pair of angels complete this heavenly orgy. One is in a reclining position on his back as his loincloth thinly covers a large erection. Below him, his companion reaches to unmask the angelic loin.

Remember, that all of this is depicted as if in the air so the "aboves" and "belows" are marvelously psychedelic and agile as if in a dream and more as we'd like it to be, having none of the grinding-around-on-crumpled-sheets look.

My impression in viewing the Chapel as a whole, is the yearning upward of the fisherboys toward the activity transpiring above them. This quality of lifting the eye and spirit upwards in church decoration is age-old. But what inspires one here, as he lifts his head heavenward, is the total abandonment and joy of the love-play of the male angels. If God is "love", then Cocteau has certainly captured an aspect of its multiplicity.

Behind the altar, and in the very center, is a beautiful youth that obviously is a companion to the scene of Christ walking on the water while Saint Pierre attempts to do the same. The youth is sinking, showing only his wide shoulders, beautiful throat, and upturned mouth and eyes as he pleads for help from the angels above. A group of startled and bemused fish view all these happenings and show various stages of disgruntlement and astonishment over these gods and mortals "walking" about their domain.

But the youth is looking up to the masculine angels for his inspiration and salvation. To be lifted up and to join these angels at play is what he appeals for.

And that becomes the overpowering wish of all simpatico people who view these wall paintings. Cocteau has placed the sinking, pleading, mortal youth center-stage behind the altar, the first thing seen upon entering the chapel and the last impression taken with us as we leave.

APPENDIX F

"Music Awareness in the Age of Enlightenment"
(One of three Programs prepared for KSCI Television, March 1978)

(Piano) "Jesu, Joy of Man's Desiring" by J.S.Bach arranged by Myra Hess (3 minuets, 45 seconds)

There's one of the favorite compositions in the world. I wonder if people ever stop to think why that music seems so inevitably right? After all, Bach wrote more music than anyone else ever has and surely there must be other pieces equally as appealing. Yet that one is the most beloved. I've discovered in the music some things which may be clues as to why this piece has all the right ingredients to produce a masterpiece. Let's first look at the hymn-tune Bach surrounds with his delicate filigree of sound. The melody was used by at least two Lutheran authors: Johann Schop in 1642 set a series of verses to it called "Be Glad My Soul". Martin John set 16 verses to the tune calling it "Jesus, Joy of my Soul," the sixth and sixteenth verses of which Bach set for chorus as we have just heard it in his 147th Cantata. In both cases, the sense of joy, of gladness as felt in the soul, is the central issue. Bach's faith was one of great positiveness. Indeed, he has even been called the Fifth Evangelist. Let's look at the chorale-tune itself in one of Bach's several harmonizations. (Piano, 45 seconds)

If we dissect it we discover that the tune is always three rising steps up the scale and return. There is not one single skip in the entire melody and its contour is always three rising notes! (Piano, melody only, 45 seconds.)

Again, if we look at the original hymn-tune, we see that it is in 4/4 time. (Play) But as Bach has placed it in this choral setting in his cantata, he transforms it into 3/4 time. (Play, 10 seconds) Yet another instance of the use of 3.

Let's look at some other Chorales as Bach has harmonized them for some more clues. In all, Bach harmonized over 400 hymns and put figured bass to many more. The hymn that he harmonized the most was "Jesu, Meine Freude", Jesus, My Joy! The relationship of words to music is of utmost importance at all times, but particularly during the Baroque era. The Camarata of Florence who invented opera at the end of the Renaissance, insisted on a "Doctrine of

Affections": that the music must convey the mood and meaning of the word. Certain musical cliches had developed by Bach's time to indicate various moods; descending minor melodies for sadness, ascending major melodies for happiness, dotted rhythms for fury and the like. Bach, through his great personal devotion to God, had devised many subtle nuances of musical expression to express his faith. His obvious liking for the verse of "Jesu, Meine Freude" is proven by the number of times they were set to music. Let me play the simplest arrangement first. (Piano: 40 seconds). Truly a lovely, serene melody isn't it! Albert Schweitzer points out in his definitive biography of Bach that Bach's favorite hymns were not those of the Pietists of the late 17th and 18th centuries, but rather the objective more sturdy chorales of the 16th and 17th centuries. Now see in this next harmonization how he begins to weave his magical inner voices accompanying the tune. Notice the frequent use of 3 rising notes that counter the point of the melody. (Piano: 45 seconds.)

Now notice in this next harmonization how he slides a passing tone, not in the original melody, into the soprano line. The words here in the first verse are "Jesu, Meine Zier", Jesus, My Lord. (Play) By placing this passing note between the two original melody notes (play) he achieves the figure of 3 rising notes as they embellish the words "Jesus" and going to the words "My Lord". Now, before you think I'm playing musical numbers, let me quote from Ernest McClain's, "The Myth of Invariance": "In antiquity, musical symbolism and mathematics were recognized spiritual languages that often were used to communicate fundamental spiritual ideas. In modern times the symbolic importance of music and mathematics has been forgotten." Obviously, Bach hadn't forgotten it. And more, the use of 3 anything for Bach would symbolize the Christian Trinity, which for him would be pure joy!

Which brings us to his simplest and most sublime harmonization of this tune. This is as it appears in the last chorus of his motet of the same name during which he harmonizes the hymn five times. Again, note the accompanying groups of 3 rising notes, and the raised 3rd at the final chord (from minor to major) giving a feeling of uplift at the end. This "Piccardy Third" as it was called, was another Baroque cliche, but in the hands of a master surpasses the commonplace. (Piano, 45 seconds.)

Note that the soprano line descends the scale for the last line in which the words, finally, are: "Jesu, Meine Freude". (Play) Bach can't alter the shape of the original melody to suit his feelings. Instead, he hands the tenor, the highest male voice, the 3 rising notes (Play) to carry upwards to meet the descending soprano on the same note in a glorious arch of joy. (Play) And it is the tenor also, that having risen upwards the 3 symbolic notes, gently lowers into the piccardy third-of-the-chord creating the serene cadence. (Piano:play last phrase twice: 20 seconds.)

Now let us return to the piano transcription of the last chorus of Cantata No. 147. We have already seen that the original hymn-tune is made up of nothing but rising groups of 3 notes and that Bach changed the meter from 4/4 to 3/4. And now for the final 3 in this Trinity of 3'ism, Bach produces the surrounding notes which buoy this serene tune along with groups of 3 rising notes (Piano: 20 seconds)

Upon hearing this, people at first think Bach has written a pretty accompaniment to a stately tune, not realizing that the accompaniment has grown from the very shape of the melody itself, as well as from the joy of the words: "Be Glad My Soul"! So we see that one of Bach's musical symbolism was the use of 3 rising notes to express the sense of joy.

Regarding figured bass—a short-hand of harmony during the Baroque—Bach wrote in the rules and principles of accompaniment that he gave his pupils: "Figured bass is the most perfect foundation of music. It is executed with both hands in such a manner that the left hand plays the notes that are written, while the right adds consonance and dissonances thereto, making an agreeable harmony for the glory of God and the justifiable gratification of the soul. Like all music, the figured bass should have no other end and aim than the glory of God and the recreation of the soul. Where this is not kept in mind, there is no true music, but only an infernal clamor and ranting."

Albert Schweitzer writes: "For Bach the tones do not perish, but ascend to God like praise too deep for utterance." PIANO: "Jesu, Joy of Man's Desiring", Bach-Hess, 3 minutes 45 seconds.

APPENDIX G

Whitman Concert Program

SEPTEMBER 1985

VOLUME XXXIII

NUMBER 8

3340 Country Club Drive
LA 90019 (213) 735-5252

λ λλλ λ λλλ λ λλλ λ λλλ λ λλλ λ λλλ λ λλλ λ λλλ λ

The CALENDAR is published by ONE, Incorporated and sent to Members and Friends of ONE in all parts of the world. It gives the current schedule of the month for those living nearby, or planning to visit Los Angeles; for those living elsewhere it is a newsy bulletin telling what their organization is doing these days.

ONE INSTITUTE
3340 COUNTRY CLUB DRIVE LOS ANGELES, CALIF. 90019 • (213) 735-5252

PRESENTS

William Bryan, pianist

CELEBRATING

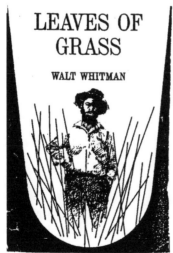

LEAVES OF GRASS

WALT WHITMAN

SUNDAY, OCTOBER 6, 1985   3 P.M.

ARLINGTON HALL

GALA CONCERT

FALL OPENING

In its longtime role as a cultural end educational center for the Homophile (Gay) Community ONE Institute is pleased to announce a brilliant piano concertwhich celebrates the poetry of Walt Whitman.

Pianist Bill Bryan is long remembered for his April 1964 concert of the music of Homophile composers which drew one of the largest audiences ONE Institute has ever had. He is on the Music Faculty at Foothill College, Los Gatos. Do not miss this outstanding event& bring your friends.

3 P.M., Sunday October 6, 1985 in Arlington Hall on the Campus. Only access is by the gateway at 12th & Van Ness; open at 2:30. Parking on the tennis court. Coffee hour afterward. Contributing & Associate Members admitted by card, all others $ 5.

WALT WHITMAN

Born May 31, 1819, Long Island, N.Y.; Died Mar. 26, 1892, Camden, N.J.
Foreword: The music does not attempt to mirror the meaning of the poems
but rather to provide an appropriate interlude for the intensity of the
poetry.

PROGRAM
I

I CELEBRATE MYSELF

"I celebrate myself,...:   Frédérick François Chopin
Prelude No. 1, C major   1810-1849

"Poets to come! ..."
Prelude No. 3, G major

"This hour I tell things in confidence ..."
Prelude No. 8, F♯ minor

"The expression of a well-made man ..."
Prelude No. 9, E major

"Whoever you are holding me now in hand ..."
Prelude No. 10, C♯ minor

"Are you the new person drawn toward me? ..."
Prelude No. 13, F♯ major

"Passing stranger! ..."   Erik Satie
Gymnopédies No. 1   1866-1925

"When I heard at the close of the day ..."
Prelude No. 17, A flat Major   Chopin

"You sea! I resign myself to you also ..."
Intermezzo, Opus 118, No. 1 (1893)   Johannes Brahms
                                                  1833-1897
"I dream'd in a dream ..."
Prelude No. 24, D minor   Chopin

PAUSE

II

I HEAR AMERICA SINGING

"I hear America singing, the varied carols I hear ..."
Excerpt, Appalachian Spring (1944)   Aaron Copland
                                            Born 1900, Brooklyn, N.Y.

"To the East and to the West ..."
Excerpt, Appalachian Spring

"A song of the rolling earth ..."
The Prairies   Ms. Ulric Cole
                                            Born 1905, New York City

"From this hour I ordain myself loos'd of limits ..."
Berceuse   Louis Moreau Gottschalk
                                            Born 1829, New Orleans -1869

"My lovers suffocate me ..."
Come Where My love Lies Dreaming   Stephen Collins Foster
(Arranged for L.H., Louis Victor Saar)   Born July 4, 1826-1864
                                            (Lawreceville, Pa.)

"O camerado close! ..."
At an old Trysting-Place   Edward MacDowell
                                            Born 1861, New York -1908

"City of orgies ..."
Prelude No. 2   George Gershwin
                                            Born 1898, Brooklyn, N.Y.-1937

"The male is not less the soul nor more ..."
Pas de deux from SOUVENIRS, Opus 28   Samuel Barber
                                            Born 1910, Westchester, Pa.

"O to make the most jubilant song!"
Springtime   Charles Wakefield Cadman
("To my young protege -- Edward Earle")   Born 1881, Johnstown, Pa.

Yamaha Piano

This program is available
for any appropriate
cause; anywhere, anytime.

APPENDIX H
LISZT LECTURE
Presented at the Langdon Cultural Center, Granbury, Texas
on Sunday, Jan. 14, 1999
Piano Introduction excerpt from Funerailles by Franz Liszt

That was an excerpt from one of Liszt's Harmonies Poetic and Religious. Liszt saw himself thusly: "My place will be between Weber and Beethoven or rather between Hummel and Onslow. I am perhaps a genius Manque, only time will show. I only know I am not mediocrity. My mission will be to have introduced poetry into piano music with some brilliance. What I attach most importance to is my harmonies; that will be my serious work. I will sacrifice everything to it. When I've finished my tour as pianist, I will play only for my own public. I will shape and elevate it."

Music, the most abstract of the arts, yet when listened to becomes the most immediately real: pulsating sound waves descending upon our own eardrums and piercing the brain. We can choose to look at a picture and "take it in" or not. But sound—if we are anywhere near, is here and now. There is no such thing as "dead music". Music plucks the lyre of sound waves and only asks to be heard...and understood.

We all stand in awe and admiration of Michelangelo's paintings on the walls and ceiling of the Sistine Chapel. We wonder how one soul could encompass so much of the Biblical experience on a flat, lifeless surface. We rush to embrace his genius and pictorial eloquence.

The same can be said of the music of Franz Liszt. To a less practiced listener than the acknowledged horde of admirers of Michelangelo, Liszt's audio descriptions of God, St. Francis and Dante coping with the throes of hell, have to be heard and understood sonically.

The first fifteen centuries of Christianity, prior to Luther and the rise of Protestantism, revolved around the religious institution known today as the Roman Catholic Church. Music evolved from a single line of chant into sophisticated harmony and polyphony, all to elevate the observance and practice of Christian ritual by the ordained religious. The visual arts also flourished at this time through ecclesiastical paintings like those of Michelangelo in the Sistine Chapel and the "holiest" of Christian art: "The Last Supper" of

Leonardo da Vinci. Thus, the evolution of the Western arts, as we know them, was begun early in the Christian Church.

With Protestantism and congregational participation in worship services, a new kind of religious music arose: The Hymn, sung by everyone, not just the ordained. Martin Luther believed in religious participation by all worshippers. Thus the vernacular of the people was introduced into worship services and Christian religious tradition was forever changed. Out of this new tradition grew the monumental religious works of Johann Sebastian Bach. His Catholic influenced B Minor Mass was but a blip on his otherwise Protestant collection of 350 Choral Cantatas, many of which were inspired by Lutheran Hymns. Bach was at the apex of the Baroque era that extended from the end of the 17th Century to the first half of the 18th.

The era of Classicism followed the Baroque and was punctuated by the works of Haydn, Mozart, and even Schubert who wrote numerous Masses for the Catholic service.

Enter the Romanticism of the 19th Century, the age of rationality, the age of secular art and music. The Church receded from the endeavors of the artistic world. Have you heard of Delacroix's religious paintings? Have you heard of Rodin's ecclesiastical sculpture? Have you heard of Liszt's body of work for the Church including masses for orchestra and chorus and soloists? You haven't heard about the former because they don't exist. But the religious works of Liszt does, our first clue as to the religious Genesis of the musical genius.

Born in the year 1811, Liszt's genesis was not limited to his old age when he took the vows and mantel of an Abbe at the Vatican. It was in evidence early on. Liszt was not unlike a bewildered Saint Simonian searching for spiritual truth while exhibiting his extraordinary technical ability at the piano. He was a Leonard Berstein type of being: pianist extraordinaire, conductor, champion of the music of others, most notably Robert Schumann and Richard Wagner, and composer of music including religious music, just as Berstein was to compose the religious Chinchester Psalms and MASS. This man of varied talents was often thought of as merely a pianistic showman.

In an age when the public was just getting used to Beethoven's music, along came this brash pianist, Franz Liszt. Beethoven was likewise first noted as a pianistic wunderkind in Vienna rather than as a composer. The Hungarian Liszt dazzled audiences with thunderous improvisations on familiar ditties by less capable composers. He was

not known as a composer of poetic or deeply felt original composi-
tions.It is left for us—one hundred and fifty years after his death in
1886, to move past the glitter and listen to the soul of Franz
Liszt...and what a lovely soul it is!

Here are some interesting figures regarding modern performances of Liszt compositions. At last year's prestigious Cliburn
International Piano Competition, 32 Liszt compositions were programmed by the 36 competitors. Four of the semi-finalists scheduled
Liszt's major work, the B minor Sonata which we will be privileged to
hear this afternoon. There were 46 compositions by Chopin who is
recognized as "The Poet of the Piano", but they might have been as
small as a Nocturne or as big as a Ballade. Of passing interest is the
fact that 11 Schubert compositions were scheduled, but none of
Liszt's countryman, Bella Bartok. Perhaps in another 100 years—as
was the case with Liszt, Bartok will receive his just dues as a fine
pianist and composer.

Today, while being recognized as a premier composer, Liszt is still
regarded as the showman of the keyboard. Let's look at his B minor
sonata from this point of view. First of all, it is a very difficult piece to
play, requiring consummate pianistic technique. That Liszt had it we
can't deny, but the technique in this composition is in the service of
the music, not of the artifice. I'm reminded of when I was a graduate
teaching assistant at the University of Colorado following my return
from France as a Fulbright Scholar. One member of the piano faculty
had studied with the incomparable French pianist, Robert
Casadesus, who was visiting Boulder to give a recital. The faculty
member asked for a private lesson with the master as he was having
difficulty getting through the horrendous octave cadenza of the B
minor sonata. The master asked his former student how long he had
been playing it and the reply was: "for several months". "But my
dear, it takes several YEARS to play that passage adequately!" said the
master.

I also recall hearing Emil Gilels perform this work to conclude his
recital at the Mozarteum in Salzburg and watched him as he nearly
fell from the piano stool upon its completion. Thunderous applause
brought him back repeatedly to the stage for bows but he was not
capable of playing one more note that evening, his energy having
been totally expended on the sonata.

Enough of the difficulties of the B minor. An understanding of
Liszt, the man, is imperative. His biographer, Eleanor Perenyi asks:

"How are we to understand an artist if we omit the life of his mind—understand and not just be grateful.?" She continues: "not until the advent of the Romantics do we begin to see a connection between a man's life and his music...and lives that are interesting in themselves."

Some insight into Liszt's personality is found in the diary of his friend, Clara Schumann, the foremost female pianist of the Romantic era. She writes: "Into our home Liszt descended, bringing his lady love, Princess Wittgenstein, and his own unique kind of non-stop uproar. Whenever Liszt comes, all domestic order is instantly turned topsy-turvy! He plunges one into a never-ending excitement...We made lots of music: Second Symphony of Robert's (Schumann)(for 8 hands); Springbrunnen and Kroatenmarsch out of the Album, then the whole Kinderball; and for the wind-up he played a new concert-piece and a few 'Harmonies'. As always, he played with a truly demonic bravura, he really mastered the piano like a devil; but alas! The compositions! They were simply too fearful stuff." That remained Clara's verdict on Liszt's best composition, the B minor sonata, dedicated to Robert Schumann. This shows how much Liszt thought of him...but of little avail to Clara!

An insightful Liszt wrote of himself: "I have often wept, and bitterly reflected in the past year...there is always in my heart an indefinable remorse that tortures me secretly , and when I'm idle—sometimes I tell myself that a thousand others have had the same experience. At other times, the storm breaks and then my sorrows and hates break out furiously...then...dreams of love, ecstasy, hopes, energy and the enthusiasm of youth return...."

Liszt's frantic search for enlightenment and insight was not a pose. His pursuit of intellectual and spiritual fashions struck many people as ridiculous. He was sneered at for his propensity to "stick his nose into every pot where the good God cooks to the future!" But for Liszt there could be nothing more important than to know who and what God intended him to be. A great artist, of course. But what kind? To find out, he investigated every movement in religious or philosophic thought available to him in the Paris of the 1830's.

A love relationship with Marie D'Agoult produced a son and a daughter, the latter destined to become wife to Richard Wagner named Cosima. Liszt writes to Marie following a sojourn with his guru, Abbe Lamennais: "Our good Father, takes his straw hat and says in a simpatico voice, 'let's go children, let's go for a walk' and we are launched into space for hours together. Really, he is a marvelous man, prodigious, absolutely extraordinary in loftiness, devotion, passionate ardor, possessing an acute mind, profound judgement, the simplicity of a child and sublimity of thought.I have yet to hear him say: 'I'. It is always Christ. Always in his mind to sacrifice for others and a voluntary acceptance of opprobrium, scorn, misery and death."

Even given his search for deeper meaning in everything, we cannot suppose that Liszt, on his own, had given serious thought to a new form of sacred music "uniting on a colossal scale the Theatre and the Church"...dramatic poetry with liturgical simplicity. But from an essay attributable to him because of the chaotic style, the underlinings, the exclamation points and the impulse behind the words, comes this quote: "Come hour of deliverance when the poet and the musician will no longer speak of the 'public' but of GOD and the PEOPLE." So we see the maturation of Liszt's religious genesis.

George Sand, (novelist and lady lover of Chopin) and her friends—the true Romantics of the era—frequently became engrossed in conversation about the right relation of art to nature. As reported by the biographer Eleanor Pereny, they had daily discussions that went like this:

"What connection could there be between Beethoven and a nightingale?"

"The nightingale is useful in that it gives a realistic base to art, and prevents the artist from losing himself in the indefinite spaces of the ideal."

George, smoking calmly, (usually a cigar) would say:

"You are wrong, my masters, art is creation."

"Agreed, with restriction..." went the conversation.

"With no restriction whatever..." was the retort. "Art creates as literally and totally as any power that brings forth something from nothing."

Liszt published an open letter to George Sand: "The work of certain artists is their life. The musician above all, who is inspired by nature but without copying it, exhales in the sound his life's most intimate mysteries. He thinks, he feels, he speaks in music; but because his language, more arbitrary and less definite than all others, lends itself to a multitude of diverse interpretations....it is not unprofitable for the composer to give, in a few lines, the psychic sketch of his work...to explain the fundamental idea of his composition. The critic is then free to praise or blame the manifestation of his thought."

I am taking the liberty of giving, in a few lines, the psychic sketch of Liszt's masterpiece, the B minor Piano sonata:

The opening notes—motif—are not unlike the opening of Beethoven's famous 5th symphony. Not that they are at all the same, melodically speaking, but rather that they have similar usage as a Fate Motif. Beethoven used his motif to thread together an entire four movements.

The first theme, rather like in a Classic Sonata-form, emerges as an heroic, aggressive, powerful theme after which the bridge (using the opening motif) leads to a majestic yet sublime second theme that appears but gives only a glimpse of itself...of paradise? As Maharishi says: "When we glimpse the palace, then we know we are on the path!" This is the essence of Liszt's composition: at the first, a glimpse of paradise—of Nirvana—but then the earthly distractions commence. The interlude immediately following is seductive in its sensuousness. Beautiful even as the women with whom Liszt continually surrounded himself: lovely, pastoral delights heralded by ecstatic upper register trills. But life's vicissitudes and turbulence spill over into a frantic, many-keyed change of difficulty until the terrible truth of the Fate Motif bellows forward in demonic chords only to be answered by sky high abolutions from the piano's treble, indicating, as always, a reminder to remember "the path"..the palace..."do not get caught up in the vicissitudes of life."

A peaceful interlude follows, not unlike the typical classic slow movement, as it soothes the soul of the poet-seeker as he continues the arduous path to enlightenment. As if by magic, the sublime "palace" theme reappears, reminding us that this is what the struggle is for. The beautiful theme attempts to hang on but the fate motif reappears in the left-hand trying to negate Nirvana , but the "Path" theme reasserts itself and calm ensues...but only for a while. The opening motif (First theme proper) reappears ominously: the soul is not yet ready for Nirvana. More ordeals and trials must be met. It is written in a fugatto style which means that there is much imitation between many voices on the piano. It is also very difficult. Cascades of octaves (the passage Cassadesus referred to as taking years to master) and arpeggios indicate the overwhelming struggle taking place. Finally the third and most magnificent statement of the "Path" theme triumphs in its radiant splendor. The fate motif insistently echoes in the bass as this monumental musical Sistine chapel of sound comes quietly to a close...way up in the treble, softly, serenely. If this were the composition of only a showman, it would never end like this...Dona Nobis pacem.